CHRISTIAN
HIGH SCHOOL
RELIGION SERIES

COMMITMENT

God's Plan for Engagement and Marriage

Student Book

By Diane Christian Boehm

CONCORDIA PUBLISHING HOUSE • SAINT LOUIS

Concordia
Publishing House
www.cph.org

This publication is available in braille, in large print, or on cassette tape for the visually impaired. Please allow 8 to 12 weeks for delivery. Write to the Library for the Blind, 1333 S. Kirkwood Rd., St. Louis, MO 63122-7295; call 1-800-433-3954, ext. 1322; or e-mail to *blind.library@lcms.org*.

Manufactured in the United States of America

8 9 10 11 12 13 14 15 14 13

Contents

To the Student

To the Student

What do you do with a textbook when the course is over? Throw it out? Pass it on to a friend? Lose it?

As the author of this Student Book, I would like to make a radical suggestion: Keep it! Place it in your personal library.

"Keep it? Are you kidding? Why should I keep it?"

You are not "finished" with the topics in this book. In fact, you may never be "finished" with some of them! Two years, five years, fifteen years from now, you may decide to marry—and wish you could recall what elements make a marriage stable and strong. Or you may be getting ready for your first child and wonder—what were those characteristics of a strong family, anyway? Taking a second look at this Student Book at such times will allow you to see clearly how much you've grown—and what God has been doing in your life!

Though this Student Book centers around the subject of Christian marriage, this book is *not* limited to the future. Instead, it begins with *who you are now*, for that is the foundation for *who you will become* as you prepare for future commitments and relationships.

The wonderful truth we Christians share is the good news that *who we are* was totally and completely changed when Jesus said, "It is finished." His death made it possible for corrupt, sinful, selfish people like you and me to be made new! We are new creatures because Jesus made it so. There is no more important lesson to be learned. God made us His own. This good news we share today we will celebrate together when we meet around His throne in eternity!

The Author

Chapter 1

Relationships—Where It All Begins

Chapter Preview

Chapter 1 will help you answer the following questions:

- Why are loving relationships important?
- What differences exist between the Christian's understanding of love and the world's attitude toward love?
- What is the basis for a right relationship with God? with ourselves? with other people?
- How can we grow in our ability to establish loving relationships?

1. Wanted

Wanted: one good friend with whom to share good times or bad; may be male or female; late teens preferred. Must be able to care about the real me.

Wanted: Parent or other caring adult who has time to listen to my fears and concerns, and who sees my potential as a person. Must like teenagers.

Will trade: One brother or sister (any age); seeking one with whom it is possible to get along. Bonus if he or she likes to play *Scrabble*.

Do any of these ads sound like something you might have written? Which comes closest to describing a need in your own life? Write a fourth ad describing specifically a relationship you would like in your life. (If you prefer, you may write two ads, one which is just for you, one which you would feel comfortable sharing with the class.)

The Importance of Relationships

When God created man and woman, He also created relationships. He created people in such a way that they would need each other. We all have many kinds of relationships: with our parents, our brothers and sisters, our grandparents and other relatives, our friends, our neighbors, members of our church. Human connection is a fundamental need. We need to feel that we belong, that someone cares about us, that our life has meaning to someone besides ourselves.

How can someone abandon a helpless baby, we ask? What will happen to this helpless child?

When we are born, we need another person if we are even to survive. From that person, a mother

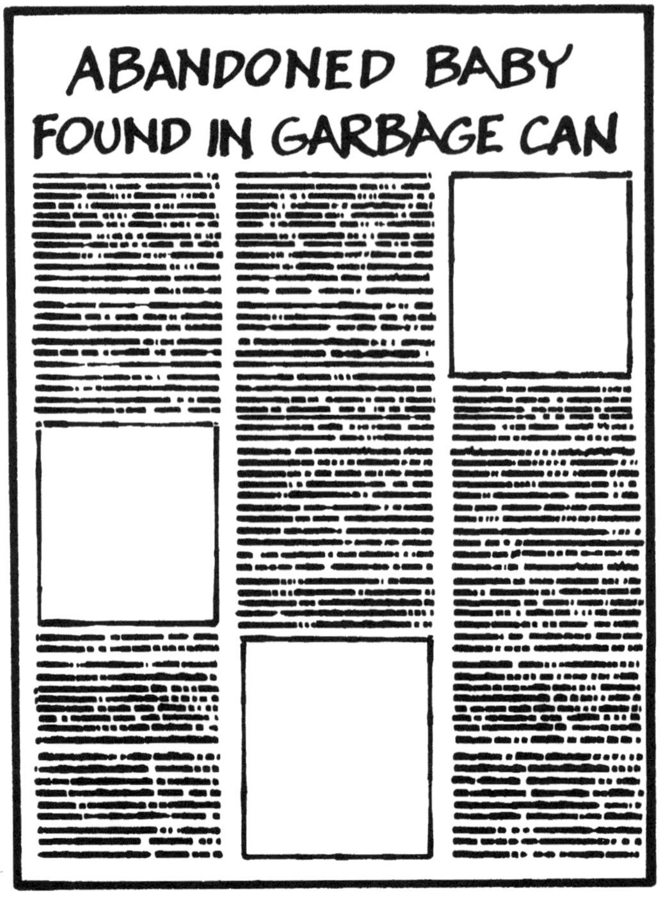

or a mother figure, we receive not only the food we need to live and grow. We also establish our first human bond, the bond that shows us what it is to be a person, the bond that teaches us how to love.

If someone did not love and nurture us when we were helpless infants, we would never be emotionally whole. In fact, abandoned infants, even if they are placed in institutions where they are fed, often develop a condition known as "failure to thrive." If no one takes the time to hold them, to speak to them, to let them feel the warmth of human affection, they will gradually withdraw. They will stop developing in a normal pattern. Without someone to love them their physical growth will be stunted; their emotional growth will cease; they may become mentally retarded; they may even die.

Loving relationships are necessary throughout our lives. God made us that way. He works through our relationships to nurture us and help us grow. In love He created us. In love He sent Jesus to bring us back to Him. In love He gives us the power to love others. We demonstrate our love for God by loving the people He has given us in our lives.

We give love through the relationships we establish with other people. Love is a necessity if life is to be rewarding and fulfilling, lived according to God's design. It is not only babies who fail to thrive if they are deprived of love. An old proverb says, "No one can stand the awful knowledge that he is not needed."

You and I need to know that someone cares for us—and we need to care for someone else. Anyone who works in a nursing home can tell you about people who have died, not because they had a terminal disease, but because they no longer felt needed or loved. If no one cared about them, they no longer had any reason to live. Without loving relationships, life is empty, lonely, and without purpose.

What is a relationship anyway? What does that term mean to you? Think of all the people you know well. You have a relationship with each of them.

Write a definition for what the word *relationship* means to you.

How does your definition compare with those of other students in your class?

Choose one of the pictures and write a caption or title which tells something about the relationship it illustrates.

Not only is each of us unique as an individual. Each of us is also different in terms of the relationships we have. Our personality, our sex, our age, our personal history, all play a part in determining the relationships we establish.

Some of us may want many friends; others may prefer just a few to whom they are really close. Some of us are happiest when we are with other people; others of us may value time alone. Some will come

from a large family group with its many established relationships. Others may have few immediate family members but establish close ties with people from their school or church families.

Relationships may be equality-based, as with two friends who equally value each other. Or they may be dependency based, as is the case in the parent-child relationship until the child reaches maturity.

Our lives will continue to present us with an infinite number of possibilities for relationships. God's gift of human relationships gives our lives meaning—and opportunities to serve others in love.

Each of us has three kinds of relationships in our lives:

- A relationship with God
- A relationship with ourself
- Relationships with other people

Everyone has a relationship with God. Even unbelievers have a type of relationship; though they may choose to separate themselves from God, He still offers His mercy and forgiveness. Most of us can also count dozens of relationships with other people. Perhaps you've never thought about the second kind of relationship, the one with your self. Your relationship with your self is based on your self-esteem: do you see yourself as a unique, valuable person? Each type of relationship is interwoven with the other relationships.

As the Father has loved Me, so have I loved you. Now remain in My love.

John 15:9

2. We Love because He First Loved Us

As we look more closely at our relationships with God, ourselves, and other people, we will begin to see how God is at work in our lives. Our relationship with Him, which forms the basis of all other relationships, is the place to begin.

Read **John 15:12–27.** Suppose you wanted to explain to someone who is not a Christian what this text means. Consider the following questions.

1. How do you know God loves you? How is it possible for God to love you?
2. How is it possible for you to love God?
3. How is it possible for you to love others?
4. What is the greatest kind of love **(v. 13)?** Give an example or two of this kind of love from people you know or have read about.
5. Perhaps you've seen the slogan, "If God seems far away, guess who moved?" What does that slogan say about our relationship with God?
6. Give several examples of ways in which you have experienced God's love in your life.
7. How has your relationship with God changed since it began? What things can a Christian do to strengthen his or her relationship with God?
8. Based on this passage, describe the kind of love you think Jesus wants you to show to others. Tell briefly about a time when God's love gave you the power to love someone in this way. Write a prayer which expresses your feelings about the text and discussion above.

The Truth about Me

Our relationship with God forms the basis for all our other loving relationships, including our relationship with ourselves. Self-esteem—how we feel about ourselves—is a vitally important factor in the kinds of relationships we build with others.

Our self-image is created bit by bit as we grow up. It is based on a number of things: the abilities and talents God gave us; the faith He created in us; the body He made for us; the people in our lives; the things they say to us and about us, and the ways they treat us.

Those of us who have a high self-esteem feel good about ourselves most of the time. Those of us who have a low self-esteem worry about ourselves a lot. But God has something important to say to those of us who sometimes suffer from low self-esteem.

One way to reflect upon our relationship with ourselves is to answer questions such as the following:

1. Write three adjectives which describe how you felt about yourself as a child. (You need not share these with anyone.)
2. Write three adjectives which describe how you see yourself now. (You need not share these with anyone.)
3. If you were the only person on earth, would Jesus have died for you? (See **Luke 15:3–7** if you are not sure.) Share this answer with everyone!
4. What experiences have most strongly influenced your life?
5. What things do you value most about yourself? What things which can be changed would you like to change?

If the three adjectives you listed above in number 2 were positive, you probably have a positive self-image. If they were all negative, you may have a negative self-image.

Low self-esteem makes us feel ugly and unloved. It may make us afraid to trust other people, afraid they would reject us if they knew "the real me." It makes us wonder why everyone else seems to have more talent or friends or success than we have. It may make us dislike everything about our-

selves and wish desperately we could be someone else. We may be constantly searching for abilities, possessions, or people to help us feel worthy and loved. Every person must feel that he or she has something worthwhile to share with others to be able to respect himself or herself.

Messages

Listed below are a number of statements you may have received about your looks, personality, and talents. Which ones have you heard said about you?

- ☐ You've got a good head on your shoulders.
- ☐ When will you ever grow up?
- ☐ You're just like your father (or mother).
- ☐ You're pretty (or handsome).
- ☐ You're clumsy as an ox.
- ☐ You're terrible with figures.
- ☐ Children should be seen and not heard.
- ☐ You've got what it takes.
- ☐ Your smart mouth is going to get you into trouble one of these days.
- ☐ You're a good athlete.
- ☐ You have a great laugh.
- ☐ Big boys don't cry (but girls may).
- ☐ We've had to make a lot of sacrifices for you.
- ☐ You're never going to make it in this world with that attitude.
- ☐ You're dependable; I can count on you.

What other messages about *you* do you hear a lot? Write these down on a piece of paper.

Healthy self-esteem is very important to happy and healthy adult relationships. What are the benefits of a positive self-concept? When our self-image is positive—when we feel lovable, competent and deserving of happiness—we are likely to choose friends who will nurture us. We are also likely to nurture them. We will treat our friends well and expect them to treat us well. We will have the strength to make good decisions and withstand peer pressures when we know what the crowd is doing is wrong. If we marry, we are more likely to marry someone with whom we can establish a relationship of mutual respect and support. We will be willing to meet new challenges and able to accept responsibility. We will be able to accept those things about ourselves which cannot be changed, and seek to grow in areas of weakness.

If, on the other hand, we have a negative self-image, that too will affect our life and our relationships. We are likely to choose friends based on what we hope to get from them to meet our own needs. Our fear about losing our friends may make us excessively dependent on them. We may be willing to sacrifice our principles just to stay on good terms with them.

The more we give in and go against our own values, the worse we will feel about ourselves and there is likely to be little mutual nurture in our relationships, if any. We may spend much time and energy searching for someone or something to make us feel good. When we feel insecure and needy, we will most likely establish relationships with others who are also insecure and needy. If we marry, we may choose someone who is not able to nurture our growth as a Christian person. If we don't value ourselves, the verdict is usually unanimous.

Self-esteem is *not* egotism. Egotism causes a person to live for self. Healthy self-esteem, on the other hand, provides inner strength to serve others. In order to choose wisely our friends and the person we may someday marry, we must feel that we are worthy of love; that we have special qualities to bring to a relationship; that we have the potential to grow; that our love can nurture growth in the other person.

What if our self-esteem is low? Does that mean we are doomed forever to unhappy relationships? Of course not! Sometimes our problem is that we value ourselves according to the world's standards, rather than as the unique person God made us to be. The world assigns importance to people on the basis of what they do and what they have: money, beauty, power, control over others, possessions. But these are *not* the things that make us valuable or worthy. God assigns importance to people on the basis of who they *are*—His redeemed children.

Someone has said, "A person can stand a lot if he can stand himself." Because God has forgiven us in Jesus, we can stand ourselves. Because we live under the umbrella of God's love, we have both the power and the freedom to make changes in our lives. In fact, the life of every person who belongs to Jesus has been changed! When we were baptized, we received the gift of the Holy Spirit. His power remains available for us to draw on every day of our life as Christians. Maturity enables us to unlearn old behavior and concepts; we can make decisions to set goals for new behavior.

Look back at the negative messages you checked on the messages inventory. Which one(s) reflect a person you no longer are—or want to be? What areas of your life need changes? Each day in a believer's life contains a potential situation for Christian growth. You have several options.

1. You can continue to follow the negative messages—and give up on making any changes in yourself.
2. You can resolve to no longer be the kind of person who caused that negative message—and hope for the best.
3. Because you are a Christian, you have an even better option. You can (a) recognize past sins; (b) seek forgiveness from God and those people with whom you may have had a problem; (c) forgive those people whose negative messages may have hurt you; and (d) ask for and receive God's power to grow in your Christian life.

Indeed we are "poor, sinful beings," as we confess when we worship each week. But that is *not* the last word on our condition! God has made us new in Christ Jesus! The powerful tools we have available—prayer, God's Word, Holy Communion, Christian fellowship—will help us grow!

If the Lord Is My Shepherd, Why Do I Still Feel Like a Bedraggled Sheep?

We all face bad days and hard times when our self-esteem nose-dives. At those times it might be helpful to remember some important things about yourself.

Read the following Bible references and then write in your own words what each has to say about the person you are:

- **Gen. 1:27**
- **Ps. 139:13–16**
- **1 Cor. 12:4–6**
- **Matt. 18:12–13**
- **Gal. 5:13**

You are a valuable person because God made you to be so. You are His precious child—so precious that He sacrificed His own Son for you. He can remove your poor image of yourself and give you the power to change. In Christ, God makes you a new person! He created you with unique abilities—and unique opportunities to use them. Each of us has been given talents to share with other people. God is working in the world through you every time you invest your gifts and abilities in service to others. God loved you enough to sacrifice His own Son so that you could be His person. We Christians truly have cause to celebrate the personhood God has made for us, and then re-made for us through Jesus!

1. Write a slogan which celebrates the person God made you to be. Share that slogan with at least two other people today.

2. List three strengths or abilities God has given you. For each ability listed, write one way in which you can use that gift to build a relationship with a friend or family member. Try to use each ability *every day for one week* to build your relationships.

You may wish to record your results in the following way. Create a diary page on which you list the seven days and under each day list your three abilities. At the end of every day, make a notation to show how you used those abilities during that day. Write a summary of your experience.

3. Share yourself with people around you. Practice affirming someone *twice a day for one week*. (Affirming means telling someone something you value or appreciate about him or her. Try to do this with people who are not members of this class so that your affirmation will be "honest" and not "canned".) Write a paragraph about your experience.

We love because He first loved us.
1 John 4:19

3. Nobody? Or Somebody?

Cipher in the Snow

It started with tragedy on a biting cold February morning. I was driving behind the Milford Corners bus as I did most snowy mornings on my way to school. It veered and stopped short at the hotel, which it had no business doing, and I was annoyed as I had to come to an unexpected stop. A boy lurched out of the bus, reeled, stumbled, and collapsed on the snowbank at the curb. The bus driver and I reached him at the same moment. His thin, hollow face was white even against the snow.

"He's dead," the driver whispered.

It didn't register for a minute. I glanced quickly at the scared young faces staring down at us from the school bus. "A doctor! Quick! I'll phone from the hotel . . . ."

"No use, I tell you, he's dead." The driver looked down at the boy's still form. "He never even said he felt bad," he muttered. "Just tapped me on the shoulder and said, real quiet, 'I'm sorry. I have to get off at the hotel.' That's all. Polite and apologizing like."

At school the giggling, shuffling morning noise quieted as the news went down the halls. I passed a huddle of girls. "Who was it? Who dropped dead on the way to school?" I heard them half-whisper.

"Don't know his name; some kid from Milford Corners," was the reply.

It was like that in the faculty room and the principal's office. "I'd appreciate your going out to tell the parents," the principal told me. "They haven't a phone and, anyway, somebody from school should go there in person. I'll cover your classes."

"Why me?" I asked. "Wouldn't it be better if you did it?"

"I didn't know the boy," the principal admitted levelly. "And, in last year's sophomore personalities column I note that you were listed as his favorite teacher."

I drove through the snow and cold down the bad canyon road to the Evans' place and thought about the boy, Cliff Evans. "His favorite teacher!" I thought. He hasn't spoken two words to me in two years! I could see him in my mind's eye all right, sitting back there in the last seat in my afternoon literature class. He came in the room by himself and left by himself. "Cliff Evans," I muttered to myself, "a boy who never talked." I thought a minute. "A boy who never smiled. I never saw him smile once."

The big ranch kitchen was clean and warm. I blurted out my news somehow. Mrs. Evans reached blindly toward a chair. "He never said anything about bein' ailing."

His stepfather snorted. "He ain't said nothin' about anything since I moved in here."

Mrs. Evans pushed a pan to the back of the stove and began to untie her apron. "Now hold on," her husband snapped. "I got to have breakfast before I go to town. Nothin' we can do now, anyway. If Cliff hadn't been so dumb, he'd have told us he didn't feel good."

After school I sat in the office and stared blankly at the records spread out before me. I was to close the file and write the obituary for the school paper. The almost bare sheets mocked my effort. Cliff Evans, never legally adopted by stepfather, five young half-brothers and sisters. These meager strands of information and the list of "D" grades were all the records had to offer.

Cliff Evans had silently come in the school door in the mornings and gone out the school door in the evenings, and that was all. He had never belonged to a club. He had never played on a team. He had never held an office. As far as I could tell, he had never done one happy, noisy kid thing. He had never been anybody at all.

How do you go about making a boy into a zero? The grade-school records showed me. The first and second grade teachers' annotations read, "sweet, shy child," "timid but eager." Then the third grade note had opened the attack. Some teacher had written in a good, firm hand, "Cliff won't talk. Uncooperative. Slow learner." The other academic sheep had followed with "dull," "slow-witted," "low I.Q." They became correct. The boy's I.Q. score in the ninth grade was listed at 83. But his I.Q. in the third grade had been 106. Even shy, timid, sweet children have resilience. It takes time to break them.

I stomped to the typewriter and wrote a savage report pointing out what education had done to Cliff Evans. I slapped a copy on the principal's desk and another in the sad, dog-eared file. I banged the typewriter and slammed the file and crashed the door shut, but I didn't feel much better. A little boy kept walking after me, a little boy with a peaked, pale face; a skinny body in faded jeans; and big eyes that had looked and searched for a long time and then had become veiled.

I could guess how many times he'd been chosen last to play sides in a game, how many whispered child conversations had excluded him, how many times he hadn't been asked. I could see and hear the faces and voices that said over and over, "You're a nothing, Cliff Evans."

A child is a believing creature. Cliff undoubtedly believed them. Suddenly it seemed clear to me: when finally there was nothing left at all for Cliff Evans, he collapsed on a snowbank and went away. The doctor might list "heart failure" as the cause of death, but that wouldn't change my mind.

We couldn't find 10 students in the school who had known Cliff well enough to attend the funeral as his friends. So the student body officers and a committee from the junior class went as a group to the church, being politely sad. I attended the services with them, and sat through it with a lump of cold lead in my chest and a big resolve growing through me.

I've never forgotten Cliff Evans nor that resolve. He has been my challenge year after year, class after class. I look for veiled eyes or bodies scrounged into a seat in an alien world. "Look, kids," I say silently, "I may not do anything else for you this year, but not one of you is going to come out of here a nobody. I'll work or fight to the bitter end doing battle with society and the school board, but I won't have one of you coming out of here thinking himself a zero."

Most of the time—not always, but most of the time—I've succeeded.

("Cipher in the Snow" by Jean Mizer, taken from *Student Peer Counselling Training* by Barbara B. Varenhorst. Used by permission.)

Discussion Questions

1. How did Cliff Evans become a nothing?
2. How did his family fail him? How did his school family fail him?
3. How could the cycle of rejection have been broken? How important are loving relationships?
4. What would Jesus have done with Cliff Evans? Find a Bible passage to support your answer. Who saved you from total rejection by God?
5. Think of the person you know who is most like Cliff Evans. How will you as Jesus' disciple treat that person?
6. Your relationships now are the training ground for the future. As Jesus' disciple, how will you treat the people in your own family? your school family? your church family?
7. Where will you find the power to treat others with understanding, love, and compassion?

Our relationships with others are the third kind of relationships to be explored. As the story above illustrates, our relationships with other people have tremendous impact on our lives. From the time we were born, we have had relationships with other people.

The experience of being loved must always come before the experience of loving. We cannot learn to love unless someone first loves us. We will never learn to trust others unless that fundamental human bond was established. We grow as persons, not in spite of others, but because of our relationships with other people.

God designed us, the creatures He made in His own image, to need human relationships. We must create relationships with people if we are to demonstrate love for them. We can never love "people"—we can only love individual persons. When we see the image of God in the people around us, it changes our relationships.

God created Eve because He saw it as not good for Adam to be alone. We need other people, not just so someone can save us from loneliness, but *so we will be saved from living only for ourselves!* People who are isolated cannot love—and do not fulfill God's plan for their lives. Their lives are incomplete. Wholeness is becoming a channel for God's love to reach out through us to other people.

Love began with God. It is His very being! The new life He created for us in Christ is a life of love—love for Him and love for our fellow beings. A personal relationship with Jesus Christ is the cornerstone of all other relationships; it gives meaning and purpose to every aspect of life.

Questions for Reflection

1. What are the most important relationships in your life right now?
2. How do those relationships affect your life?
3. How will these relationships change in the future?
4. What new relationships do you think you will develop in future years?

Myths, Fables, and Wrong Impressions

People who do not know God can never reach a full understanding of love. They may experience love in their lives, but they cannot know the *source* of love. God can love us only because Jesus' death paid the price for our sins. We can love God only because Jesus sacrificed His life to restore the friendship between God and man which sin had totally destroyed.

We did not go out looking for Jesus; He went out searching to find us. God knew that He would have to pay the greatest price possible—He would have to sacrifice His own Son, a part of Himself. It was the only possible way we could be brought back to Him. It was truly the most heroic deed in history. It was the only way we could truly love ourselves or other people.

We need power in order to be truly loving to other people. Our power source is God's perfect love for us in Jesus. His power comes to us through His Word and His sacraments. It is free and available for us to draw upon at any time. His love is the basis for all our caring, loving relationships.

The world around us, operating without this source of power, has many conflicting ideas about love. We all "buy" some of the myths, fables, and wrong impressions with which we are bombarded. The world of advertising is a prime example. Advertisers know we all seek loving relationships. So, what better way to sell a product? We will all have more love in our lives (they imply) if only we will use the right deodorant; drive a certain car; take up jogging—while wearing the most expensive type of shoes; change our hairstyle; buy a new brand of cologne.

The ads teach that we must *make* ourselves lovable by consuming the right products. The ads teach that it is possible to measure how lovable we are on the basis of our image, our popularity, our sex appeal. In our minds and even in our hearts, we know that these are not the basis for love. Yet it is all too easy to believe that these superficial standards and external coverings will increase our chances to be loved.

Bring to class three examples of ads or commercials which use some aspect of love to "sell" a product. What implied statement about love is made in each?

Our ideas about love are shaped by four main influences:

- The love we have experienced from God
- Our past experiences with love
- What our family and friends say and demonstrate to us about love
- What our culture and our culture's media (TV, movies, modern music, magazines, books, newspapers) say and demonstrate about love.

These influences are powerful, for we absorb them without even thinking about it. They form impressions which enter the subconscious levels of our thinking and subtly influence our behavior. For example, by the time a teen graduates from high school, he or she will have watched 18,000 hours of television, according to the National Parent Teacher

Association. If you're "average," that's more than two years of your life spent in front of the TV. Memory is not easily erased. Our subconscious stores all this input; it becomes part of our "program," where it shapes our attitudes and decisions. Whether the impressions we have stored are right or wrong, they may still influence us. Ask any child what he or she wants for Christmas, and you are likely to get a complete list of all the toys advertised on TV that are "in" this year. Unless we have a clearly defined Christ-centered concept of love, we may find ourselves "programmed" by outside influences. It seems as though people who stand for nothing fall for anything.

Most of us carry around in our minds an image of what a love relationship between a man and a woman "should" be. This image is a combination of ideas drawn from our knowledge of God's love, our past experiences, our friends and family, our culture and the media. These sources exert a strong influence which affects what we think is appropriate and acceptable for male-female relationships.

For example, would you date someone you thought was quiet but interesting if your friends thought he or she was "hopeless"? Have you ever dated someone just because he or she was attractive, or had a terrific car and lots of money—without thinking about the kind of *person* he or she is? Have you ever dated someone just to prove to your parents that you could go out with whomever you liked?

On what basis do you choose the people you date?

To understand what attitudes about love between a man and a woman you may have developed, think about the following questions.

Discussion Questions

1. What have your past experiences led you to believe about man-woman relationships? Summarize in one sentence.
2. What ideas about man-woman relationships are shown by your family? Summarize in one sentence.
3. How do your friends feel about such relationships? Summarize in one sentence.
4. Do you think your present image of man-woman relationships is realistic? Do you think it will change in the future? Is your image one on which you could base a healthy marriage? Why or why not?
5. List three ideas about man-woman relationships which you have observed in TV shows, movies, modern music, magazines, books, newspapers. Bring specific examples to class if possible.Write a sentence summarizing the attitudes toward man-woman relationships shown by each example.
6. How would the love you have experienced from God play a part in your relationships with the opposite sex?

Each of us has been exposed to an incredible variety of ideas and definitions and concepts of love. Some of them are valid; many are not. Some of them are God-pleasing; many reflect our selfish sinful natures. What we think about love will control our behavior in relationships with other people.

Our beliefs about love will affect the way we treat other people—our family, our friends, the man or woman we may someday marry. *Our beliefs about love will shape the relationships we build.* We must do much weighing and sifting to define for ourselves a healthy, realistic, Christ-centered concept of love!

The truth is that we are only lovable when God's presence gives us the power to love others. The love we have experienced from God becomes part of us. When Jesus lives in us, we have the power to overcome selfish wrong notions of love. Instead, we can rely on His power to love others as He has loved us!

And so we know and rely on the love God has for us. God is love. Whoever lives in love lives in God, and God in him.

1 John 4:16

4. God's Definition

"When I was a child, I talked like a child, I thought like a child, I reasoned like a child. When I became a man, I put childish ways behind me," said the apostle Paul (**1 Cor. 13:11**). To be able to put into practice the kind of love Paul described, we must grow to Christian maturity. How can we measure our Christian maturity? How do we know if we are loving as God wants us to love? One way is to look at some of the signs of Christian maturity.

On the scale below, rate yourself from 0 to 10 on each sign of Christian maturity listed. 0 is for childish; 10 for mature. (You need not share your rating with anyone.)

My Christian Growth

1. I can forgive others who have hurt me because I know God has forgiven me.
2. I can control my anger and settle disputes without becoming violent or destructive.
3. I think about and respect the feelings of others.
4. I can deal with frustration, discomfort, or defeat without complaining or falling apart.
5. I can stand up against the group when they are doing something wrong.
6. When I face a decision, I seek God's will through prayer and His Word.
7. I accept responsibility for my own behavior.
8. I can give up immediate pleasure for future goals.
9. I can admit my mistakes without making excuses for them.
10. I do my work conscientiously, honestly, and on time.
11. I contribute to the good of my family in a cheerful, dependable way.
12. I think about how something will affect others before I do it.
13. I can face people even after I have sinned, because I know for sure that, because of Jesus, God has forgiven me.
14. I can accept people who are different from me without putting them down.
15. I have set goals which will allow me to serve others with my life (rather than striving for money or power or possessions.)

(Adapted from *Sex Respect* by Coleen Kelly Mast, copyright 1986. Respect, Inc., P.O. Box 349, Bradley, IL 60915. Used by permission.)

Questions for Reflection

1. Look at the two statements on which your score was highest. These marks of Christian maturity which you have attained are cause for celebration. (Why not thank God for these the next time you talk with Him?!)

2. Look at the two statements on which your score was lowest. These are areas in which you need to grow.
3. On a note card or small sheet of paper, write three things you plan to do to further your growth in each of these areas of weakness. Keep these three statements posted on the mirror in your room or in another place where you will be reminded of them. Strengthen your relationship with God through your use of Word and Sacrament, pray for His power, and remind yourself of your goals. As you do, you can be sure that growth will happen!

"God is love!" the Bible tells us. Jesus, His love-in-the-flesh, gave us a clear and simple formula for love. "Love others as I have loved you." But how can we make that kind of love happen in our lives? The apostle Paul answered that question in **Gal. 2:20.** What is his answer? Write it in your own words. Paul also wrote an entire chapter to the Corinthians to answer a second question: How does love behave?

Have you ever heard the expression "the more things change, the more they stay the same"? That is certainly true for people. No matter how sophisticated we may think our culture to be, we are still subject to the same temptations and problems in our relationships which plagued Christians centuries ago. You probably discovered this when you rated your own Christian growth. The Corinthians had been playing the game of one-upmanship with each other. "My spiritual gifts are greater than your gifts," was a commonly heard refrain. Bragging, one-upmanship, and put-downs among Christians—do these happen today?

How Love Behaves

Paul lays out a clear pattern explaining how to show love. Read **1 Cor. 13,** concentrating especially on **verses 4–7.** Then make two lists of characteristics, listing what love is not—and what it is.

1. Look again at the characteristics you have listed under "Love Is Not." Then think of the people with whom you have close relationships. Which of these characteristics is the greatest temptation for you? Write a sentence about what you will do, with God's help, to work to overcome that temptation.

2. Reread the aspects of what "Love Is" which you have listed. Which of these aspects could help you strengthen one of your relationships? Write three specific ways in which you might practice that aspect of love in that relationship.

Billy Graham once said that the smallest package he ever saw was a person totally wrapped up in himself. If we truly wish to demonstrate God's love, we must wrap ourselves up in other people, not in ourselves. Growing in love is an ongoing process throughout a Christian's lifetime. We change. Our relationships change. But God's command to "love others as I have loved you" does not change. Thank God for Jesus, whose love is never self-seeking and never keeps score! Because of what He has done for us, we can grow throughout our lifetime in our ability to love others.

Grown-up Love

Our level of Christian maturity determines the kinds of relationships we are capable of having. Many of the people we loved as children we loved because of what they did for us. Some people never grow beyond this kind of "what's in it for me" relationship. Unfortunately, our self-centered, materialistic culture and our own selfish human nature seem to say that's all right.

Think again about your own attitude toward love. Do you see love as *giving* or as *getting?* Do you see relationships as something to *use* for your own welfare, or do you see them as opportunities to *nurture* the welfare of others? Is your love for other people *conditional,* based on doing (what does he or she do for me)? Or is it *unconditional,* based on being (I love that person because of who he or she is)?

These questions are not easy to answer, are they? No matter how loving we may think we are, our sinful selfishness always gets in the way. "Look out for number one," says the world—and off we Christians go to fall into the same trap.

If something no longer serves our purposes, or seems like too much trouble to fix, we throw it away. We have disposable diapers, disposable eating utensils, even disposable clothing. Use it up and throw it out, we say. What about people? Do we treat them the same way? Do we use them until we no longer need them, then throw out the relationship? Is our throw-away attitude encouraging the swelling number of disposable relationships, disposable marriages, even disposable babies?

List the five most important relationships in your life. Then look at the diagram below.

Conditional love .... Unconditional love
(using others) (giving to others)

Examine each of the five relationships you listed by writing the name of the other person in that relationship somewhere along the line. Which relationship is the most conditional? Do you need to make some changes in that relationship? Which of these relationships would you like to move farther toward the right of the line? Where would Jesus' love for you be on this line? Write His name in also.

Only God is capable of truly unconditional love. His love for us in Jesus is totally giving, totally unconditional. It gives us the power to grow, and to make our relationships more giving, less using. Unconditional love does not depend on what the other person *does*. He or she does not need to *earn* our love.

Unconditional love is *given with no strings attached.* Growing up to this kind of Christian maturity does not depend on our size or our age. It depends on our values; on our willingness and ability to truly care about others; on the strength to control our own impulses. We mature as Christians when we are nourished by the love God provides through His Word and Sacraments.

Discussion Questions

1. Read how St. Paul describes Christian maturity in **Eph. 4:14–16.** In your own words, how does Paul describe our goal as Christians?
2. Read **1 John 3:11–24.** What model are we to follow in our relationships with others? How do we follow that example?
3. Some people say marriage is a 50-50 proposition. Would such people see married love as conditional or unconditional?
4. What percentage would accurately describe God's love for us? What percentage would accurately describe the kind of love we are to give a marriage partner?

From the Greeks

The people of Jesus' day were able to think and talk about love with more accuracy than we, because their language had more words for love. Each word described a different type of relationship, so each word represented a different kind of love. When Jesus used the word *agape* to describe God's love for us, His hearers knew exactly what kind of love that was. The word itself helped them picture the kind of love Jesus wanted them to give to others.

The Greeks had three words for the kinds of love demonstrated in different intimate relationships:

1. *Phileo.* This type of love is described in **Gal. 6:10** and **1 Sam. 18:1, 3–4.** What kind of love is described? What are its characteristics? How have you experienced this kind of love? In which relationships does *phileo* play a part?

2. *Eros.* This type of love relationship is described in **Gen. 2:18–24** and **Song of Songs 2:10–13.** What kind of love relationship is described? What are its characteristics? Have you experienced this kind of love? In which relationships now or in the future would *eros* be important?

3. *Agape.* This love is described in **John 3:16** and **Rom. 5:6–8.** What kind of love is described? What are its characteristics? How have you experienced this type of love? In which relationships would you experience *agape?*

As you have probably discovered, our most important relationships will often express more than one type of love. In a loving, committed marriage, for example, how many types of love would be present? How could all three types of love work together to build that strong bond which unites husband and wife?

Only God is capable of pure *agape,* totally unconditional love, love with no limits, love with no strings attached. But His *agape,* living in us, cannot help but come through us to the people we love.

This is how we know what love is: Jesus Christ laid down His life for us. And we ought to lay down our lives for our brothers.

1 John 3:16

5. 70 Times 7

How often, when a relationship is going well, we wish we could do something to keep it just that way. But in any long-term relationship, sooner or later the other person will do or say something that angers or hurts us. Suddenly the relationship is no longer the same.

The most difficult part of maintaining relationships is being able to deal with the wrongs and hurts that occur. How we handle them determines whether the relationship dies or continues. How much are we expected to be able to forgive? And how often? Hosea came face-to-face with this painful dilemma in his life.

The Love Story of Hosea

I, Hosea, have been called the prophet of the broken heart. But I would rather be remembered as the prophet of love and hope. I am Hosea, prophet of God to Israel, my homeland.

I began my ministry during the reign of Jeroboam II. Those were prosperous years; the trading caravans brought wealth and many fine goods to our country. But the traders also brought their idols—idols my people began to serve.

My ministry has always been hard. When I began preaching that Israel would be crushed by the mighty Assyrian army if our people did not repent, my words fell on deaf ears. I knew my people were destroying themselves, selling themselves, bodies and souls, to false gods. I spoke hard words of judgment to them.

■ Read **Hosea 13:2–8.** I pleaded with them to return to the Lord.

■ Read **Hosea 6:1–3.** For 10 long years I preached. My words had no impact on their hard hearts.

Then my life changed. I met Gomer. She was a strikingly beautiful woman. Suddenly I realized how lonely I had been. There were things about her that worried me. She seemed to be so worldly, to have experienced so many things about which I knew little. And she craved expensive clothing and jewelry. But I loved her. I was certain that my love would be enough to make her happy. When I received a message from God to marry Gomer, I was overjoyed. Gomer responded to my love for her and we were married.

Love filled my days with joy and hope for the future. In our second year of marriage, our son Jezreel was born. How proud I was! But something in Gomer began to change. She no longer responded to me as she had in the early days of our marriage. Perhaps it is the new responsibilities of motherhood, I thought.

I continued to travel through the land, preaching and pleading with my people. Our daughter was born. Gomer drifted farther away from me. Now, after putting the children to bed, she would often be gone all night. When she returned, she would be haggard, rebellious, harsh with the children. I tried to reach her, but with no success. When our third child was born, my heart was broken. What I had suspected about our daughter I now *know* to be a fact about our new son. This baby was not mine.

Then Gomer left—and did not return. I became both father and mother to my three little children. I was bitter and angry. My ministry no longer seemed worthwhile. My prayers seemed empty and meaningless.

In spite of my pain, I still loved Gomer. I searched for many days until finally I found her. Her freshness and beauty were gone. She was now poor and gaunt, living in the filthy house of a disreputable man. When I begged her to return, she laughed at me. She would not listen when I tried to tell her about the children. I went home heavy-hearted.

But I couldn't erase Gomer from my mind. Finally I came up with a plan. I took all the money I had and bought her beautiful clothes and jewels. Privately I went to see her lover. He laughed at me! But I could not bear to see her so poor and worn. I would provide for her, I told him, everything she needed. Let her think they came from him. I would know she was cared for. We shook hands on the deal, and he went off to give her the beautiful things I had bought for her. I followed at a distance. I could hardly bear to see the joy with which she greeted him and his gifts.

She went inside to wash and change, and came out looking radiant in the beautiful new clothing. But when her lover reached out to embrace her, she pushed him away. "I must thank the god Baal for what he has sent me!" she said. "I will serve as a priestess at his high place."

I felt as if I had been struck down. Because of my gifts, she had deliberately chosen to serve an idol! I spent days in confusion and pain. I heard from others that Gomer had dedicated herself fully to her new life. Eagerly she prostituted her body to the worshipers of Baal. How could God let this happen, I wondered. Time passed.

Then one day I was led to go to Samaria and I found myself standing in the slave market. As I turned away, sick with disgust, I saw her—Gomer—being led to the auction block. She was naked, dirty, broken, emaciated. Her hair was matted and streaked with gray. Madness flashed in her eyes. Then I thought I heard God's voice. What could He possibly have in mind now?

The bidding began. Suddenly I heard my voice, raising each bid that was offered, until the bidding was done. She was mine.

(Adapted from a dramatic sermon by Dr. John W. Reed. Used by permission.)

Discussion Questions

1. If you were Hosea, what would you have done when you saw Gomer on the auction block?
2. Put yourself in the place of Hosea; write a paragraph to conclude the story.
3. Read **Hosea 3:1–3.** Based on this story of Hosea, how would you define the word forgiveness?
4. Tell about a time when you had to pay a high price to forgive someone. Tell about a time when someone had to pay a high price to forgive you.
5. What hurts and wrongs seem hardest to forgive?
6. How do the words of the Lord's Prayer, "Forgive us our trespasses, as we forgive those who trespass against us" apply here?
7. Why is forgiveness essential to maintaining relationships?
8. Why are you able to forgive others?

When we are hurt or angry because of someone's words or actions, our human nature tempts us to hold a grudge. We may become resentful or seek revenge against that person. Only the power of forgiveness can restore broken relationships. That power is available to the Christian through his new nature in the Spirit. Because we are forgiven, we are forgiving. As each day we seize God's forgiveness for our sins, we become more and more able to forgive others.

Forgiveness in the Christian life has three parts:

- We admit our sin.

- We receive God's forgiveness.
- We offer forgiveness to others.

How many times are we to forgive the person who sins against us? Jesus gave us the "formula" in **Matt. 18:21–22**. Jesus drew people to Him because everything about Him spoke of love. He was able to see into their souls, to understand all the guilt they were carrying, and then offer them that greatest gift, forgiveness.

The Bible records many stories of Jesus' healing. To many of these suffering persons, Jesus spoke the comforting words, "Your sins are forgiven!" **(Mark 2:3–12; Matt. 9:2–7)** First He healed their souls; then His compassion moved Him also to heal their bodies. As His forgiveness moves us to forgive others, our relationships can be healed.

What Is This Thing Called Love?

Poets have created countless word pictures of it. New songs are written every year which attempt to capture its essence. It's a word we use every day. We use it to describe our feelings for persons or objects as different as a beloved grandfather; a favorite food; a friend's new car. It is one of the most widely used verbs in the English language.

There lies the problem. What is this thing called love? How can we think clearly about the strong emotional bond in a relationship when we use the same word in so many different contexts? How can we focus clearly on the core meaning of that overused word, *love,* to describe the essence of Christian relationships?

Since love is such a prominent word in our culture, does that mean we are a loving people? A glance at newspaper headlines will quickly dispel that notion. We will discover, however, how great a need for love so many people have!

Listed below are 10 synonyms for the word love. Choose the 3 which you believe express the meaning of the word most clearly. Are there any other synonyms you would like to add?

- ☐ liking
- ☐ affection
- ☐ empathy
- ☐ devotion
- ☐ cherishing
- ☐ attraction
- ☐ sympathy
- ☐ acceptance
- ☐ desire
- ☐ attachment

Which of the words above best communicates the meaning of the word love as it is expressed in the poem below?

Rx

Love
is getting into
the other fella's shoes
and finding out
where they pinch
then doing
whatever must be done
to correct the fit.

(Pollyanna Sedziol. Used by permission)

Think for a moment about someone you love. What is going on in his or her shoes? Where do they pinch? What can you do to correct the fit?

What does the sign language symbol tell you about the word *love?*

Love in Action

If our relationships are truly to be based on love, we need to clear our minds of the many myths about love and *incorporate into our lives* some basic Christian principles of love which have been discussed in this chapter.

1. *Love is a choice, not just a feeling.* Feelings are hard to control; they come and go. Can we still love someone even if we don't "feel" loving? Because of God's love for us, we can *choose* to be loving, even when the other person is unlovable and we don't *feel* like loving. Love is a choice we make, not something

which is conditional upon what someone else does for us. Read **Acts 10:1–28.** How did Peter demonstrate this principle of love?

What is one situation in your life in which you can choose to love, even if you don't feel like it? How will you choose to love in that situation? Write your answer as a declaration: "I will . . ."

2. *Love must be demonstrated by action.* Warm, fuzzy feelings do not benefit the other person. Love must be demonstrated if the other person is to know it is there and so that he or she responds to it. Action is more important than feeling. When we *act* loving, we can restore the feeling of love.

Read **Gen. 22:1–12.** How did Abraham demonstrate this principle of love?

What is one situation in your life in which you can demonstrate love for the other person? How will you demonstrate love? Write your answer as a declaration: "I will . . ."

3. *The power of love lies in giving it to others, not in getting it from them.* We become lovable by loving (giving), rather than by straining to attract love (getting). Being loving is more important than being loved. By our own ability we cannot love others. Getting God's love gives us the power to give love to others. With His power, we can sustain relationships with others, rather than living for ourselves.

Read **Luke 7:36–50.** How did the sinful woman demonstrate this principle of Christian love?

What is one situation in your life in which you can give more love than you are giving now? How will you give more love? Write your answer as a declaration: "I will . . ."

4. *Love reaches out to the other person's needs.* It wants the very best for the one we love. It is willing to discover the other person's needs, and it cares enough to find ways to meet those needs.

Read **Luke 10:30–35.** How did the Samaritan demonstrate his love by meeting the other person's needs?

Who is someone you know who needs to feel love from someone right now? How will you reach out to that person's needs? Write your answer as a declaration: "I will . . ."

Write a prayer which you could use when you try to apply these principles of Christian love in your everyday life.

Loving relationships help us weather inevitable social and personal changes. They give us the support we need during hard times, such as job losses or transfers; adjustments to new inventions and technologies; or changes in our family roles, our communities, or our churches.

God gives us people who strengthen us to cope with personal changes beyond our control, such as illness or disability. And because joys shared are joys doubled, loving relationships enhance our good times. When we choose to give ourselves in love to others, we become for each other a mutual support system. This support makes us stronger and more able to deal with social changes effectively.

Loving relationships are also an essential part of the changes within ourselves. God works through people. Our relationships are a part of who we are. He can use a loving relationship to provide the reason we need to make a necessary change in our behavior. He gives us other people so we can feel His love for us in a tangible way—so we can believe it and experience it through the people He gives us.

When we are able to begin to love others as He does, not only for who they are but for the persons they want to become, then our relationship will nurture their growth. Such relationships will also nurture our own growth as Christian persons. Our lives thus become, under God's direction, a means He uses to bring other people into fellowship with Him.

As Erich Fromm puts it, "To love somebody is not just a strong feeling—it is a decision, it is a judgment, it is a promise."

Chapter Summary

God's love is the basis of all our relationships—with Him, with ourselves, and with others. We love Him because He first loved us. We love ourselves because we are His creation and re-creation. His love makes it possible for us to grow in our ability to love others.

God's gift of relationships gives our lives meaning and purpose. Each day of our lives, our relationships provide us with opportunities to serve others in love!

Dear children, let us not love with words or tongue but with actions and in truth.
1 John 3:18

Chapter 2

Your Family of Origin

Chapter Preview

Chapter 2 will help you answer the following questions:

- What is a family of origin?
- How does it influence the person we become?
- How does it influence our relationships?
- How does it influence the marriage relationship?

1. Where Did You Get That Script?

Aaron and Lynn had been chosen to play the two characters in a new drama. Each was given a script and the instructions, "Learn all the lines as soon as possible and begin to identify with the character you play." Both of them worked hard. When they came to the first rehearsal, they were eager to see how the play would unfold with the two of them interpreting the characters. The director gave them staging suggestions and the rehearsal began.

Aaron's character came on stage first and spoke his opening lines. Lynn entered and began the play's initial conversation. Almost immediately Aaron interrupted her: "That's not right. You're supposed to say . . . "

"What do you mean, it's not right?" Lynn retorted. "I memorized my lines exactly the way they were written in the script."

"You couldn't have! See? The script says . . . "

As Aaron and Lynn began to compare their scripts, the rehearsal came to an abrupt halt. Each had been given a different script! It was the same play, but each had a different version, with different wordings, different staging, even some different scenes. What were they to do now? How could they enact a drama if they were working from different scripts?

Each of us is likely to have had some experience trying to communicate with someone who is working from a different script. Perhaps you have heard the story of the politician who threw a sheaf of papers on the desk of his harried secretary with the instructions, "Do these immediately." The secretary immediately dropped what she was doing and began to feed the papers into the paper shredder. Just as she was finishing, the politician rushed in with the question, "Are my copies ready yet?"

No two people will ever be able to understand each other completely. Differences in age, in sex, in education, and in past experience make that impossible. "All of us are combinations of our past home lives, the personalities of our parents and dozens of others with whom we have come in contact, and accumulated learnings and traditions and values, all woven together in a unique way by our own individual gifts and genes. Morever we are constantly changing and interacting under the influence of present persons and experiences."

These differences always enrich but also complicate our relationships. Think of one or two examples of real-life problems caused by people "working from different scripts." Possible real-life examples include: a time when you and your parents were not "on the same wavelength"; a time when you and a friend had entirely different expectations about how something should be done; or a time when you thought you were communicating with someone, only to discover he or she completely misunderstood what you were trying to say.

What caused the problem?

In what way(s) was your script or expectation different from the other person's?

Was the problem resolved? How? (If not, why not?)

In chapter 1 you explored the many types of relationships you have had in the past, have now, and expect to have in the future. Many of you anticipated marriage in your future. Marriage is the most intimate of all human relationships. When a man and woman marry, they join together to form a lifelong partnership in which they will enjoy an emotional, spiritual, and physical intimacy that no other relationship can provide. Perhaps that is why about 95 percent of people marry. A loving Christian marriage is indeed a wonderful relationship.

Let's review what we already know about family relationships.

1. Who created the family?
2. For what purpose was marriage created? **(Gen. 2:18)**
3. What great gift did God share with Adam and Eve? **(Gen. 1:28)**
4. What happened to God's plan for families after the fall into sin? **(Gen. 3:16–19; 4:1–12)**
5. What new relationship did God provide for His people? **(1 Peter 1:3)**
6. How do Christians live with one another? Why are they able to live that way? **(1 Peter 1:22–23)**

If you enjoyed fairy tales about love as a child, you will remember the way many of them ended: "And they lived happily ever after." What the fairy tale didn't include was how to achieve this happily-ever-after goal! The fairy tale seemed to assume that once two people declared their love for each other, all the adjustments would take care of themselves. But we know from living in our own families that living "happily ever after" isn't as easy as it sounds. Differences among family members sometimes create serious problems in relationships.

When a young couple makes a commitment to each other in love, invariably they find themselves in the same predicament as Aaron and Lynn above. As they set out to write the drama of their lives together, they discover that each is working from a different script. In essence, the person we marry is a "foreigner." Even if he or she comes from a similar background and we have a lot in common, he or she will still come from a different family culture.

Why does this happen? Because each of us comes from a different family of origin. Sociologists use the term *family of origin* to describe *the family in which we grew up, which shaped our attitudes and values*. Our origins or beginnings as persons come from our families.

In our families we learned about life. We learned to enjoy favorite family foods; we learned how to get along with other people; and we learned to communicate in the language our family used. Our family of origin shaped most of our values; it developed our attitudes; it established the routines and rituals which are part of the fabric of our everyday lives.

Our family relationships are a part of who we are. Many of the things we learned within our families stay with us throughout our entire lives. Most likely we will pass on to our children the way in which we received love when we were growing up. The way our parents communicated with us is the way we are likely to communicate with our spouses and children. Our family of origin provides a good portion of the script we use to understand and organize our lives.

My Family Script

What type of script have you received from your family of origin? Listed below are 10 statements describing a family. Give each statement the number which most accurately describes your family.

1	2	3	4	5
Almost Never	Once in a While	Sometimes	Frequently	Almost Always

1. Family togetherness is very important.
2. Family members ask each other for help.
3. Family members consult other family members when making decisions.
4. Different persons share leadership in our family.
5. We shift household responsibilities from person to person.
6. Family members like to spend free time with each other.
7. Our family changes its way of doing things from time to time.
8. Family members feel very close to each other.
9. Rules change in our family.
10. Family members support and encourage each other.

Adapted from materials developed by PREPARE/ENRICH premarital counseling program. Permission granted by David H. Olson (www.prepare-enrich.com)

After you have examined your personal script, compare it with the scripts of your classmates. (Our purpose is not to judge our family or its members, but to explore how different family systems develop and operate.)

Discussion Questions

1. In what ways is your family similar to the families of your classmates? How is it different?
2. How might your family differ from the family of the person you may one day marry?
3. If you gave one of the statements above a 1, and

the person you planned to marry gave it a 5, what would that tell you?

4. Do you think it is possible for two people with different scripts to live in harmony with each other? What would make it possible?

The statements above have probably started you thinking about the way your family operates. Each family is unique; each has its own way of doing things. Although one way of operating is not necessarily better than another, each family creates its own system based on the people who are part of that family. Think again about the way your family functions. How do you think your family would handle each of the following situations?

- A child in the family requires major surgery.
- Your mother, who has spent many years as a homemaker-mother, gets a job.
- You want to go to college, but your parents can't afford to send you.
- Your family is planning its next vacation.
- A child in the family gets put on probation for a behavior problem at school.
- Your father is facing a possible lay-off at his job.

Families come in all varieties. Your family may be just you and a parent or guardian. It may be two parents and several children of assorted ages. Your family may include a grandparent or other relative who lives in your home. You may be part of an extended family, with grandparents, uncles and aunts, and cousins who have influenced your life. Whatever type of family you have, it provides a portion of the script you have been using to govern your life.

Think again of Aaron and Lynn. Imagine them as a young couple setting out on a lifetime together. Each will have favorite foods—but they may be entirely different foods. Each will have learned how to relate to others—but they may have learned entirely different ways of doing so. Each will have developed values and attitudes which determine how hard they work; how they spend their time; how they use their money; what goals are important to them. But their values and attitudes about each of these important questions may be entirely *different*.

Differences in background can provide lively and interesting variety in the marrriage relationship. But they can also be potential sources for some very hard-to-resolve conflicts. Will they be able to stage a successful production when each is working with a different script?

Each family has a distinct personality and a unique family system. If you were to describe the personality of your family of origin, you would need to examine characteristics such as the following: spiritual life; work and interests; goals and priorities; problems; fun times; types of individuals in the family unit; places and names; rules and systems; celebrations. The family culture which we inherited has had a powerful influence on our lives.

Our family was our training ground for relationships with *God, ourselves,* and *other people.*Many of us established and grew in our relationship with God by the power of the Holy Spirit through our family of origin. Some of us may first have come to know God through others if our own family did not have a relationship with God, but our family's attitudes have probably still influenced us.

Our relationship with ourselves also had its origins in our families and personal histories. These influenced the way we feel about ourselves and about life. The love and acceptance we received from our family, together with the forgiveness we have received from God, played a large part in the development of our self-esteem, as we saw in chapter 1.

Our family of origin also gave us our first experiences in relationships with others. As family members cared for each other's needs and reached out to care for people outside the family, we learned to do so also. If we grew up in a home with healthy family relationships, we learned how to establish such relationships in our lives. Our home is where we first learned to communicate and respect others.

From observing our parents, we learned about adults and how they function. We developed many of our ideas about man-woman relationships, including marriage. From brothers, sisters, and other relatives we learned about getting along with other people. Many of the things we learned we will carry on to our own family in the future. Our children will carry on what we teach to them, teaching it to our grandchildren. Each family carries a great responsibility to the future!

Construct a "family tree" based on your family of origin in the following way:

1. Under the heading *My Family of Origin,* describe at least three things you think are most significant about your family. What is something you would like to retain from your family of origin in your own family if you marry? What is one thing you might wish to change? (You need not share those things which are personal and private. However, since our families do shape us, we can learn a lot about ourselves by reflecting about our families.)

2. Ask your parents or guardians about *their* families of origin. Under the heading *My Parents' Families of Origin* describe at least three things your parents feel are significant about the families in which they grew up. What things did they retain from their families of origin? What things did they change? Why? (You may choose to describe the family of origin of each of your parents separately.)

3. If you are able to, confer with as many of your four grandparents as possible, and follow the same procedure.

Summarize what you have learned from your family tree in a concluding paragraph. How has God blessed you through your family?

Know therefore that the Lord your God is God; He is the faithful God, keeping His covenant of love to a thousand generations of those who love Him and keep His commands.

Deut. 7:9

2. Building on the Past

Have you ever seen a little boy who walked just like his daddy walked and talked just like his daddy talked? Do you know a little girl who loves to dress up in her mommy's high-heeled shoes, wear her mommy's dangling earrings, or smell of her mommy's perfume? As little children, we repeated the behavior of our parents because it was the most natural to us. We believed that all dads and moms were—or should have been—like ours. As little children, we "took the course" about life which our families gave us and lived the way in which we were taught.

As we grew up, we began to observe that all families were not like ours. While we were no doubt envious of some families, perhaps other families made us thankful for our own.

As we reach adulthood, we face choices. Will we keep the patterns we have learned? Or do we wish to change some of those patterns and find other ways of doing things?

Questions for Reflection

1. What attitudes does your family have about money?
2. How do your parents feel about school and education?
3. How does your family deal with sickness?
4. How are discussions about sex handled in your family?
5. How does your family feel about the role of women? The role of men?
6. When things go wrong in your family, how are family members most likely to react?
7. What does your family do for fun?
8. Describe *your role* in your family in two sentences or less (as son/daughter, brother/sister, oldest/middle/youngest, good student/good athlete, most responsible/ most fun-loving, etc.).
9. How important is Christian faith and life-style in your family?

Every family has its own culture or personality. Evaluating our family culture allows us to see the strengths which are there, and to build on them. It may also point up weaknesses, things we will desire to change in our own relationships as we grow in Christian living.

Every family also has a system, a way of operating, with roles for each person in the family. There are rules and behavior patterns for how things are to be done. These include all aspects of the give-and-take which are part of family relationships. The rules may be spoken or unspoken. Either way, you know what the family expects.

My Family System

Every family has rules or expectations about the following:

1. Showing love and affection. How are love and affection shown in your family? How do your parents (include step-parents or guardians, if they are part of your family) demonstrate love toward each other? How do they show love to you? Is affection shown openly (hugs, kisses, "I love you") or is it mostly implied? Do you feel loved by your family?

2. Behavior. What is your family's attitude toward work? How do you know what behavior is acceptable and what is not? What kind of discipline is used in your family? Who is responsible for disciplining? Is discipline loving or harsh? Is your family strict? permissive? in between? Is your independence encouraged or discouraged?

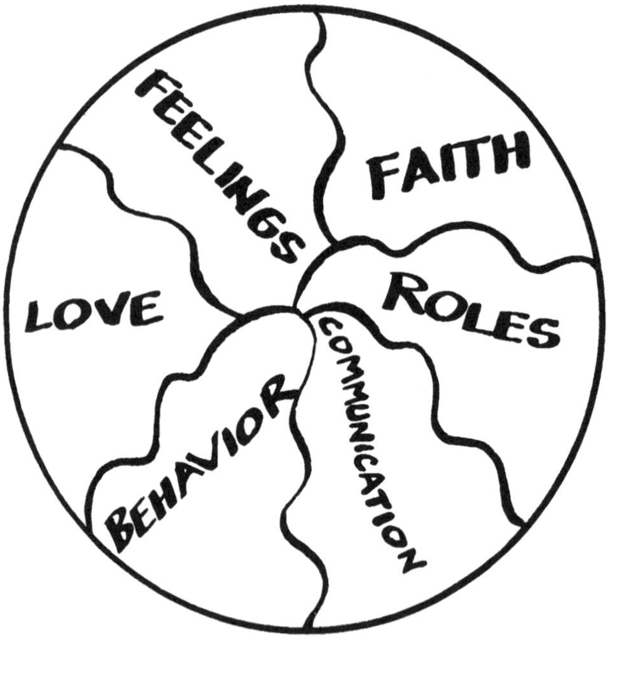

3. Communication. How much do family members share ideas or feelings? Do you talk a lot? Is conversation usually limited to everyday concerns about living, or do you spend time talking about faith, goals, attitudes, and the future? How are disagreements handled?

4. Feelings. Can you express both positive and negative feelings in your family? How are emotions such as anger, fear, or sorrow expressed? Is there a difference in the ways males and females express their feelings? How are discussions about sex handled? Are bad feelings buried or allowed in the open?

5. Roles. How are children treated in the family? How are adults treated? What is the mother's role? the father's role? Who has the most authority in the family? the most responsibility? Who makes most of the decisions? How are decisions about money handled? Is your family usually authoritarian or democratic.

6. Religious faith. What type of relationship with God do the members of your family have? How does your family talk about God and spiritual concerns? Do family members pray together? share their faith? build each other up?

(Adapted from *Newly Married and Before* by Wayne Rickerson. Used with permission. © 1985 David C. Cook Publishing Co.)

After you have thought through the above questions about your family system, write each of the six headings below across a sheet of paper: *Love, Behavior, Communication, Feelings, Roles, Faith.*

1. Under each heading, write three words or phrases which sum up your family's system for that category. Under the heading *love,* for example, you might write words or phrases like the following: parents love each other; hugs and kisses when I was little, but few now; I know they care.

2. Circle those words or phrases which describe things you will want to keep when you establish your own family in the future.

3. Look at those words which were not circled. Which two would you most like to change in the future? Write a sentence telling how you would make those changes, either in your family of origin now or in your own family in the future.

If you marry and establish your own family, you will marry not only a person. You will also "marry" a family of origin. That person will bring to your relationship all the attitudes and values which he or she learned from a family of origin. Your partner's personal history is part of him or her—so it will become part of your relationship. You will bring with you all the attitudes and values you learned from your family as well.

Both you and your partner will also bring a set of "built-in" relationships. You will each have to forge new relationships with each other's parents, brothers and sisters, relatives and friends. Partners who get to know each other's families well before marriage have a great advantage, for they have already begun to understand the culture, customs, and language of their partner.

Discussion Questions

1. How can two people who come from very different family backgrounds handle these differences?
2. What are two things you could do now, with God's help, to make it possible for you to someday establish with your spouse a happy family?
3. What are two things you would want to do when you are preparing to make a marriage commitment?

Together with the other members of your class, choose a TV show which is based upon family life and which most class members would be able to watch. Using the six family characteristics listed above, describe the TV family's method of dealing with each characteristic. Then write a paragraph (or more), contrasting and comparing the TV show family's six characteristics with your own ideal of how you would like your family to be someday.

May the God who gives endurance and encouragement give you a spirit of unity among yourselves as you follow Christ Jesus, so that with one heart and mouth you may glorify the God and Father of our Lord Jesus Christ.
Rom. 15:5–6

3. The Family Circle

Examining all these aspects of our family life is bound to uncover some feelings that might be hard to cope with. Though nearly all parents love their children, want the best for them, and are willing to make sacrifices for them, we know that some families are happier than others. Some of us have had easy, carefree childhoods while others have had to deal with disappointment and pain from the time they were very young. We may have both positive and negative feelings about our families.

These feelings are the natural reactions to the things that have happened to us and to our families. The sinfulness that created suffering in the family of Adam and Eve is part of our families, too. Jesus' redemption was necessary in order for these sins to be forgiven.

How do we deal with our feelings when sin creates pain and trouble in our families? The feelings in themselves do not necessarily destroy relationships. It is what we *do* about our feelings that has consequences for our relationships. We cannot control our feelings. But we can control what we do about them. With God's power at work in us, we can control *how we act upon our feelings*.

We all know families who have suffered the pain of divorce; the death of a loved one; the bitter sorrow of a son or daughter wasting his life. Perhaps you suffer from low self-esteem partly because of things that happened in your family. Maybe you have only one parent, or only one active parent; you may never have a strong mother or father figure in your life. Perhaps someone has hurt you as deeply as Gomer grieved Hosea.

What should we do with the hurt and anger we feel? What do we do about those feelings?

Sometimes we are able to forgive and go on with our relationships as before. Some problems resolve themselves over time. But most families encounter some conflicts which create bad feelings, some of which may last a long time. We can choose to handle these feelings in *destructive* ways—and live with the consequences. Or we can seek God's power to handle problems and bad feelings in *constructive* ways, ways which build up relationships rather than tear them down.

What are some *destructive* ways to handle problems and deal with our feelings of anger or hurt?

1. We can *bury our feelings* deep inside—and hope they will go away. The problem with this reaction is that our anger and hurt go into a memory bank that never forgets—where they usually lead to resentment. If the feelings continue to build within us, sooner or later they will affect our lives. We may become sick, either emotionally or physically. We may lose our self-control over a trivial incident. We will have to continue to live with the feelings because the problem has never been dealt with, and therefore remains unresolved.

2. We can *seek revenge* if we "keep score." Rather than attack the problem, we may attack the person and attempt to get back at him or her for the pain we are feeling. This may make us feel better for awhile, but it will destroy the relationship, and it cannot resolve the issue that caused the problem in the first place.

3. We may try to *escape* our feelings, to block them out through various means, including alcohol, drugs, or other destructive behavior. Since we are seeking to escape the problem, rather than seeking to resolve it, this approach will bring no satisfying results either.

4. We may *take it out on others*. We have all seen cartoons similar to the one which shows a man, who has had a fight with his wife, stomping out, kicking the dog, and yelling at the kid who left his bike in the driveway. Obviously, this approach does not resolve the problem. Instead it usually makes us feel worse about ourselves.

Do you recognize any of these destructive behaviors from experiences with others? In yourself?

Are there better ways to deal with problems and bad feelings? What methods can help us to maintain or rebuild our relationships with other people? What are some *constructive* ways to handle problems and deal with our anger and hurt?

1. We can *share our feelings* with the other person by expressing them in a caring way. When we make the effort to explain our feelings and the reason why we feel as we do, we are creating an opportunity for understanding. We are opening a window and allowing the other person a glimpse of what is going on inside us. When we do this with humility and honesty, admitting that we too contributed to the problem, we open the door to empathy.

Empathy allows each person to feel some of what the other person is feeling. (Is there ever a conflict between two people in which we don't share *some* responsibility?) Sharing our feelings is the only method which will increase understanding between people. It thus allows the relationship to deepen and continue. This is the only way forgiveness can be offered and received. It is the only way a problem can finally and truly be resolved. If you are coming to worship God, Jesus said, and remember that your brother has something against you, **"first go and be reconciled to your brother; then come and offer your gift" (Matt. 5:23–24).**

2. We can *pray* and share our feelings with God. Sometimes we may simply not be able to share our feelings with the other person—but we need to share them with someone. God invites us to bring our burdens to Him. **"Come to Me, all you who are weary**

and burdened, and I will give you rest" (Matt. 11:28). Sometimes we may not know how to go about solving a problem. When we turn it over to Him, we are putting ourselves in the hands of a God who was willing to sacrifice His own Son for us!

3. We can *talk it over with a friend.* The listening ear of a friend may provide the outlet we need to unburden some of our feelings. Often when we talk things over with a friend, we obtain clearer insights into what we could do to resolve the problem. **"A friend loves at all times, and a brother is born for adversity" (Prov. 17:17).**

4. We can *find an outlet.* If we are dealing with a problem that cannot be resolved easily, at least not now, we may be able to cope much more easily if we expend all that anger and energy in exercise, in tackling a project we've been putting off, in helping someone who needs help. After our anger has passed, we may feel refreshed enough to be able to cope with the situation.

Many people spend much time and energy trying to change things which cannot be changed. We cannot change other people, for example. (The only person we can change is ourselves—and we need God's power to accomplish this.) We cannot change the socioeconomic status of our family. We cannot change the past history of our family members. We cannot plan to change the lifelong habits of another person. If we try to change any of these things, we are likely to end up frustrated and bitter. But most of us can identify some things we *can* change in our families.

If we concentrate our efforts on changing those things which can and should be changed (including ourselves), with God's help, our efforts may bring results. Chapter 7 will provide further insights into effective ways to resolve conflicts.

Questions for Reflection

Think of a problem that has occurred recently in your family.

1. Which of the methods listed above have you used thus far to deal with the problem? What results have you had?
2. What new approaches could you try, based on what you have just read?
3. How often does your family use a Christian approach in handling family conflicts?
4. Where do you see a need for forgiveness in your family?

Discussion Questions

1. How can Christian families resolve family problems in ways different from non-Christians?
2. Why is it hard to forgive? What do we gain or lose when we forgive?
3. Why is it hard to ask for forgiveness from a family member? Why are we able to forgive?
4. What promise have we received from God? See **Matt. 9:2.** On days when you feel confused about the problems and frustrations of family living, the Serenity Prayer might help you:

   God, grant me the serenity to accept the
   things I cannot change,
   the courage to change the things I can,
   and the wisdom to know the difference.

"Bear with each other," St. Paul says, **"and forgive whatever grievances you may have against one another. Forgive as the Lord forgave you" (Col. 3:13).** Just as God's forgiveness offers us new possibilities and hope in our lives, so forgiving each other offers new hope and possibilities for family life together. As St. Peter reminds us, **"Love covers cover a multitude of sins" (1 Peter 4:8).**

From the first family, which consisted of Adam and Eve and Cain and Abel, to the present, families have been under pressure. The stresses on families are especially great today. Think for a moment about problems faced by your family and other families you know. List the three greatest stresses on families, as you see them.

The family you may one day create will face stresses also. For the first time in the history of the United States, the "traditional" nuclear family of a mother, a father, and one or more children is no longer in the majority. In fact, we have had to create new words to describe the many kinds of family relationships that exist. We have single parent families; blended families; commuter families; families whose members may live apart from each other, and many other types of families.

Economic pressures have played a part in creating family stresses. Other problems include teenage pregnancies; no-fault divorce; selfishness and greed; and the "anything goes" philosophy of the world in which we live.

Many aspects of our society do not always reward nurturing parents or families. Neither does it always reward self*less*ness and sacrifices made out of love for others.

If the family is to be the school for love, the place where God's love comes through us to those with whom we live, the place where children are nurtured and valued as they are prepared for healthy adulthood, then we Christians must do everything we can to build up and strengthen our families! We Christians have God's plan for building nurturing families.

Look up the following Bible references. What does God's Word tell us about families?

1. **Ps. 68:6**
2. **1 Tim. 5:8**
3. **Prov. 3:33**
4. **Deut. 6:5–7**
5. **Eph. 2:1–10**
6. **1 John 1:8–9**

Since our society does not nurture family relationships as God intended, we in the Christian community have a special calling to families. Members of the Christian community must support each other when families do not support each other. In addition to our families of origin, we are also members of a school family and of God's family, the church. In each of these settings, we can be "family" to someone whose own family is not able or not willing to provide what he or she needs.

Questions for Reflection

1. What is one thing you could do to build up a member of your family?
2. What is one thing you could do to build up a member of your school family?

Discussion Questions

1. What are some things you can do in your school family to support Christian families?
2. What are some things your church is doing now to support families? (If you are not aware of anything, ask your pastor or a leader in your church about it.)
3. What are some things we Christians need to be doing to help families in need?
4. Imagine yourself as a parent sometime in the future. If your family has problems, where will you go for help?

Chapter Summary

Our family of origin has an important role in shaping our values and attitudes. Each family is unique and has its own culture and operating system. When two people marry, they will have to learn to live with someone who comes from a different family culture and system.Our relationship with God does not exist in a vacuum. When God created human beings, He placed us in families. These family relationships touch all aspects of our lives and influence our relationships with others. Every family has strengths and weaknesses. In every family, we need forgiveness both from God and from other family members. Because God has forgiven us, Christians have the power to forgive each other and to restore and maintain loving relationships. To quote Jesus, **"Freely you have received, freely give!" (Matt. 10:8).**

Be kind and compassionate to one another, forgiving each other, just as in Christ God forgave you.

Eph. 4:32

Chapter 3

On Your Own

Chapter Preview

Chapter 3 will help you answer the following questions:

- Can a Christian live a happy, fulfilling life without being married?
- What skills and attitudes are necessary to live a satisfying, God-pleasing single life?
- How does a single person meet his or her needs for fulfilling relationships and for love?

1. A Table for One

Time: the Future.

You've had a demanding day on the job. You had to give a major presentation and iron out a problem with several other employees, in addition to all your usual responsibilities. You've decided to treat yourself to dinner at a fine restaurant you heard about recently.

You're already wearing your best suit, so after a quick check in the mirror you're ready for a leisurely meal. As you enter the restaurant, you notice that it's nearly full. Most of the tables nearby are occupied by chattering groups of people. A few have romantic couples who seem more interested in each other than in the food before them.

You approach the head waiter. "I'd like a table for one, please."

■ Where in the restaurant would you expect to be seated?

■ What kind of service would you expect to receive?

■ How would you feel if yours was the only single-person table in the restaurant?

In chapter 2 we explored family relationships. Our families truly are a special gift from God. Many of the things we learned from our families will remain with us, even as we establish an independent life. However, as we grow up and become independent, we begin to separate from our family of origin. Some of us will marry and create our own families. Some of us will not. Most of us will spend at least part of our life as a single adult.

Listed below are statements about single adults. Tell whether they are true or false.

1. Nearly half of all Americans over 18 are single.
2. More women than men are single.
3. Single adults over 18 outnumber married couples in America.
4. On the average, wives outlive husbands by almost eight years.
5. Women who live alone are generally happier than men who do so.

The growing number of single adults has changed our society in many ways. Statistics show that single adults are the fastest-growing segment of our society. Eleven percent of American adults now live alone. One-person households account for 24 percent of all households. Singles over 18 presently number about 46 percent of the total adult population in our country. Some people welcome the solitude and freedom that a single person often enjoys. Others, accustomed to the noise and activity of family life, find living alone a difficult adjustment. Many adults were not prepared for life as a single person.

Some adults remain single by choice. Others lose a spouse through death or divorce. As the average age for marriage has gone up, many young people have spent at least some years as a single person. And because women can expect to outlive men, many once-married women (and smaller numbers of men) must suddenly confront single life and cope with an entirely different pattern of life than they may have expected. Understanding the single life-style, then, has great importance for us as Christians. Many of us will spend at least a part of our lifetime as a single person. We need to know how to live a Christ-centered life whether we will live as a single person or marry someday. We will need to understand the needs and life-styles of single persons to minister effectively to each other as Christians.

To understand how various life-styles differ from each other, answer the following questions:

1. What are the advantages of living as a single person? What are the disadvantages?
2. What are the advantages of living as a married person? What are the disadvantages?
3. How would each of the activities listed below differ if you were single instead of in a family?
   - Moving into a third-floor apartment
   - Celebrating Christmas
   - Cooking dinner
   - Having your car break down
   - Planning for retirement

Facts or Misconceptions?

Which of these statements do you believe are generally true? Which are generally false?

1. Singles and marrieds have little in common.
2. All singles want to be married.
3. Singles have fewer financial worries than married persons.
4. Since they have fewer responsibilities, single persons have more potential than married people for service to the church.
5. God approves of singleness.
6. Married people are never lonely.
7. Single parents in our society have more freedom and fun than married parents.
8. The rapid rise in the singles population is detrimental to the church.
9. Couples are better "prospects" to join the church than are singles.
10. Singleness has been accepted as an appropriate way to live.

Value to God

1. Though the number of single persons has greatly increased in just the past generation, some people still have the attitude that a single person is somehow incomplete. Which of the following terms have you heard used to describe single persons? Which terms are derogatory and express a negative attitude toward single persons?

- old maid
- eligible bachelor
- widow
- swinger
- divorcee
- little old lady
- never married
- unclaimed treasure

2. What other similar expressions have you heard?

3. If you were a single adult in your early thirties, how would you answer the question, "How come a nice young man (or woman) like you isn't married?"

4. The spirit of **Col. 3:11** would allow us to add "married or single" to the contrasts mentioned there. What do Paul's words say to all of us—what has happened to *all* Christians?

Here there is no Greek or Jew, circumcised or uncircumcised, barbarian, Scythian, slave or free, but Christ is all, and is in all.

Col. 3:11

2. Where Am I Going? How Do I Get There?

Life Goals

As you approach independent adulthood, you have probably been giving thought to goals for your life. Listed below are some possible life goals. Which are most important to you? Rank them

1 for the very important;
2 for the somewhat important;
3 for the not important.

Rank what is really important to you, not what you think other people expect your answer to be.

_____ accomplishment in education
_____ a successful, fulfilling career
_____ self-acceptance
_____ emotional stability—peace of mind
_____ a fulfilling, satisfying marriage
_____ material possessions (house, car, vacations, etc.)
_____ an intimate relationship with a special person
_____ involvement in social concerns—helping to make my community or the world a better place
_____ sexual fulfillment
_____ a happy family with children someday
_____ openness to change
_____ being admired and respected in the community
_____ growing in my Christian faith
_____ having many friends

A clear focus on our life goals helps give us a sense of direction. When we have clearly defined goals, we know where to invest our time and energy. Many people find it difficult to know what is really important. They have not learned what to put first in their lives.

Whether we live all or parts of our adult lives as single persons or married, each of us confronts basic and universal questions when we become adults:

- Whom or what shall I serve?
- What shall I do with my life?
- With whom shall I share my life?

Think about these questions.

1. For a Christian, which question will always be answered in the same way?

2. The other questions may have different answers at different times in our lives. How do you find answers to these questions? Write out a Bible passage that would provide guidance for you when you are wrestling with these questions.

Direction for Life

God's Word provides answers to life's difficult questions. There God gives direction to our lives.

Out of His great love for us God has provided for us the way to find true joy and purpose in living. Read each word from God below and answer the questions that follow.

Mark 8:34–38—Does it matter what kind of goals a Christian chooses for his or her life? Explain your answer.

Matt. 6:33—Jesus says that our first priority should be to ____________.

1 Cor. 6:19–20—Why do we serve God? What Source of power lives within us?

Matt. 6:24—What is likely to happen if we try to "fit God in" among our other goals, but do not put Him first?

1 Peter 2:9–12—To whom do we belong? Why—what happened to cause such a situation? What is the purpose of our life?

Having heard God's Word for you, what changes might you want to make in your original ranking of life goals above? Where will you find the power to keep your priorities straight?

How could you use the passages above to help people you know in the following situations?

1. A single person you know loves money a lot and has chosen to remain single so she can use all her money for herself.

2. A single person you know avoids commitment to another person because he enjoys the sinful aspects of life as a "swinger."

3. A married person you know judges single persons as sinful and incomplete, and is always trying to push them toward marriage.

Write a prayer that would help you or any person who is struggling to define goals for his or her life. Keep that prayer in your notebook or another accessible place and use it on a regular basis during this school year. Perhaps your class might wish to collect the prayers to copy and exchange as you support and encourage one another to choose Christ-centered life goals.

You are a chosen people, a royal priesthood, a holy nation, a people belonging to God, that you may declare the praises of Him who called you out of darkness into His wonderful light. Once you were not a people, but now you are the people of God; once you had not received mercy, but now you have received mercy.

1 Peter 2:9–10

3. Universal Needs

The Mate Wait Game

Some single people have not learned how to lead a productive, fulfilling life on their own. Some spend years "on hold," waiting to find the right person who will rescue them from their solitary state and create a "happily ever after" life for them.

Imagine for a moment that you are a single person over the age of 25. Which of the following statements would be a likely reflection of your attitude toward your life-style?

- It's silly to decorate my apartment attractively; I might get married and move.
- I don't need a long-range financial plan; I can always take care of that in the future.
- Married couples work more effectively in church, so I won't get involved.
- I will feel better about myself when I find a marriage partner.
- What's wrong with partying? I don't have any responsibilities.

Living "on hold" is usually a waste of both time and talents. When Jesus said, **"I have come that they may have life, and have it to the full" (John 10:10),** He was describing the potential He provides for every type of person, including single and married people. Whatever our life-style, He surrounds us with His love and forgiveness and with opportunities to glorify Him by serving others.

Universal Needs

Each one of us, regardless of the life-style we choose, has the same human and spiritual needs. Of course we need the basic necessities of food and shelter. But because God created human beings to be unique, we have uniquely human needs for those things that will make life meaningful and satisfying. *We need . . .*

■ **Love.** We need to love others and to be loved by them in return. We need to know someone cares about us and that we are important to someone else.

■ **Self-esteem.** We need to value and love our own selves, to recognize we are unique persons, and to feel that we are worthwhile human beings.

■ **Community.** We need to feel we belong somewhere, that we are part of some kind of community.

■ **Purpose.** We need to feel that our lives have meaning and purpose, that we are growing in life and love, and that the person we are has a reason for being.

No matter how many different roles we have in our lives, or how many changes we will meet, these needs remain. Depending on the life-style we have, however, we might meet these needs in different ways. Single persons may meet some of these needs in ways different from married persons.

Choosing a Life-style

Deliberately choosing a single life-style is a relatively recent phenomenon. Throughout history certain religious orders have always offered special opportunities for a celibate life of service to God and others. But only in the past generation has the number of single persons grown so rapidly. A number of social factors have caused these changes: lower birth rates, high divorce rates, longer lives, later marriages. These changes have affected people's lives in many ways.

Our society is still adjusting to this change. As a result, many single persons are deprived of the traditional support system that has helped people during times of change or difficulty. Single persons often lack the extended family living nearby, with its many built-in relationships. They may have few or no familiar neighbors to help with emergencies or with whom to just chitchat. In many cases they will not have the variety of social opportunities that churches or business-related groups offer to couples. Single parents may find the heavy responsibilities they carry almost overwhelming. Growing numbers of elderly single people often feel left out of the mainstream of life.

Does that mean the single person must lead a lonely, unsatisfying life? Of course not! A single person may experience as much love, joy, and satisfaction in life as a married person. Single persons may lead *more* fulfilling lives. The richness and fullness of a person's life depends upon the presence of God in his or her life and upon fulfilling personal relationships. Someone has said that people can endure almost anything if they do not have to carry their burdens alone. God's love binds us to Him and to other people.

1. Identify three people in your community who face problems of loneliness, lack of support, etc. Without naming the individuals, describe their problems. Determine ways you might help each of these people on your own or through your class, school, or congregation. How can the love of Jesus flow through you?

2. Think again of the universal needs listed earlier, and the ways people would meet those needs in their lives. First of all, think of a married person.

■ What is the the married Christian's most important goal in life? (Refer back to **1 Peter 2:9–12** if you are not sure.)

■ If you marry in the future, what part would your marriage play in meeting your needs for

- love?
- self-esteem?
- community?
- purpose in your life?

■ What needs would the marriage relationship not be able to meet completely?

3. Now think about the needs of a person who does not marry.

■ What is the single Christian's most important goal in life? (Refer back to **1 Peter 2:9–12** if you are not sure.)

■ If you live as a single person, how would you meet your needs for

- love?
- self-esteem?
- community?
- purpose in your life?

■ How would a single person meet some of these needs in ways different from a married person?

4. Though we may know all about universal needs and may be able to identify them easily, we still feel unloved at times. Sometimes we feel helpless and hopeless in the face of our needs. How do we handle ourselves during those times? Do we go off and brood? feel sorry for ourselves? get angry that life is unfair? blame God?

Brainstorm this with your class: What are some things you can do when you don't feel loved

- by God?
- by family?
- by friends?

Solitary? Or Lonely?

Each of us will spend some time in our life being alone. A single person is likely to spend more time alone than a married person, but each of us can learn to use time alone well. To many people the word *alone* implies loneliness. But the words have different meanings.

1. What does the word *alone* mean to you? How is being alone different from being lonely? Tell about a time when you felt lonely even though you were in a crowd.

2. How do you feel about being alone? Which statements below apply to you? When I am alone I

- feel lonely;
- use that time for reflection;
- realize I can't handle it;
- get busy to keep my mind off being alone.

3. What are some effective ways you have discovered to get benefits from time alone? Maybe you enjoy being alone at times—so much so that you sometimes plan ways to be alone. If so, how do you arrange to be alone?

4. How do you know you are never really alone? Which promises of God keep you from being lonely? Share them with your classmates.

Loneliness is not related to the number of people around us or to the place we are. You can feel very lonely in the midst of a group of people if you feel no one cares about *you.*

Loneliness is a problem of our time for several reasons. People frequently move away from family and friends. Families are smaller—and busier. Divorces and separations occur more often than a generation ago. Lonely people often turn on the TV as soon as they come in the door to avoid the silences. They may frequently go to shopping malls or other places with lots of people. They may run ads in personal columns to meet people.

Our loneliness (or lack of it) really depends upon how close we feel to God, how we feel about ourselves, and how satisfying our relationships with other people are. The Christian who has God for his or her companion and thereby receives the power to reach out in love to others may find both blessings and opportunities from being alone.

A Full Life

Though it may seem contradictory, building a full life for yourself as a single can contribute a good foundation should you marry.

1. What are some things you would learn from a single life-style that would prepare you to establish a good marriage?

2. What are some habits from a single life-style that you might need to change if you marry?

3. Interview a single person 25 or older whom you admire. Ask him or her to share with you some of his or her experiences of living as a single person. If the person is comfortable answering some questions, you might ask the following:

- How does the single life-style affect your relationship with God?
- How do you meet needs to love and be loved?
- How do you meet needs to belong to a community?
- What purposes or goals do you have for life?
- What do you do with time alone?
- What actions by others in God's church help you feel part of the body of Christ?

[Jesus said,] "I have come that they may have life, and have it to the full. I am the Good Shepherd. The Good Shepherd lays down His life for the sheep. . . . I will not leave you as orphans; I will come to you."

John 10:10b–11; 14:18

4. The Priceless Gift of Friendship

You met Ben the first day of your part-time job. The two of you hit it off and enjoyed working together. Though you didn't get together outside of work, you enjoyed kidding around together. Several months later Ben no longer comes to work, but no one knows why. You begin to ask around. Several people say he's sick. One says he's in the hospital. You hear a rumor that Ben was arrested for drunk driving after being involved in a near-fatal accident.

Nearly a month goes by. Then one evening, just as you are about to punch out, Ben appears.

- What will you say?
- What will you do?
- Has an awkward situation ever developed in any of your friendships? What did you do? Share your experience if you are comfortable doing so.

In chapter 1 we discovered the many types of relationships that are part of our life. Family relationships are important in many ways, as we learned in chapter 2. Friendships are vitally important relationships as well. Friendships outside the family circle are especially important for most single persons.

For people who have few family relationships or who live far away from family members, friendships may serve many of the same purposes as family relationships. Friends may *become* "family" as they support and nurture each other through good times and bad. Friends can be a lifeline to someone who is struggling to recover from illness, to one facing the pain of loss due to death or divorce, or to one coping with an unexpected problem.

A well-balanced life needs a variety of relationships. No one person can fulfill all our needs for relationship, no matter how much we love that person or that person loves us. Even a marriage partner whom we deeply love cannot meet all our needs. We need different kinds of people for different relationships.

Listed below are several statements about friendship. Tell whether you *agree* or *disagree* with them.

_____ It is easy to be a friend.
_____ I don't need friends for me to handle my life.
_____ Women generally have more and deeper friendships than do men.
_____ A friend should always be ready with good advice.
_____ Friendships with members of the opposite sex are easier to maintain than friendships with my own sex.

Friendships in My Life

Think for a moment of the role friendship plays in your life now, and what part it may play in the future.

1. (For reflection.) What does friendship mean to you? How important do you think it is to develop and maintain friendships?

2. (For reflection.) Did you choose your friends or did they become your friends by accident?

3. (For reflection.) In what ways do you show friendship?

4. In what ways is Christian friendship different from friendships among non-Christians?

5. Which type of friendship (Christian or non-Christian) provides the greatest support during times of trouble? Why?

6. Which type of friendship best nurtures your total growth? Why?

7. How does the change described in **Eph. 2:3–5** affect your friendships?

8. How do we build friendships that will nurture our growth, both as Christians and as persons? How can we develop relationships with friends who will support us during times of trouble and rejoice with us during good times?

9. Which three qualities on Varenhorst's list do you think are most important? Did she miss some important qualities? If so, what are they?

10. Think of someone you know who is a good friend to you or others. Which of these qualities does he or she possess?

11. God empowers *you* to give this priceless gift of friendship to people around you! What qualities listed above do you have that would make you a good friend? (You need not share your answers with anyone unless you wish to.)

12. Which qualities do you need to develop further? Choose two of these qualities and write two statements showing how you will work to grow in these areas. Begin with the words, "With the help of God I will grow in my ability to be a Christian friend by . . ."

Characteristics of Christian Friends

Following are important qualities for a person to be a Christian friend. He or she

1. doesn't make fun of other people or use put-downs or labels, is careful not to hurt others;
2. likes people and is interested in them;
3. respects and trusts others;
4. has sound Christian values and remains committed to them;
5. is able to accept others in spite of their flaws;
6. can share his or her feelings in an open, honest, caring way;
7. is able to admit his or her own problems or faults;
8. is willing to make sacrifices or be inconvenienced for others;
9. can be trusted to keep personal matters confidential;
10. is able to share joys without being jealous, and can share problems without trying to run the other person's life.

What Friendship Can Be

In **1 Samuel 18, 19,** and **20** we find the account of David and Jonathan, a powerful account of Christian friendship. Note that both David and Jonathan were men, while in our culture we tend to find more close friendships among women. (Perhaps because more women than men in our society find it easy to share their feelings and to be sensitive to the feelings of others.)

As a young man, David had slain the giant Goliath. King Saul had taken him into the royal household, where David became a friend of Saul's son Jonathan. Read **1 Samuel 18, 19,** and **20** for the story of their friendship.

1. Though the story does not tell us how they became friends, what common bonds may have linked David and Jonathan together? How were their backgrounds different? (What common bonds do you and your friends share?)

2. What type of relationship did they have? List several verses which describe their friendship. (How would you describe your most important friendships?)

3. What great barrier did their friendship have to overcome? (See **15:28** and **16:12–13**). (What kinds of barriers have your friendships had to overcome?)

4. What risks did Jonathan take for the sake of David? (What risks have you had to take to be a true Christian friend to someone?)

5. What vow did David and Jonathan make before David was forced to flee **(1 Sam. 20:41–42)?**

6. After Jonathan was killed by the Philistines in battle, how did David fulfill that vow? (See **2 Sam. 9:1–10.**)

7. What one quality in the friendship of David and Jonathan would you like to develop in a relationship with a friend? With God's help, what one thing could you do today to begin to develop that quality?

I no longer call you servants, because a servant does not know his master's business. Instead, I have called you friends, for everything that I learned from My Father I have made known to you. You did not choose Me, but I chose you and appointed you to go and bear fruit—fruit that will last. Then the Father will give you whatever you ask in My name. This is My command: Love each other.

John 15:15–17

5. Singles in the Church

A Sunday morning conversation began, "Good morning! Are you new here? What's your name?"

After the visitor answered, the conversation continues, "Where do you live? What do you do? Are you married?"

For many single people in the church today, a Sunday morning conversation will end with the last question—or shift quickly to a discussion of the weather.

1. How might the congregational member have caused the visitor to feel by asking that last question?
2. Do you agree or disagree with the following statements? Give reasons for your answers.

- The rapid change in our society will call for a new ministry with singles.
- Singles fit into the church best when they serve in such roles as overseeing the nursery or singing in the choir.
- Maturity and responsibility are linked to being married.

3. Who do you think church leaders should be?
   a. Married people
   b. Divorced people
   c. People who have never heen married
   d. Widows or widowers
   e. All of the above
4. How should the church respond to the needs of the 59 million single persons in America (and to the large numbers in many other countries as well)?

The social changes we have discussed in this chapter have left many churches scurrying to catch up with the needs of its people. In some churches, unfortunately, members treat single persons as second-class citizens, as "incomplete" or less important than married people. The "Noah's Ark syndrome," which implies that all people come in couples or families, still seems to persist there. Those churches may have a rich ministry to families—but nothing for single persons.

Single persons often find it difficult to attend events like family reunions, weddings, and funerals.

Many family members or old friends feel free to ask questions about their future, dating, and relationships, without thinking about how the single person might feel about answering these questions. These people often feel free to ask a single person questions about his or her personal life that they would never consider asking of a married person. They seem to assume that something is missing in the single person's life—and that marriage is the something missing. Sometimes a single person may feel pressured into marrying the next available partner just because society gives the impression that he or she would be better off married.

Jesus did not say that to follow Him a person must first go and get married. Nor did the apostle Paul preach such a message. As a matter of fact, in **1 Cor. 7:8** Paul said, **"Now to the unmarried and the widows I say: It is good for them to stay unmarried, as I am."** Paul was, of course, speaking to people during a time of persecution; he was not promoting a rebellion against marriage (see, for example, the rest of **1 Cor. 7** and **Eph. 5:22–33**). Nevertheless, Paul uplifts the condition of singleness, both in his advice and his personal state.

When we became sons and daughters of God in Baptism, He called us to serve Him in our individual lives. This call is valid regardless of whether we are single persons or married. Each of us has a mission and ministry, regardless of marital status. Single persons may have opportunities to serve God and others which are not available to those who have the responsibilities of married life.

One single man in his 30s, active in his church in Illinois, remembers a member saying, "For a single person, you are really showing a lot of dedication and commitment to this church." Should we be surprised that on a typical Sunday morning 85 percent of the single members of The Lutheran Church—Missouri Synod are not in church?

"Instead of emphasizing completeness in Jesus Christ, we have emphasized completeness in marriage," says one pastor.

Married or single, it is in Christ that we, the people of God, find our identity and sense of self-worth. St. Paul makes it clear: **"There is neither Jew nor Greek, slave nor free, male nor female, for you are all one in Christ Jesus" (Gal. 3:28).** We could add, "There is neither single person nor married in Christ Jesus."

(Adapted from "Lutheran Singles: Finding a Place in a Family Church" by Christine Scheele. *The Lutheran Witness,* June 1987, 1–3.)

5. How are Jesus' words in **Matt. 28:18–20** related to a congregation's ministry to single persons?
6. Suppose you know a congregational leader who has treated singles as second-class citizens. What words of hope can you give that leader about a proper relationship with God? (You might base part of your remarks upon Peter's denial and reinstatement **(John 18:15–27; 21:15–19.)**

A True Story

After several years of teaching, Laurie had decided to return to school. She had just finished a master's degree program in counseling. As she was preparing to interview for jobs, she discovered that her widowed mother had cancer. She decided to put her career plans aside for a few months to nurse her mother through her final days. One Sunday morning the pastor announced that unless someone volunteered to organize the youth program, the church would have to cancel all youth activities for the year.

Laurie thought about her training and the time she had available. After the service, Laurie went up to speak to the pastor to offer her services with the youth program.

"Thank you very much," said the pastor, "but we were looking for an adult or maybe a married couple."

This incident actually occurred in a church; it is not fiction. Probably similar incidents have occurred in churches of all denominations throughout the country.

1. What message was that pastor sending to single persons in his church?

2. Compare the potential for ministry that single and married persons bring to a position of youth group leadership. What are some qualities of a leader that are more important than being married or single?

3. Churches often use the following terms to describe events or ministries. Which terms present single persons in a better light?

- family night or church supper?
- pairs and spares or fellowship meeting?
- broken homes or single-parent homes?

4. What are some other terms or practices within congregations that can help singles feel like something better than second-class citizens?

5. Suggest a response to the suggestion (often spoken in a spirit of kindness), that a person "find a nice young woman (or man) and settle down"?

6. Interview your pastor, director of Christian education, or another prominent leader in your congregation to discover ways your congregation is ministering to singles. Ask questions such as the following:

- Describe this congregation's ministry to single persons.
- How does this congregation help to meet a single person's needs for fellowship? the need to grow in life and love? the need to have meaning and purpose in life?
- How are singles encouraged to use their spiritual

gifts in this church? (*You may wish to re-read* **1 Cor. 12** to review what St. Paul says about the spiritual gifts each of us receives, and how we are to use them to build the body of Christ.)

Single and In Ministry

We do not know what direction our lives will take in the future. Many of us will marry. Some of us will not. Most of us will probably spend a part of our lives as a single adult. How will you spend those years? Following are some suggestions for single persons:

1. Celebrate your singleness. God loves you just like He loves all His children. His promises are your promises.
2. Volunteer, go, do, participate, enjoy, be involved in your congregational life.
3. Let your needs be known to the pastor and church council.

(From *43 SAMS* (Single Adult Ministry Suggestions), Bulletin 65180, Board for Youth Services, The Lutheran Church—Missouri Synod. Used by permission.)

Chapter Summary

■ God gives us value as persons; we need not be married to work effectively in His kingdom.

■ Single persons may have special opportunities to use their gifts to serve God and others.

■ Single persons can lead a happy, fulfilling life.

■ Single persons can establish rich, satisfying relationships.

■ Each of us has a story to tell. God is at work in each of our lives. Whether you are a single person or married, share your story with those around you who need a living model of God at work in the lives of people!

There is neither Jew nor Greek, slave nor free, male nor female, for you are all one in Christ Jesus.

Gal. 3:28

Chapter 4

Dating and Mating

Chapter Preview

Chapter 4 will help you answer the following questions:

- What are the purposes and stages of dating relationships?
- What common bonds should a Christian look for in a dating partner?
- What is the difference between infatuation and love?
- What does the Bible say about the gift of sexuality and how we are to manage it?

1. The Perfect Mate

From the time we are children, many of us carry in our minds a mental image of the kind of person we may someday marry. Often that image is a composite drawn from many sources: the best qualities of our mother or father; TV or movie stars; someone we may once have had a crush on; the kind of person our friends seem to admire.

1. Create a word collage of your dream mate by listing in the following way 10 qualities you think would make someone an ideal mate for you.

First list five words or phrases to describe your ideal mate's *physical appearance*. (Include qualities more important than "great build" or "gorgeous face.")

Next list five words or phrases to describe your ideal mate's behavioral characteristics; describe his or her *personality*.

2. Take another look at your word collage. Do you think it could describe a real person? Why, or why not?

3. Now think of yourself as a potential marriage partner for someone someday. Create another word collage, this time of yourself.

First of all, list five words or phrases to describe aspects of your *physical appearance* that would make you attractive to the opposite sex.

Next list five words or phrases to describe aspects of your *personality* that would be attractive to someone of the opposite sex.

Was it easy or difficult to find 10 attractive characteristics you possess? (If you got stuck after one or two, review the section on self-esteem in chapter 1. God made you—and God doesn't make junk. You are so important that He sent His only Son to die for your sins. God has given you traits and qualities to share with other people in relationships.)

About 95 percent of us will marry, and the process of choosing a marriage partner demands an enormous amount of time and energy in most of our lives. Most of us begin with casual dating for fun and recreation. At some point we begin to move toward courtship or serious dating, the process by which we get to know members of the opposite sex well enough to determine their potential as a future mate. The relationship that develops during courtship may lead to future marriage.

The dating/mating process is an important part of our development as mature men and women. Whether we marry or live our whole life as a single person, the things we learn from close friendships with the opposite sex contribute greatly to our personal growth. Some of us may begin the process in our early teens; others of us may not find it important until years later. Some of us may date many people; others may prefer just a few close relationships.

Our personal dating pattern grows out of our own goals and personality. One person's pattern may be totally inappropriate for another. Whatever our personal dating pattern, establishing close relationships with the opposite sex provides experiences in social discovery of ourselves and others in a number of ways.

The Purposes of Dating

1. Socialization. We learn more about our sex roles, and about what it means to be a man or a woman by contact with members of the opposite sex.

2. Building understanding. By dating we learn to get along with the opposite sex. Do men and women think differently? Do they have different approaches to life? Dating helps us understand some of the God-given differences between males and females and teaches us how to establish and maintain relationships with members of the other sex.

3. Personality development. Developing relationships with other people develops our character and personality. We get to know ourselves better as we establish relationships with others including persons of the other sex.

4. Ego satisfaction. We feel good about ourselves when we know someone truly cares about us and finds us special.

5. Selection of a mate. As we develop relationships with a variety of members of the other sex, we begin to define for ourselves those qualities that are important to us. We identify the qualities of a person we could love and could continue to love for a lifetime. Dating allows us to get to know and value the other person so we can make a wise decision about whether or not that person would make a good marriage partner.

Arranged Marriages

In our country and culture, the dating-courtship process is the means by which people find a suitable mate and establish the deep love relationship which preceeds marriage. When two people marry, a strong bond of mutual love and affection has led them to want to make a lifetime commitment to each other. We can hardly imagine people building a happy life together if they marry for any other reason.

In other times and other cultures, however, marriages were not based on two people falling in love with each other. Marriages were taken very seriously as a bond between two families, and so they were arranged by the parents or a go-between. People in some countries still use this process today.

Perhaps you cannot even imagine marriage to a partner you did not choose. Perhaps you think it would be impossible to love someone if you did not choose that person. In our minds love comes before marriage. Did you know that throughout the centuries of Bible history in both Old and New Testament, marriages were arranged? Often we are told that a strong bond of affection linked the couple before their marriage, but the final decision usually remained with the parents. Let's look at a few examples.

1. Read the following passages and answer the questions that follow.

Gen. 24:37–67. How did Rebekah become the wife of Isaac? Which came first, love or marriage? How did their relationship develop after their marriage?

Ruth 3:1–4:10. How did Ruth become the husband of Boaz? Why was the marriage arranged? From what we know about them in the narrative, how would you expect their relationship to develop after their marriage?

2. In spite of the fact that arranged marriages were the custom, what is the Biblical directive for how husbands and wives are to live together? See **Prov. 5:18** and **Eph. 5:33.** According to **Eph. 5:25,** where do we get the power to live this way?

3. How does the love that maintains a marriage differ from the love in courtship? Explain your answer.

Discussion Questions

1. Think about the process by which you would find a mate; then think about how your parents would find a partner for you if that were their responsibility.

- List three advantages of mate selection by mutual affection. What disadvantages might there be?
- List three advantages of parental mate selection. What disadvantages would there be?

2. Imagine for a moment that you live in a culture in which it is the parents' responsibility to arrange marriages for their children. Then ask your parents or guardians to describe the kind of person *they* would choose if it were their responsibility to find a mate for you. (Remember: you are asking for the kind of mate they would choose for you, not the kind of mate they think you should choose.) You may ask them to write out their description, or you may prefer to jot down what they say.

3. Think about the kind of person *you* think you might one day marry. Describe the kind of mate you imagine you will choose if you marry.

4. How are your and your parents' descriptions alike? How are they different? Write a paragraph or two discussing the similarities and differences you discovered.

Husbands, love your wives, just as Christ loved the church and gave Himself up for her to make her holy, cleansing her by the washing with water through the Word, and to present her to Himself as a radiant church, without stain or wrinkle or any other blemish, but holy and blameless. In this same way, husbands ought to love their wives as their own bodies. He who loves his wife loves himself.

Eph. 5:25–28

2. Whom Should You Date?

What kinds of questions do we need to ask ourselves before becoming involved in a long-term relationship that might lead to marriage? Tell whether each question listed below is

- very important (VI);
- somewhat important (SI);
- not important (NI).

1. Can I respect as well as love this person?
2. Do I know this person really well?
3. Is this person emotionally mature and socially well-adjusted?
4. Do my parents approve of this person?
5. Can I trust this person?
6. Does this person have realistic goals and is he or she willing to work to attain them?
7. Does this person treat me with respect and consideration?
8. Does this person demonstrate faith in God?
9. Is this person responsible about money?
10. Does this person like children?
11. How does he or she get along with his or her family and friends?

Be prepared to discuss why you think each is or is not important.

Since the dating-courtship process is part of our growth, whom to date becomes an important question, especially when we talk about serious dating that could lead to marriage. This question is a frequent source of conflict between young people and their parents. The apostle Paul understood something important about relationships. In **2 Cor. 6:14** he said, **"Do not be yoked together with unbelievers. For what do righteousness and wickedness have in common?"**

The last three words provide a key. What do you *have in common* with the person you're dating? That question is crucial for establishing a relationship with someone who might eventually become a marriage partner.

What Should We Have in Common?

1. Do you share the same *faith?* Do you both believe in Jesus as your Lord and Savior? Do you share the same understandings about the importance of God's Word and the sacraments?

Even if it will be years before you are ready to marry, remember that *a healthy relationship should nurture our total growth as Christian persons.* If the other person is not a Christian, he or she will not be able to nurture that vital part of our growth. It's never too early to have a faith standard when you start dating. It will help you keep the right priorities for your life, and it may save you a lot of pain and disappointment later.

What are some ways you can determine if you and another person share the same faith?

2. Do you share the same *values?* Do you have a common understanding of appropriate behavior? What about alcohol? drugs? sex? R-rated movies? Do you have the same expectations of each other? If you must compromise your Christian values to have a relationship, you are paying too high a price for that relationship. You may be jeopardizing your relationship with God and with the people who truly care about you. *If you can't be your own person—if you can't be God's person—then you're in the wrong relationship!*

What are some ways you can determine if you and another person share the same values?

3. What other things do you have in common? Do you have similar *goals* for your life? Do you share interests? If you are able to share things you have in common, you have a better chance of developing a strong friendship. Friendship is a vital part of a lasting marriage relationship. You can waste a lot of energy trying to maintain a relationship with someone with whom you don't really have much in common.

What are some ways you can determine what you and another person have in common?

We can call these the "big three," the three bonds a Christian should share with his or her dating partners: shared *faith* in Christ, Christian *values,* and Christ-centered *goals* for life. A relationship built on these three common bonds will nurture our growth as Christian persons. Compromise is part of every relationship, but we cannot compromise our Christianity! To do so may destroy our most important relationship—our relationship with the God whose gift is eternal life!

(Adapted from "How About a Date." LYF supplement, March 1985. Board for Youth Services, The Lutheran Church—Missouri Synod. Used by permission.)

The Chain of Intimacy

Josie had always loved to sing and had been blessed with a beautiful voice. When other kids asked for fancy bikes or expensive clothing for birthday or Christmas gifts, Josie wanted only to be able to continue with her voice lessons. She had sung in church many times and had always known what she wanted to be: a professional singer with time enough to direct church choirs and give voice lessons to kids who might not be able to afford it. She knew she would need a scholarship to go on with her training, but she had prayed about it a lot and knew God would help her make the right decisions.

Carefully Josie saved her money so that she could attend a summer music camp. There she met Gabe, a trumpet player who lived in a town not far from hers. She was attracted to him the first time she saw him playing with the band. She could hardly believe that someone as sure of himself as Gabe would be interested in her.

Josie knew Gabe didn't really care about music; he had come to camp to get away from his parents. She worried sometimes because Gabe had some pretty wild friends—but he always treated her well. They started eating meals together, going for long walks, and soon Josie could hardly think about anything else.

They'd had a big fight when she had invited Gabe to go to church with her; Gabe had told her he didn't need some preacher telling him what to do. But most of the time they got along wonderfully. By the end of summer camp, they had become nearly inseparable. When Josie was in Gabe's arms, nothing else seemed important.

Though Josie was nervous the first time Gabe came to her house and met her parents, she was relieved that her parents didn't ask Gabe a lot of questions but just told them to have a good time. However, when Gabe began coming over several nights a week, and Josie's grades started to slip, her parents expressed concern. Her choir director was disappointed, too, when Josie followed Gabe's suggestion that she just didn't have time to sing with the church choir anymore.

One night Josie and Gabe went to a party with some of his friends. It wasn't the kind of party she had expected, and she was hurt when those friends started to tease her and call her "Miss Perfect," be-

As a couple spend more time with each other, a chain of intimacy will develop in a pattern similar to the following:

1. Mutual attraction. You invite each other's affection by paying attention to each other. You protect yourself, however, by revealing only a little about yourself and your feelings; you may hide behind a "line." Getting to know each other seems like a game with each of you taking a turn moving the pieces.

2. Lover's quarrel. When you reach the point where the game has gone on long enough so that you want to get below the surface to know the real person, one or both of you begin to risk sharing your real feelings. If you discover you don't have a common bond, the relationship will end. If you are able to move the relationship to a deeper level, it will lead you to further involvement with each other.

3. Common interests. Further involvement leads to deeper sharing of the things you have in common. You feel more sure of each other and begin to trust and depend on each other.

4. Increased intimacy. You begin to express your affection with verbal and physical gestures of affection. You begin to trust each other. The words "I love you" may be spoken, establishing a deeper bond than existed previously.

5. Idealization. Your affection for the other person may lead you to overlook flaws and concentrate on how wonderful he or she makes you feel.

6. Couple unity. You begin to develop a private culture, a world for just the two of you. Your relationship gives you a sense of belonging and meets your needs for love and attention. You may exchange a symbol of unity, such as a ring or other jewelry, or treasure "our song" or "our favorite place."

cause she wouldn't get drunk with them. When couples started sneaking off to other rooms or their cars, she asked Gabe to take her home. But Gabe grabbed another drink and told her it was about time she loosened up and had some fun. In tears, she ran out to Gabe's car; when he followed, they drove home in icy silence. But the next day he called and apologized, and Josie was so relieved.

Somehow Josie's parents found out about the party, and told her she could not see Gabe for two months. When she called Gabe to tell him, he laughed. "Your parents are hopelessly old-fashioned," he said, "so just don't tell them! Tell them you're going to the library or a game or something, and we'll find a place to meet."

What would you do if you were Josie?

The question of what kind of person to date is crucial, because romantic relationships often take on a momentum of their own, as the story of Josie and Gabe illustrates. Suddenly we may be confronted by the need to make a decision about the future when we aren't prepared for it.

A romantic relationship generally follows a predictable pattern. This pattern may vary somewhat with individuals; not all couples will experience all steps; and the sequence of steps may vary. Sometimes relationships go back and forth between steps.

The six steps of the chain of intimacy usually occur over a period of months, or even years. If you are both mature adults, the relationship that has developed will cause the people around you to begin thinking of you as a "couple." You may start to hear questions about engagement or marriage. Step by step you've reached a point of decision.

Each step along the chain leads to further intimacy. Each step requires increasing commitment. The relationship has assumed a central importance in your life.

1. How does the story of Josie and Gabe illustrate the chain of intimacy which develops in a relationship?

2. How does it illustrate the importance of the three common bonds discussed previously?

3. What needs to happen for Josie to continue to be her own person if she continues the relationship with Gabe? What needs to happen for her to be God's person?

4. If Josie were to abandon her music and eventually marry Gabe, how do you think she might feel 10 years from now? How would her feelings affect the relationship?

The steps in the chain of intimacy are exciting and affirming. We may feel better about ourselves than we have ever felt before. The entire process is highly emotional; our feelings may be so deeply involved that we don't bother to spend much time thinking about the relationship from a logical perspective.

Unfortunately, some people get caught up in the process and don't know how to get out. Once their emotions get so involved, they find it hard to look at common values realistically, common goals, or shared faith. As the story of Hosea and Gomer in chapter 1 illustrated, our personal relationships affect our ability to serve God and others.

Let's Talk about It

1. Maybe you want to date a really great guy or gal. Maybe you like nearly everything about that person—except for the fact that he or she drinks. Does the abuse of alcohol rule out all the seemingly good things about him or her? Is it worth the risk to you?

2. Or perhaps there's a person whose life is a mess, but whom you think you can help. You get involved in a relationship. Will you be able to change that person's life? Is it worth the risk to you? Will that relationship nurture your growth as a Christian person?

We need to think about these things at the *beginning* of a relationship, when our thinking is less clouded by emotional involvement.

3. If the three criteria above for sharing faith, values and goals don't fit, should you invest yourself in the relationship? What could happen if you invest yourself in a relationship with someone with whom you could not build a good marriage? What dangers arise if you invest yourself in a relationship with someone who cannot nurture your personal and spiritual growth?

A close relationship with someone who doesn't share your faith or values could gradually begin to undermine both faith and values. If you want a Christian marriage someday, you must marry a committed Christian.

Lovers tend to be idealistic. Many believe they will be able to change the person they love. Many believe that the heartbreak and pain that come from investing in wrong relationships cannot happen to them. Often they do not realize until they've already been hurt that this was a relationship they should have avoided. If you make a decision about your standards *before* engaging in close, intimate relationships, your emotions will less drastically distort your judgment. Think with your head *and* your heart!

4. Maybe someone says to you, "Those are nice, pious words, but they just don't fit 'real' life." How can you respond? Read **2 Cor. 5:14–15, Rom. 6:4,** and **Eph. 2:3–5** as you plan your response.

All of us also lived among them at one time, gratifying the cravings of our sinful nature and following its desires and thoughts. Like the rest,

All of us also lived among them at one time, gratifying the cravings of our sinful nature and following its desires and thoughts. Like the rest, we were by nature objects of wrath. But because of His great love for us, God, who is rich in mercy, made us alive with Christ even when we were dead in transgressions—it is by grace you have been saved.

Eph. 2:3–5

3. Is It Love?

Falling in love is a wonderful experience. When it happens to us, we feel so ecstatic we hardly seem to need food or sleep or anyone else but the one we love. *Eros,* or romantic love, brings out the best in us; we want to be the best person we can possibly be!

Yet we know, from observing people around us and perhaps from our own experiences, that falling in love is not the same thing as remaining in love. What kind of love can last for a lifetime?

We can easily confuse love with our emotional feelings for someone (infatuation). Infatuation, like other aspects of the dating/mating process, is not bad. It can provide valuable experience in relationships. It is not, however, the kind of love that can last for a lifetime.

INFATUATION IS A DOUBLE HOT FUDGED SUNDAE WITH LOTS OF CREAM AND A BIG CHERRY ON TOP.
LOVE IS A NOURISHING, WELL BALANCED MEAL.

Infatuation or Love?

1. Tell whether the statements below describe *infatuation* or *love.*

- May be described as being "in love with love."
- Gives the freedom to grow as a person.
- Is a growing relationship based on shared values, interests, and goals.
- Makes you feel tense, worried, and insecure about the relationship.
- Describes the way God feels about you.
- Takes time to grow and develop.
- Is based on fantasy and romantic dreams.
- Grows deeper through trials and separations.
- Makes you feel possessive or selfish.
- Is based on external attraction.
- Cares enough to accept the other person's weaknesses.
- Delights in giving of yourself to bring joy to the other person.
- Can happen with someone you hardly know.
- Finds beauty in the other person even if he or she does not look attractive at the moment.

2. Based on this activity, what do you think are the most important differences between love and infatuation? State them in your own words.

3. Is infatuation the same thing as lust? What is the difference between love and lust?

As we learned in chapter 1, we need a clear concept of love in order to establish lasting relationships. The sexual, sensual, and romantic feelings that the world around us calls love are not enough to last for a lifetime. Those feelings will not last unless there is more to the relationship. Passion or a desire to have someone to love are not enough.

Our desire to be close to someone, to find someone with whom we feel secure and important, can create a strong attraction between two people. This may provide a foundation on which to develop a love relationship, but it is not enough to carry two people through a lifetime of joys and sorrows, victories and defeats.

Love means that you are as concerned about the welfare of the other person as you are about your own, and wish to nurture the other person's personal and spiritual growth as much as you do your own. It means that you can communicate your feelings to each other and work together to achieve a common goal.

That kind of love will provide a sound basis for marriage. It cannot happen in a short time. It will take effort and commitment. As God's love nurtures you, the love between you and your partner will grow. Romantic attraction is wonderful; it is a vital part of the bond between a man and a woman—but alone it is not enough to make a marriage strong.

4. Read **1 John 4:7–12.** How does God's love for us affect our love for another person?

The Right Questions

If you are presently in a dating relationship, how can you evaluate that relationship to determine whether it has the potential to lead to a lasting love? A checklist such as the following can become a helpful tool to allow you to look at a relationship realistically and evaluate it honestly. Review what we learned earlier in this chapter about the three important common bonds.

Evaluating a Relationship

If you are presently in a romantic relationship, use the checklist below to evaluate that relationship. Tell whether each statement is true or false. (If you are not in a romantic relationship, read the statements carefully as a guide for future relationships and a way to help friends who may be trying to sort out questions in a relationship.)

1. This person often pressures me to do things I'd rather not do.
2. I'm afraid that if this person knew certain things about me, he or she wouldn't like me anymore.
3. I'm often embarrassed by this person's language or behavior.
4. This person continues to remind me of mistakes I've made in the past and seems unable to forgive.
5. One of the things that attracted me to this person was the fact that he or she was so different from most of the other people I know.
6. I'm afraid to ask this person to go to church with me; I'm not sure what reaction I might receive.
7. I feel uncomfortable around this person's friends.
8. Since we started seeing each other, my grades have gone down.
9. My parents do not approve of this person.
10. I avoid telling this person what I really think about many things because I don't want to start an argument.

1. What things can you learn about a relationship by evaluating it with questions such as those in the box above?

2. What would you tell a friend who answered "true" to several of the statements in the box? (Counselors believe that if more than one or two of the statements above are true, the present relationship has many risks for you, because it is not based on shared values and goals. It probably cannot lead to a successful marriage.)

3. How can you get out of a relationship if you discover it's wrong for you?

4. Which question is more important to ask: Is this love? or, Is this the kind of love on which I can build a lasting marriage?

When St. Paul reminds us, **"Pray in the Spirit on all occasions with all kinds of prayers and requests" (Eph. 6:18),** he is giving us a powerful tool to use whenever we face decisions in our lives. Choosing and building God-pleasing relationships is surely one of those occasions when we will pray for God's direction for our lives.

5. Write a prayer you could use to ask God's will for a present or future relationship.

Dear friends, let us love one another, for love comes from God. . . . This is love: not that we loved God, but that He loved us and sent His Son as an atoning sacrifice for our sins. Dear friends, since God so loved us, we also ought to love one another.

1 John 4:7a, 10–11

4. Male and Female

When God created human life, He immediately placed people in relationships. **"It is not good for the man to be alone,"** the Lord God said. **"I will make a helper suitable for him" (Gen. 2:18).** Without female companionship and a partner in reproduction, the man could not fully realize his humanity.

The male-female distinction is basic to all relationships and forms the foundation for the creation of the family. Our male-female identify shaped us even before we are born; at the moment of conception we already became male or female. Early in our fetal development hormones were already shaping our sexuality and creating the sex organs with which we would be born. Our sexuality is part of every aspect of our lives.

Our sexuality displays a wonderful part of God's plan. Man and woman were not designed to be the same; they were designed to complement each other. Men and women are different anatomically, emotionally, psychologically, and physiologically.

Many people think of sexuality only in terms of gender—being physically male or female. But sexuality is much more than just our physical make-up. It involves our total being—body and spirit. The fact that we are male or female shapes everything about us, our whole life experience and character. All our relationships are based upon our sexuality. God brings great joy and richness to our lives through this blessing.

Questions for Reflection

1. How does the fact that we are created male and female enrich human life?

2. How does it complicate our life?

Because we are sexual beings, being in love awakens not only an emotional response, but also a physical, sexual response. As the chain of emotional intimacy develops, gestures of love and affection become an integral part of expressing our love to the other person. In fact, touch is one of the most powerful links between human beings. Whether it be a mother holding and stroking her infant, or lovers holding each other close, touching is part of the expression of love. The embrace of a loved one is one of the greatest pleasures we experience. Sexual intercourse is a special and unique expression of our giving and receiving love.

As two people grow progressively closer to each other in love, their physical attraction to each other grows also. The way we deal with these feelings of sexual attraction has important consequences for our present relationships and may influence the rest of our lives.

The world around us presents many conflicting ideas about managing our sexuality. It exerts strong influences that shape many people's sexual decisions.

3. List at least four factors that influence the sexual decisions of young people today.

4. How many of these factors are in harmony with God's will for our lives?

About Sexual Relationships

You have probably heard most of these statements about sexual acts—acts of sexual intercourse or acts leading to intercourse. Tell whether you *agree, disagree,* or are *uncertain* about each of them.

1. Sexual acts are all right if they express your real feelings.
2. God designed sexual union to be part of the marriage covenant between husband and wife.
3. Sexual acts are all right if they don't harm anyone (including you, the other person, or possibly an unwanted child).
4. Sexual acts provide experience necessary for marriage.
5. When it comes to being sexually active, everybody is doing it, so I can do it, too.
6. Sexual responsibility demonstrates Christian love.
7. Sexual acts have few, if any, long-term consequences.
8. It is the woman's responsibility to set the standards for sexual behavior in a relationship.

Our morals and ethics are not simply a matter of personal taste. God is in charge of the world, and His Word clearly condemns some things as wrong and establishes other things as right. Our actions and decisions matter, for they affect our relationships with God and with other people.

Unfortunately, sin has corrupted God's gift of sexuality, just as it has invaded every other part of our lives. Rather than following God's plan, designed for our joy and fulfillment, many in the world prefer to ignore God and abuse God's gift of sexuality. As the examples in chapter 1 show, when sex is used to sell products ranging from deodorants to cars, that which should be special is soon reduced to the commonplace.

Our culture is saturated with the idea of sex. Yet the beauty of our sexuality is often lost in the loveless and dehumanizing sexual relationships with which we are bombarded in the entertainment media, the press and magazines, and in everyday conversation. According to the American Academy of Pediatrics, research of sex on television revealed that of all sexual acts displayed, only 6 percent are with spouses! Another 40 percent of sexual acts are with friends; 29 percent are with strangers. Young people on television are portrayed in a state of continual sexual crisis; sexual relationships develop easily and quickly. Nearly every romantic relationship moves quickly to the bedroom.

Some of our sexual attitudes may also be based on fear. The great increase in sexually transmitted diseases, for example, has further devalued God's gift.

Because the world does not value God's gift of sexuality according to His purposes, even Christians sometimes tend to see their sexuality as evil, as a dimension of themselves which must be denied or hidden. Of course, the very way in which we are created makes it impossible for us to deny or hide our sexuality. All our contacts as human beings are sexual, for every other person's sexuality is also a part of that person. Our sexual behavior affects the development of our personal life and our relationships with others. Furthermore, understanding our sexuality is an important part of growing into mature men and women.

Few young adults can put sexuality out of their minds for any length of time, for the hormonal changes in their bodies have brought them to a sexual peak—usually at a much younger age for men than for women. Questions, fantasies, and sexual desires occur naturally as we mature. God's gift of sexuality can be a great source of happiness in our lives—or a great potential for pain and unhappiness if we abuse it.

Recent years have seen a "sexual revolution," characterized by the easy availability of contraceptives, "free" love, and sexual relationships based purely on human drives. The sexual revolution promised joy, liberation, and good health. Instead, many received broken dreams, rootless or uncommitted relationships, disease, and now even death. It satisfied some people's drives temporarily—but it left their basic needs as human beings unfulfilled, for it was contrary to God's plan.

Christians are not immune to sexual temptations. Most of us reach physical maturity long before we are ready for marriage. Our sexual drives may reach a peak before we are ready to make a lifetime commitment to share our lives and sexuality with another person. So we must learn how to handle our sexuality to make it the blessing God intended it to be.

Because of the many temptations we face—from our own sexual drives, the world system, and the devil—we must have a clear understanding of God's plan for our sexuality. Based upon God's plan, we can establish clear standards of sexual conduct for ourselves before becoming involved in close relationships. Then our emotional involvement will not need to distort our judgment.

Following God's plan by drawing upon His

power will bring blessing to our lives and strengthen our ability to be faithful to our marriage vows in the future. Left to our own power, we would continually give in to all types of temptations. But God has for Jesus' sake forgiven us our repented sins of yesterday! The power of His Spirit living within us can create the power we need today to obey God's will for our lives.

What is God's plan for our use of this special gift? What does His Word have to tell us? What perspective does the Bible provide to enable us to manage our sexuality according to God's will? How can we conduct our lives now so that we may enjoy happy, healthy marriages in the future?

Searching for Answers

Think about the story of creation and God's pronouncement about everything He had created, including human sexuality.

1. Skim **Genesis 1.** What phrase is used seven times in this chapter to describe every aspect of God's creation?

2. Read **Gen. 1:27.** What do the words *male and female* have to say about our sexuality?

3. Men and women were designed to participate in God's creation of human life. What command does God give them in **Gen. 1:28?**

4. Read **Gen. 2:24.** Which words describe the sexual bond between man and woman? What do those words mean to you?

As these passages illustrate, God intended sexuality to occupy a positive and important place in human life. It is part of our total life as a child of God. God's gifts are always good. His love for us—His creation—is so great that He created the pleasure and joy of the sexual bond as His gift to make the love relationship between men and women different from every other relationship.

Our new life in Christ affects this aspect of our day-to-day life also. His forgiveness of our past sins brings us joy and peace. Our new life in Christ provides the power for us to grow in our understanding and management of our sexuality.

The Bible is never bothered by the question of whether sex is good. Everything God created was good! To make it a power for good in our lives, to give it the potential to create great happiness for us, the Bible shows us how to use our sexuality in harmony with the will of God.

5. Read **2 Cor. 5:17.** How does God enable Christians to manage their sexuality so that every aspect of their lives brings glory to Him?

6. Read **1 Thess. 4:1–8.** What difference exists between Christians and unbelievers in the way they manage their sexuality?

7. Read **1 Cor. 6:15–20.** What does this passage suggest about sexual relations outside of marriage?

8. Based upon this study, how would a Spirit-filled Christian answer the eight statements listed under **"About Sexual Relationships"** above?

As the passages from St. Paul illustrate, sex is not just a private act. It is not merely a physiological drive. The sexual act is a unique, intimate union of giving and receiving. Love and commitment bring meaning and fulfillment to sexual activity. Sex is part of the total relationship, not merely an end in itself. The sexual bond between man and woman is a special gift of God for building and sustaining love in a marriage. Sex becomes the means whereby husband and wife, two different beings, become one in sexual intercourse. When it is used in harmony with God's will in marriage, it brings great joy and happiness.

(Adapted from "Sex—A Positive Perspective," by John F. Johnson. *The Lutheran Witness,* August 1987.)

The Lord God said, "It is not good for the man to be alone. I will make a helper suitable for him."

Gen. 2:18

5. What About Living Together?

A friend of yours is contemplating moving in with her boyfriend. She comes to you for advice. What would you tell her?

Many people today live together in a sexual relationship without any marriage vows. They give many reasons for their actions:

- "We want to try out the relationship before we get married."
- "How can one vow be expected to apply through all the changes and experiences of 50 or 60 years of life? It's totally unrealistic."
- "We don't need marriage to make a commitment to each other."
- "Too many marriages break up; if we can't get along, it will be much easier this way."

You will likely encounter all of these reasons and more during the years ahead. Drawing on what you have learned thus far in this chapter, how would you respond to each of the statements above?

Whenever the Bible talks about God's gift of sexuality, and the "one-flesh" relationship for which God designed sexuality, it does so in two contexts:

1. The bond of marriage, for which the gift of sexuality was given.
2. Sexual immorality, any sexual relationship outside of marriage.

God does not provide a third category for "casual sex," living together, or any other kind of sexual relationship! For example, in **1 Cor. 7:9** Paul advised, **"If they cannot control themselves, they should marry, for it is better to marry than to burn with passion."** Having sexual intercourse with someone outside of marriage is a sin against God and against the other person. No matter what reasons people may use to justify it, sexual intercourse outside of marriage comes down to people putting their own pleasure first—before obedience to God, or before the deeper relationship of committed love that God intended marriage to be.

Living together violates God's plan for the sexual bond. He designed sex to be more than physical satisfaction. As we learned from **Gen. 2:24–25,** in marriage husband and wife are united as one flesh.

Not only are their bodies united, but their minds, emotions, and spirits are joined as well. The sexual union is only one aspect of a total relationship. Without lifetime commitment to each other, sexual union will always be less than God designed it to be.

The vow of commitment underpins the marriage relationship. A man and woman who choose to live together without marriage are really saying they are not willing to make a commitment to each other; they are taking the merchandise home "on approval." The act of holding back from true commitment detracts from their relationship. Because they are choosing a short-term relationship, their behavior and expectations are likely to be different from those of marriage partners. They are still putting up a front. The complete trust and total intimacy of marriage cannot exist in a "trial" relationship.

Furthermore, in a committed marriage, husband and wife accept responsibility for each other and for a child which could be conceived. Since no method of birth control is 100 percent effective, every time a couple has intercourse they should be ready to assume full responsibility for a child. If a couple is not able to commit to each other, how will they be able to commit to the huge responsibility of nurturing a child?

Discussion Questions

1. Who created our sexuality? For what purpose was it created?
2. In addition to sexual pleasure, what occurs in sexual intercourse? (See **Gen. 2:24** and **1 Cor. 6:13–20**).
3. In Biblical times, fornication and adultery were often associated with the worship of idols and were seen as disloyalty to God. What "idol" is the reason behind much of the sexual promiscuity of our day?
4. In what way does sexual responsibility demonstrate Christian love?
5. What part do self-respect and self-control play in a Christian's management of his or her sexuality?
6. How does a Christian develop sexual maturity of the mind and emotions? What are some things you can do to develop maturity in this area of your life?
7. How could you use what you have learned from this chapter to respond to statements such as the following?
   - Everybody is doing it.
   - I never buy a car without driving it first.
   - I take precautions to prevent pregnancy.
   - Who am I hurting if I have a sexual relationship?
   - Why should I be deprived of fun in my life?

"Good" Sex

Sex *is* a big deal—it is the means God uses to bind a man and woman together and create new life. But sex is only one part of a total relationship. Thus, God's purpose makes the term *casual sex* a lie, for sexual acts are not casual. They are part of the one-flesh relationship which God instituted in marriage.

In a human being *eros* causes more than a desire to satisfy a physical need. A man wishes to cherish one particular woman, his beloved. The same is true for the woman. "Casual sex" dehumanizes people, for it sees them only in terms of their sexual functions. Sex partners become interchangeable; they are no longer valued as unique persons created by God, people whom we are to love with a love patterned after Jesus' own sacrificing love for us.

When our sexual drives are uncontrolled by mutual love, they threaten constantly to break out and disrupt our lives. As with every other aspect of our Christian life, we can live according to God's will only when His Spirit lives within us.

We Christians need not rely upon our own strength when facing sexual temptations. We need not be a slave to sexual passions; we have the freedom to make responsible choices about this aspect of our lives also! With the Spirit's power, we are forgiven for past mistakes and now can make decisions based on God's will for us, based upon what is right rather than what is easiest.

Questions for Reflection

1. In what ways will God's plan for sexual relationships be a limit in your life?
2. In what ways will it expand and enrich your life?

Discussion Questions

1. List four ways Christian people can avoid the pressures to have premarital sexual relationships.
2. List four blessings or benefits (physical, emotional, or psychological) you may receive *now* as a result of following God's plan for saving sexual acts for marriage.

3. List four blessings or benefits for your future life that can result from following God's plan.
4. Temptation is not sin; we sin when we *give in* to temptation. How can St. Paul's words in **1 Cor. 10:13** help you when you are facing sexual temptations?

Overcoming Temptation

Sexual temptations will continue through much of your adult life, whether you marry or not. With the power of the Spirit living within you, you can overcome temptations by using the tools God has given you:

- Remember whose you are! (You are God's redeemed person.)
- Pray! (God's power is available for the asking.)
- Study the Scripture! (God works in us through His Word.)
- Choose Christian friends. (They can help affirm your Christian values).
- Follow Christian role models for your life (rather than the latest TV star).
- Avoid situations which are likely to lead to temptations.
- Be informed about your own body and how it works. (You are one of God's unique creatures; His Spirit lives in you.)
- Establish plans and goals for your life. (They will help you remember your priorities.)
- Develop the potential God has given you; get involved in working with others and serving others in clubs, church activities, sports, volunteer groups, etc.

Chapter Summary

Through the power of the Spirit and the guidance of God's Word Christians

- can learn what types of dating relationships will nurture their personal and spiritual growth;
- can choose and build God-pleasing dating relationships that may lead to marriage;
- can grow in the abilty to follow God's plan for managing His gift of sexuality;
- can as they mature, choose what is right in God's eyes, and then live by their beliefs. (One young Christian had the courage to put it this way: "When someone asks me why I do not get involved in sexual relationships, I tell that person that I already have a central relationship in my life. My relationship with Jesus Christ determines the kinds of relationships I have with everyone else.")

No temptation has seized you except what is common to man. And God is faithful; He will not let you be tempted beyond what you can bear. But when you are tempted, He will also provide a way out so that you can stand up under it.
1 Cor. 10:13

Chapter 5

Vows and Promises

Chapter Preview

Chapter 5 will help you answer the following questions:

- For what purposes did God institute marriage?
- How can a couple know if they have the kind of relationship which will lead to a good marriage?
- What does the marriage vow really mean?
- How does the church conduct marriages?

1. Will You Marry Me?

Each section of this chapter will contain a hymn stanza. You may read them thoughtfully alone, or you may speak or sing them with your class.

O perfect Love, all human thought transcending,
Lowly we kneel in prayer before Your throne
That theirs may be the love which knows no ending,
Whom You forevermore unite in one.

Reflect for a moment. What does this stanza say about marriage?

Ready for Marriage?

Scene 1

Time: Christmas Eve, some year in the future
Place: 1406 Rockwell, Hometown, U. S. A.

Marcia and Rick had dated off and on for nearly two years. It had been a rocky courtship. They had met in a college class and been attracted to each other right from the start. Before meeting Marcia, Rick had not dated much. He had always been a quiet, studious person, and he loved Marcia's easy-going, fun-loving nature. She encouraged him to do lots of crazy things he'd never done before.

Every time Rick tried to talk seriously about the future, Marcia would begin to joke around and then change the subject. Though she went to church with him once in a while, she said it made her uncomfortable. But Rick was sure he could change her feelings about it in time. He had heard that Marcia occasionally went to parties with other guys, but whenever he asked her about it, she laughed and said the other guys were just friends.

Rick knew that graduation was only five months away. He planned to go into business with his father, and he had already begun making plans for a new product he hoped to develop. He knew his parents questioned whether he and Marcia were right for each other, but he was ready to get established and begin building a future. He hoped Marcia was ready, too. He had chosen a simple but expensive diamond ring for her Christmas gift. He was nervous but determined as he prepared to ask the question, "Marcia, will you marry me?"

Scene 2

Time: Christmas Eve, some year in the future
Place: 1406 Stonewall, Anytown, U.S.A.

Brad and Katie had met at a youth gathering while they were seniors in high school. Gradually they had become "best friends." Because they shared many of the same interests, they always had things to talk about. When Brad's job training took him out of town for long periods of time, they exchanged letters. But it was not until Brad was sent to England for eight months that Katie realized how much she really missed him. When he returned, Katie knew he had missed her too.

Their relationship deepened and became more serious. They began to go to church and family gatherings together. Gradually, as they talked about the future, they began to include each other in their plans. Katie already felt close to Brad's mother, and she knew her parents liked Brad. She also knew that Brad's job training would take another year to complete.

When Brad's sister began to tease them and ask what their plans were, both of them realized they were ready to make the decision to spend their lives together. After they had gone to church together on Christmas Eve, Brad had gone to Katie's home to share the family celebration of Christmas. After everyone else had turned in for the night, Brad pulled Katie close and, after a loving embrace, asked, "Katie, will you marry me?"

Signs of Readiness for Marriage

How do you know when you are ready for the commitment to marry? What guidelines can a person use to determine whether a dating relationship has progressed to the point of permanent commitment? Christian marriage and family living counselors have identified signs a person can use to evaluate a relationship's potential for permanent commitment:

1. A bond of faith. The two of you share a common bond of faith in Jesus Christ. Your lives demonstrate your commitment to serving your Lord.

2. Deep friendship. You are each other's best friend. You enjoy being together and care as much about each other as you do about yourselves. You laugh together and enjoy many of the same things. You sense that there is a good fit between the two of you at many levels.

3. Good communication. You communicate freely and easily. You can tell each other anything without worrying about being put down or misunderstood.

4. Ability to resolve differences. You know how to resolve differences and conflicts. You know how to handle the inevitable disagreements. After you have resolved a disagreement, you feel closer to each other, not angry or resentful.

5. Mutual commitment. You both think of marriage as a lifetime commitment. You understand that commitment to one another is an essential part of love, because it holds a relationship together even when feelings come and go.

6. Intimacy and trust. You feel your partner knows you well, and accepts and values you as the person you really are. You have given yourselves plenty of time to really get to know each other. You know you can trust each other.

7. A support system. Your family and friends are supportive of the two of you as a couple.

8. A stable relationship. You feel romantic about each other much of the time, but feel comfortable and content together nearly all the time. Your relationship feels safe and stable.

The words *Will you marry me?* generally mark the end of the courtship stage of a relationship. If the answer is yes, the couple are now considered engaged to be married. (Of course the answer may also be no, in which case the relationship may end.)

During the dating process we discussed in chapter 4, a man and woman get to know and love each other and, if the relationship continues, they move toward commitment. When they agree to marry, their relationship takes on a different character than it had when they were just dating. Their friends and relatives now begin to think of them as a couple, and they begin to work out the details of arranging a marriage and a life together.

1. Both couples in the stories above reached a point of decision. On a scale of 1 (least likely) to 10 (most likely), how likely is it that Marcia and Rick will establish a successful marriage? What score would you give to Brad and Katie's chances? Explain why you rated their chances as you did.

2. Look at "Signs of Readiness for Marriage." How many of these signs do you think are essential for a couple before they become engaged to be married? What other signs of readiness (if any) do you think should be on the list?

3. How many of these signs of readiness for marriage are present in the relationship of Marcia and Rick? How many are present in the relationship of Brad and Katie?

4. You studied **Eph. 5:25–28** in chapter 4. Review: Where do you get the power to display the desirable characteristics mentioned in these signs of readiness? How does forgiveness affect *ability to resolve differences?*

Defining the Term

We have only to look around to realize that the term *marriage* means different things to different people. A clear, Scriptural definition can help us understand what the marriage relationship is intended to be. When God created each element of the universe, He put His seal of approval on every aspect: **"God saw that it was good" (Gen. 1:4, 9, 10, 12, 18, 21, 25, 31.)**

We might be startled, therefore, to hear God say in **Gen. 2:18** that something was not good. What was *not* good? **"It is not good for the man to be alone."**

God cared about Adam's aloneness. He wanted Adam to have more than a lonely, isolated life. God solved man's aloneness with His creative act. What was God's solution? **"I will make a helper suitable for him."**

The Hebrew word for *suitable helper* means much more than our English word. It conveys the idea of someone who assists another person to reach complete fulfillment. When used elsewhere in the

Old Testament, it refers to someone who comes to rescue another. God's remedy for the lonely situation of man was a woman, someone to rescue him, someone who would be there as a vital part of his life, helping him find fulfillment. God was saying, "I will give Adam someone to rescue him from his aloneness, someone to complete him, someone to give his life fullness and joy."

When Scripture says the woman would be suitable, it means she would "correspond" to him. They would fit together like two pieces in a jigsaw puzzle. Each partner was designed to be unique and distinct; they were created to need each other and therefore to find fulfillment with each other. Man and woman were created for fellowship with each other. Even as they retained their separate personalities, in marriage they became "one flesh." After God had created Eve from a part of Adam, He Himself brought her to Adam.

1. How did Adam react to this wonderful gift? Read **Gen. 2:23** in at least two translations, if possible. How would you express in your own words Adam's feelings about the suitable helper God created for him? (*The Living Bible* uses the exclamation, "This is it!")

2. You might memorize the words that follow **(Gen. 2:24),** which appear at the end of this section.

The Essence of Marriage

The **Gen. 2:24** passage, which concludes the story of the union of Adam and Eve, contains four essential elements in God's design for marriage:

- **Severance:** a man will *leave* his father and mother
- **Unity:** and be *united* to his wife (some translations use the word *cleave*)
- **Permanence and intimacy:** and they will become *one flesh*

3. Look at each of the four words in "The Essence of Marriage" and the part of the text on which each was based. Then write in your own words

a. what the term means;

b. why it is (or is not) a necessary part of marriage.

On the basis of this passage, we can formulate a definition of Christian marriage based upon God's directive for the relationship:

> Christian Marriage is the union of one man and one woman, entered into by mutual consent, pledged under God for life, to know and honor one another in a one-flesh relationship.

Making a commitment to marriage according to God's plan is one of the most important steps you will ever take. When you commit to sharing your life with another person, every aspect of your life changes. When a man and woman marry, they are setting themselves up for something wonderful—or something horrible. If the other person is right for you and your relationship is centered on Christ, the years of life you share will be rewarding and enriching. If you marry someone with whom you do not share the bonds mentioned above, of if you leave God out of your marriage, you may be setting yourself up for years of pain and unhappiness.

Every marriage is unique. A good marriage partner can strengthen your relationship with God. As husband and wife become one flesh, they also become joint heirs of the kingdom of God. An unsuitable marriage partner, on the other hand, can undermine both your faith and your Christian life. The choice of a marriage partner is so critical to the future pattern of our lives that it makes the choice of a career seem insignificant by comparison.

4. Give an example or two of people you know (do not give names) or have read about that illustrate one of the following:

a. A marriage in which each partner strengthened the other's relationship with God

b. A marriage that contributed to one partner falling away from the faith

For this reason a man will leave his father and mother and be united to his wife, and they will become one flesh.

Gen. 2:24

2. Why Do People Marry?

O perfect Life, be now their full assurance
Of tender charity and steadfast faith.
Of patient hope and quiet, brave endurance,
With childlike trust that fears no pain or death.

Falling in love and getting married are part of the natural sequence of the lives of the majority of people. Yet the reasons for marrying vary from person to person. Many set themselves up for troubled marriages by marrying for the wrong reasons. Though they may not admit or even be consciously aware of all the reasons they are marrying, many young people marry for reasons such as the following:

- They wish to escape from their parents and believe marriage will help them achieve the independence they are seeking.
- They want to be taken care of. They see marriage as a safety net, a way to find security.
- They feel lonely and empty; they believe marriage will meet all their needs to be loved and valued.
- They believe marriage will enhance their social position, making them more important and able to get farther ahead in their lives.

1. Which of these reasons will lead to a strong, lasting marriage relationship? Why?

2. Which of these reasons will make it difficult for a couple to build a strong marriage partnership? Why?

3. Which of these reasons demonstrate conditional, self-serving love?

4. What do you believe to be the most valid reasons for marrying? Why?

5. Read **Gen. 2:18–24; Matt. 19:4–6;** and **Prov. 5:18.** What does the Bible say about the first purpose of marriage, sometimes called the relational purpose of marriage?

6. Read **Gen. 1:28; Ps. 128:3–5;** and **Eph. 6:4.**

Three Purposes of Marriage

God reveals three purposes for which He created marriage:

- Companionship (mutual love)
- Procreation of children
- Restraint of sin (Since the time Adam and Eve fell into sin).

What does the Bible say about the second purpose of marriage, sometimes called the procreative purpose of marriage?

7. Read **1 Thess. 4:3–5; Heb. 13:4;** and **1 Cor. 7:2–5, 9.** What does the Bible say about the third purpose of marriage, sometimes called the healing purpose of marriage?

8. Read **Matt. 6:33; 22:37–39;** and **Mark 12:24–25.** Which relationship has priority even over the marriage relationship?

9. What key to marital happiness do you find in **Eph. 5:19–20?**

Engagement

When a young couple commit to marriage, their relationship enters a new phase. The engagement period has some very important functions. When a couple are dating, both are usually on their best behavior, trying to impress the other person. Sometimes that relationship changes drastically when they become engaged and feel sure of each other. Take the case of Rhoda:

When Joe and Rhoda became engaged. Rhoda felt happier than she had ever been. Joe was handsome, drove a great car, and always took her to wonderful places when they went out. Rhoda couldn't believe how lucky she was. They had agreed not to get married for another year and a half; they both wanted to save some money first.

For awhile everything was fine; they decided who the wedding attendants should be, what kind of apartment they wanted, where they wanted to go on their honeymoon. But gradually, as the months went by, Joe seemed to become more distant. He started going out with his buddies on the weekends.

When Rhoda asked for his opinions about plans for the wedding, he told her she should just go ahead and take care of it. And she didn't know what to do when he started to pressure her to begin a sexual relationship. Rhoda pretended that everything was fine. She paid the deposit on her wedding gown, and her parents made the reservations for a reception hall.

On the night that marked the one-year anniversary of their engagement, Rhoda planned a special surprise for Joe. However, at 9:30 p.m. he called and told her that one of his old school buddies was in town; could they go out together the next night instead? When she hung up, Rhoda was in tears.

If Rhoda were your friend, what would you tell her?

The engagement period is a preparation for marriage. There is a lot of excitement and anticipation as a couple make plans for their wedding and their future life. But this is also a time of adjustment. Important and far-reaching decisions must be made.

Sometimes a young man or woman who had been madly in love several months before begins to wonder, "Is this someone with whom I can spend the rest of my life?" The romance may begin to fade when the realities of planning a future must be faced. Differences begin to appear and may lead to serious conflicts. The two may disagree entirely about what type of wedding to have. Financial pressures become real when a couple begin to anticipate the expenses they will encounter as they begin to set up their home. Their two families may have very different expectations and traditions to be incorporated into the wedding.

Unless these conflicts can be resolved, the marriage may be in trouble even before it begins. For most couples, the engagement period is a time of hard work!

Discussion Questions

1. What options do Rhoda and Joe have in their present relationship?
2. Describe the kind of engagement relationship you think would lead to a good marriage.
3. List the decisions an engaged couple must make as they prepare to marry.
4. Is it wrong to break an engagement?
5. What should a couple do if they are having problems with their relationship during the engagement period?
6. How does God work through other people when we seek guidance for decisions in our lives? Tell about a time when someone's counsel helped you follow God's will for you. How might God work through other people to help you prepare for marriage?
7. How will their relationship with God affect a couple's words, feelings, and actions?

Preparing for Marriage

When we marry, the marriage relationship becomes the most important personal relationship in our lives. Yet most people prepare little, if at all, for it. Many couples spend thousands of dollars and hours preparing for their *wedding,* but invest hardly any time or energy at all preparing for their *marriage.* They work tirelessly to make sure the guest lists are complete, the gowns perfectly fitted, all the arrangements in place. Yet they may not share their faith with each other, pray for and with each other, or set realistic goals for their lives together.

The wedding lasts for one day. The marriage lasts for a lifetime. We need to be sure our priorities are in order when we are planning for marriage.

A lovely wedding can truly be a joyous beginning to life together; but how much more important it is for an engaged couple to talk and pray and work together to prepare for the lifetime, not just for the wedding day! Most couples will have a complete physical exam before marriage; most states require blood tests. A couple who wish to lay the foundation for a good marriage need to determine more than the health of their bodies. They need to evaluate the health of the total relationship and their mutual commitment to God and to each other!

Many churches have tried to meet this need by offering or even requiring premarital counseling for all couples intending to marry in the church.

Interview your pastor or the person who provides the preparation for marriage that your church offers. (To respect your pastor's many other commitments, arrange for a group interview if several of you come from the same church.) Write a two-part report on the premarital counseling program, concentrating on these two areas:

1. Of what does the premarital counseling program consist? How many sessions are involved? Does he use any questionnaires, booklets, or similar tools to help the couple determine what areas of difference need to be resolved? (If a questionnaire is used, attach a copy to your report.) What problems does the pastor or counselor most often encounter during the premarital counseling sessions? What does the counselor see as the primary purpose for these sessions? Does the counselor have enough time available to provide the kind of counseling he would like? (You may wish to add further questions of your own.)

2. Reflect upon your interview. What benefits do you see in a premarital counseling program? (If possible, talk with one or two recently married couples from your church to see in what ways they found the counseling to be helpful.) What kind of premarital counseling would *you* wish to receive if you were preparing to marry? How can couples prepare themselves so they will receive maximum benefit from such counseling? You may wish to add other observations based on your interviaw and conversations. (If you wish to suggest a change in your church's premarital counseling, talk with your pastor again to share your ideas.)

The Lord God said, "It is not good for the man to be alone. I will make a helper suitable for him."

Gen. 1:18

Since there is so much immorality, each man should have his own wife, and each woman her own husband. The husband should fulfill his marital duty to his wife, and likewise the wife to her husband.

1 Cor. 7:2–3

3. A History of Marriage

O Father, all creating,
Whose wisdom, love, and power
First bound two lives together
In Eden's primal hour,
Today to these Your children
Your earliest gifts renew:
A home by You made happy,
A love by You kept true.

Lutheran Worship 251:1

How did our customs and ceremonies of marriage develop? As we have already learned, marriages in Biblical times were different in many ways from our marriages today. In fact, marriages in Biblical times probably did not take place in a church. Scripture does not record any religious marriage ceremonies. While Scripture describes God-pleasing marriage and states its purposes, God did not set forth specific steps and precise procedures to govern marriage ceremonies.

Marriage among the Hebrews

During Old Testament times the father of the groom chose a suitable bride for his son. The process involved four steps:

1. Negotiation. The negotiations between the families sometimes involved a financial exchange, a bride price paid to the family of the bride. Though young men and women might meet each other at harvest festivals or the village well, love was not a necessary part of the transaction. Marriage was regarded as a covenant entered into by the two familes who formed an alliance through the marriage of their son and daughter.

2. Betrothal. When the transaction had been made, the young couple were said to be betrothed. Once the bride price had been paid by the family of the groom, the contract was sealed; the marriage arrangement was final and could not be broken. This covenant agreement was the basis for the Hebrew marriage. Betrothing in Biblical times was a permanent commitment, somewhat like arranging for a wife on the lay-away plan. This was the relationship between Mary and Joseph when Mary first heard the news that she was to become the mother of Jesus. They were committed to each other, though they had not yet begun to live together.

3. Coming together. Usually within a year of the betrothal, the husband would take the bride into his home. This was the culmination of the covenant that had been made. Scripture does not indicate that any kind of religious ceremony was connected with the coming together in marriage. It was a family, communal arrangement, and the ceremony was understood accordingly.

4. Consummation. Bride and groom would consummate the marriage. This act of sexual intercourse would complete the marriage. From that point on they would live together as husband and wife.

Some Hebrew marriage practices seem very foreign to us today. Many of the Hebrew men practiced polygamy; well-known people of the Old Testament such as Abraham, David, and Solomon had many wives and concubines as a way of increasing the numbers of their people. The Old Testament Scriptures gave no specific command against this practice, though they strongly imply monogamy **(Gen. 2:24).** Of course, polygamy often led to much disharmony in family life.

Marriage among the Jews

The New Testament Jews had a high ideal of marriage, but their actual practices fell far short of the ideal. Every man was expected to be married by tha age of 20, as part of his sacred duty to carry on the family.

The Jewish marriage concept considered a woman to be a legal possession, first of her father and then of her husband. She had virtually no legal rights at all; her status in the community depended entirely on her husband. She could never divorce her husband, though he could divorce her for nearly any cause. Because property and family inheritance were passed down through the male offspring, a woman whose husband died was left destitute, at the mercy of relatives (as the story of Ruth and Naomi illustrated). A woman's duties were clearly defined; she had no alternatives if her marriage brought her pain or sorrow. Though some women were deeply loved and cherished by their husbands, others were treated as a necessary piece of property.

At the time of Jesus, divorce had become common. Some young women were reluctant even to marry. Many people regarded chastity as an unreaonable restriction. With abuses of the marriage bond everywhere around, Jesus preached a radical change in the entire concept and practice of marriage. His strong teachings about marriage and divorce in **Matthew 5** and **19** admonished his followers to restore faithful commitment to spouse and family and instructed spouses to live with each other in mutual respect and love as a response to the love God had showed to them.

The Greeks and Romans

The Greek and Roman influences of that era further undermined the family bond. In the Greek world, sexual relationships outside of marriage were accepted and commonplace. In fact, prostitution was often part of their religious practices. Greek culture had a decided double standard. Wives were kept secluded so their purity would be maintained, but husbands engaged in many extramarital relationships. The Greeks regarded Christian teachings regarding chastity and faithfulness in marriage as absolutely radical.

In contrast to the Greeks, Roman society was founded on the home. The wife shared a full part in the marriage. After Rome conquered Greece, however, Greek immorality infiltrated Roman culture. The results were disastrous. Divorce became commonplace and marriage was held in low esteem.

As Paul and the other apostles preached to these diverse groups of people, they had to forcefully confront the sins that had become socially accepted. The apostles preached that Christians were *not* to conform to the world's practices but were to be transformed by the Spirit. Their lives were to be entirely different from the world's, to stand out and be noticed. Through the witness of their Christian lives, God would call more people into fellowship with Him and increase the number of those who would be saved.

Paul's concept of marriage is built on the basic doctrine of creation. We should enter marriage, an institution of God, in sanctification and honor. Though the New Testament does not set down marriage laws or state requirements for marriage, Paul made it clear that Christian principles of love, honor, and purity are to govern Christian marriages. No matter what the practices of the world around them, Paul told the Christians in **1 Thess. 4:4** to demonstrate holiness and honor, reflecting the self-sacrificing love which God had bestowed upon them in Jesus.

Discussion Questions

1. What parallels do you see between the world of Jesus' day and our own day concerning marriage?

2. How does engagement differ from betrothal?

3. Are Christian teachings about marriage considered radical in our society? Do Christians today have to forcefully confront sins that have become socially accepted? Give evidence to defend your answers.

4. Interview a person who is at least 60 years old. Ask about marriage and family life in recent history. What are the greatest changes that person has observed? What results have these changes brought? Have these changes strengthened or weakened our society, in his or her opinion?

5. Why do Christian teachings about marriage stay the same even when the customs and practices of society are constantly changing?

History Continues

Christianity, with its emphasis on the importance of every person, male or female, its teachings of monogamy and faithfulness in marriage, and its warnings against adultery, helped to hold society together after the Roman Empire began to disintegrate and on into the "Dark Ages."

During this time the first religious rites became part of the marriage ceremony, as the priests began to offer a prayer at the marriage. Gradually married couples would walk to the steps in front of the church, where the priest would pronounce a blessing on them. In 1439 marriage became a sacrament of the Roman Catholic Church.

St. Thomas Aquinas, (1224–74), one of the most influential theologians in the church of the Middle Ages, emphasized the mutual consent concept of marriage. A valid marriage needed *the mutual consent of the parties involved, the public announcement of the marriage, and consummation of the marriage in sexual intercourse.* No longer could a woman be "given" in marriage against her will.

If any of these factors was not present in a Roman Catholic marriage, it could be annulled (declared not valid). If a person's marriage was annulled, he or she could remarry with the blessing of the church. (A divorced person, in contrast, could be excommunicated and denied the Sacrament if he or she remarried.)

Though the requirement for mutual consent in marriage had its foundation in Roman law and was not really established on the basis of Scripture, it has remained a central part of the marriage covenant for nearly a thousand years. We can hardly imagine a marriage to which both parties did not give their consent.

In the centuries following Thomas Aquinas, marriage came under the further control of the church. The Council of Trent in 1545–1563 determined that no marriage of a Roman Catholic was valid unless it was contracted in the presence of a parish priest and two other witnesses.

Discussion Questions

1. How did the requirement for mutual consent change the framework for marriage?
2. Is a marriage between Christians valid today if it is performed outside of the church? Why or why not?
3. What are the legal requirements today for marriage in your state? (If you don't know, how can you find out?)
4. Historically, marriage was completed with the consummation (sexual intercourse). How does this compare with many people's sexual practices today?

From Martin Luther to the Present

By the time of Martin Luther the Roman Catholic Church held celibacy to be a higher order of Christian life than marriage. Yet Luther could find no basis for this in Scripture. He believed marriage was a heavenly, spiritual, and godly estate, but not a sacrament. His own marriage and family life provided great joy in his life, and he wrote, "Next to God's Word the world has not a more lovely and endearing treasure on earth than the holy state of matrimony which He has Himself instituted, preserving it, having adorned and blessed it above all stations, from which not only all emperors, kings, and saints, but even the eternal Son of God, though in a supernatural way, are born. Whoever, therefore, hates the marriage state and speaks evil of it, certainly is of the devil."

In further contrast to the Roman Catholic Church, Luther held that marriages not performed by a priest were still valid marriages. His explanation of the Sixth Commandment clearly stated his teachings about marriage: "We should fear and love God so that we lead a sexually pure and decent life in what we say and do, and husband and wife love and honor each other."

The subject of marriage has received much attention in the church during recent years. The large number of troubled marriages, divorces, or people living together without marriage have made it necessary for the church to invest much time and effort in educating God's people about His direction for marriage.

We honor God and the neighbor rightly when we

- regard marriage as a divine, lifelong institution, ordained by God for the good of man and woman;
- respect marriage as the typical, though not necessary, expression of our creation as male and female;
- see in our creation as sexual beings God's design for fellowship, and give thanks for the healing which God offers in marriage;
- affirm God's will that sexual intercourse be engaged in only between a man and woman committed to a complete and lifelong sharing of their lives with one another in a marriage covenant not to be broken;
- affirm that the mutual love of husband and wife, while possessing God-given meaning in and of itself, is by divine blessing ordered toward the birth of a child; and
- affirm that this union of mutual love is the only proper context for human procreation.

(From *Human Sexuality: A Theological Perspective,* The Commission on Theology and Church Relations, The Lutheran Church—Missouri Synod, 1981.)

1. Restate each of the teachings from *Human Sexuality* in your own words.
2. Write a statement that reflects your own understanding of marriage: Marriage is . . .

Marriage Customs

As we have observed through the study of the history of marriage, for many centuries no prescribed religious rites accompanied marriage. However, many elements of ceremony, some going all the way back to the Hebrews, developed as part of the marriage traditions.

Many of these are still part of our present day marriage customs. Among the Hebrews, for example, marriages included special attire. It was customary for women in ancient times, especially if they were unmarried, to be veiled when they were in public as a mark of modesty and character. At the coming together, the bride's father would raise the veil so the intended groom could see the bride's face. (A veil may have allowed Laban to deceive Jacob when Jacob married Leah, thinking he was marrying Rachel. Jacob did not realize he had married Leah until the next morning, after they had slept together—**Gen. 29:16–28.)**

The bride and groom would assemble their wedding parties in separate places and then proceed to a predetermined place; this is the origin for the modern wedding processional. The processions, like ours, were accompanied by music. After the coming together of the bride and groom, feasting was customary. In Old Testament times, it often lasted for an entire week.

The Jews and later the Romans added to the customs of marriage. When Romans wanted the blessing of Jupiter upon a wedding, they prepared a wheat grain cake to offer as a sacrifice; it was then sacramentally cut and eaten by the couple. After the marriage contract was signed and a matron formally introduced the bridal couple to each other, they then joined their right hands to symbolize their mutual consent to the marriage. When a couple were betrothed under Roman law, the contract was generally accompanied by an iron betrothal ring sent to the woman by the man. An ancient tradition held that a vein ran directly from the fourth finger to the heart; thus the fourth finger became the ring finger.

For Discussion

1. What customs in modern weddings have been retained or adapted from historical practices?

2. Many families and ethnic groups have their own wedding traditions and customs. Bring to class an example of a special wedding tradition or custom with which you are familiar. (*Optional:* Research and submit a written report on wedding traditions and customs, based on your own family history or reading you have done.)

3. Talk with someone who has recently married. What traditions or customs did he or she find most meaningful? Why?

4. What special traditions or customs might you wish to include in your wedding if you marry in the future?

5. What suggestions would you make to help married couples confess their faults and offer forgiveness to one another? How do confession and forgiveness strengthen a marriage?

"Haven't you read," He replied, "that at the beginning the Creator 'made them male and female,' and said, 'For this reason a man will leave his father and mother and be united to his wife, and the two will become one flesh'? So they are not longer two, but one. Therefore what God has joined together, let man not separate."

Matt. 19:4–6

4. Marriage: Vow or Contract?

Unless You build it, Father,
The house is built in vain;
Unless You, Savior, bless it,
The joy will turn to pain.
But nothing breaks a marriage
Of hearts in You made one;
The love Your Spirit hallows
Is endless love begun.

Lutheran Worship 251:4

When a man and woman marry, they make a solemn promise to each other. Each promises to love, comfort, honor, and be faithful to the other for as long as they both shall live. This promise is probably the most popular vow in history. Yet many people do not take it seriously.

Actually, the joining of a man and woman in marriage is more than a simple promise. Marriage is built upon a solemn vow, patterned on the covenant relationship God has established with us.

The Bible often refers to the church as the bride of Christ. God kept His Old Testament covenant with His people by sending the promised Messiah, Jesus. Jesus' death restored people to a loving, intimate relationship with God. The church, the people He has saved, are now His bride, living with Him in a relationship of love and commitment that will continue into eternity.

Through much of the early history of marriage, the contract between the two families was the most important part of the marriage. If the bride and groom spoke promises to each other, these promises merely reinforced the agreement already established. In contrast, in a Christian marriage today *the vows that are spoken are the heart of the wedding ceremony.*

Recently marriage contracts have again become popular with some people. Because of the high rate of divorce and the painful disagreements that often mark the division of property when a marriage ends, couples sometimes negotiate a marriage contract prior to the marriage. But a *contract* is not a *vow.*

Listed below are some examples of pledges people make. Tell whether each is a *vow* or a *contract.*

- becoming a citizen of a country
- purchasing a home
- agreeing to perform a job or work for a company
- becoming a member of a religious order
- leasing an apartment or car

Discussion Questions

1. What is a vow? What is a contract?How does a vow differ from a contract?

2. Which type of relationship demonstrates conditional love? Which type demonstrates unconditional love?

3. Does God intend marriage to be in the spirit of a vow or in the spirit of a contract? How do you know?

4. A common marriage vow concludes with the the words, "so long as we both shall live." A young couple who married recently decided to change the wording to "so long as we both shall love." Was their promise a vow or a contract? Explain. Is it in harmony with God's will for marriage?

A Public Commitment

The marriage vow is both *public* and *private.* It is a private vow in that husband and wife speak their words of commitment to each other. But it is also a public vow in that it is made in the presence of witnesses and is bound by the civil laws of the state. The couple announce to the world that they now share their lives and possessions and accept responsibility for any children which might be born. The vow thus has the important function of safeguarding the rights of the spouse and of future children, thereby effecting a wider circle of persons than just the two persons marrying.

Speaking their vows to each other, the essence of the marriage, takes the average wedding couple about 30 seconds. But keeping them involves a lifetime of much more than merely signing a legal contract. In a contract, two parties agree that each will provide some goods or services *in exchange* for some goods or services provided by the other. A contract is thus an "if" relationship, conditional on the performance of the other party. It is a legally enforceable "deal." It expires when the conditions set forth no longer apply.

Keeping a vow, however, does not depend on the behavior of the other person. There is no "if," for it is not based upon any conditions to be met by the other person; it is unconditional. A vow is a solemn promise under God to remain faithful to a commitment made. A vow is lifelong.

The marriage vow calls upon the power of God for its fulfillment. It recognizes that we do not have enough power on our own to faithfully maintain our commitment. If a couple merely promised mutual love to each other, they would be likely to fail at least part of the time.

Even in happy, harmonious marriages one spouse at times does not feel loving toward the other. No couple can possibly keep perfectly all the promises they have made. But a solemn vow retains its power and validity regardless of the other person's conduct, for it draws on the forgiveness and power of God for its commitment to the other person. When God is present in the relationship, sacred vows *can* be kept.

Most people assume that a couple's love for one another is the thing that holds the marriage together. Certainly love must be present for a marriage to endure. But the love of God working through the vows holds the marriage together and provides the foundation for continuing love, not vice versa.

God joins a man and woman. On their own they freely make the choice to marry, but God changes the two into one. The commitment within a marriage is more than emotion or experience. If loving feelings fade, the vows made before God call upon His power to provide continual strength and renewal, thereby restoring love. The commitment in such a vow loves the other person even when he or she is most unlovable. The *agape* that is ours through Jesus makes it possible for us to go on loving even when we receive nothing in return. We saw an illustration of that love in Hosea. Only God's power could have enabled Hosea to restore Gomer to the marriage relationship after all the times she had betrayed him.

Marriage is more than a personal decision. It is a public act that creates a new legal relationship between two people. It is also God's work. Working through the lives of each partner, God brings two people together and joins them in the relationship He established at the beginning of the human race. God is present in the marriage vows just as He is in every aspect of our lives. He works through each person's personal history to accomplish His purposes.

> The Christian marriage relationship is a *triangle: husband, wife, God.* Only God's power can enable you and me to go on loving, day after day, year after year.

For Discussion

1. One marriage vow reads, "I, [name], in the presence of God and these witnesses, take you, [name], to be my wife [or husband], to have and to hold from this day forward, for better, for worse, for richer, for poorer, in sickness and in health, to love and to cherish, until death parts us, and I pledge you my faithfulness." How is that vow similar to the confirmation vow printed below? In what ways is it different?

Pastor: Do you intend to continue steadfast in this confession and church and to suffer all, even death, rather than fall away from it?

Confirmand: I do so intend with the help of God.

Pastor: Do you intend faithfully to conform all your life to the divine Word, to be faithful in the use of God's Word and Sacraments, which are His means of grace, and in faith, word, and action to remain true to God, Father, Son, and Holy Spirit, even to death?

Confirmand: I do so intend by the grace of God.

Pastor: Give then your hand as pledge of your promise, and kneel to receive the blessing.

2. A marriage is still a valid marriage even if husband and wife no longer love each other. How does this truth affect the way we enter a marriage?

3. Most couples enter marriage with high expectations of living "happily ever after." The words of the marriage vows pledge faithfulness.

> . . . for better, for worse,
> for richer, for poorer,
> in sickness and in health.

Most couples automatically expect that their marriage will consist mostly of "better," "richer," and "health." How could the marriage vow help them in times of "worse," "poorer," and "sickness"?

4. Tell about someone you know who has been faithful to his or her marriage vows through bad times, financial problems, or illness. Where can we find the power to be as faithful to our vows as they have been to theirs?

For Reflection

1. *How far are you prepared to go* if you marry? Will you be faithful only in good times—or are you willing to go all the way, even in bad times?
2. Will you be faithful only when you are richer—or are you willing to go all the way, even to being poor?
3. Will you be faithful only in health—or are you willing to go all the way, even to sickness or death?
4. Write a prayer that could be used by someone preparing to marry, seeking God's power as he or she gets ready to make the solemn vow of marriage.

Be faithful, even to the point of death, and I will give you the crown of life.

Rev. 2:10

5. The Marriage Service

Lord, when You came as welcome Guest
To Cana's wedding feast,
The bridal pair, divinely blest,
Found all their joy increased.
Now give Your presence from above
That these, by vowing true,
May show their pledge is like the love
Between the Church and You.

Lutheran Worship 252:1

(Concordia Publishing House © 1982)

A Christian wedding is the occasion for a service of worship and praise. It is not just a ceremony for family and friends to watch. Every worship service focuses on God and what He has done for us, and that focus remains even during the excitement of a wedding. Marriage is God's gift and it shows His intention for us to live in community—with Him and with each other. We live our lives—and our marriages—in the context of the whole people of God.

A Christian marriage provides one way for us to live a life of praise to Him. If we marry, we will be joined to our partner for the sake of others. Marriage is one way to move beyond self-centeredness and selfishness; we reach out first to another person in self-giving love, and then in selfless service to others in the world.

The heart of the marriage service is the vows, the promises of lifelong commitment. The vows bind two people together for life. The pastor does not marry the two people; *they marry each other.* The pastor has a twofold role:

- To witness to the vows that are made—he serves as God's representative and a spiritual counselor
- To certify that the marriage has legally taken place—he serves as a representative of the state, an agent of the court

The pastor's words do not create the marriage; the vows create the marriage.

The ring, the veil—even much of the wedding ceremony itself—have come to us from heathen Rome, having been adopted and adapted by the Christian church. Much of what our church knows and teaches about marriage is set forth in the marriage liturgy. The wedding service includes a reverent setting in which bride and groom give their mutual consent and make their vows—the essence of marriage; thanks and praise to God for His gift of marriage; and prayers of the congregation for the marriage to be God-pleasing and fruitful.

Many people get so caught up in the spectacle of the wedding that they never really hear the words. A Lutheran wedding service is printed below. As you read it, pay special attention to the words, for they provide a summary of the church's teachings about marriage. The service assists the couple in viewing their marriage as God's institution; it instructs them on the nature of marriage as He designed it; it provides for the exchange of vows of lifelong faithfulness "in the sight of God"; and it asks God in prayer for His blessing and guidance. (The words may vary somewhat from one congregation to another, but most marriage rites will contain the same elements.)

The Lutheran wedding service consists of a processional, a recessional, and three major sections, each of which includes several parts:

A. The Preparation

1. Invocation and description of marriage
2. Holy Scriptures
3. Pastor's address
4. Congregational hymn or solo

B. The Marriage

5. Mutual consent
6. Marriage vows (joined hands)
7. Exchange of rings
8. Announcement of the marriage

C. The Response

9. Blessings, prayers, and Lord's Prayer
10. Benediction

The order of marriage from *Lutheran Worship* is printed below. Read the entire service. Then do the following:

1. Tell where each of the 10 parts listed above begins in the ceremony.
2. Write a brief description of the purpose of each of the 10 parts of the ceremony.
3. Where in the Rite of Marriage are the purposes for marriage restated?
4. How many Scripture passages are quoted? What is the purpose of each?
5. Which two parts are the essence of the marriage?

MARRIAGE

1. This rite, with adaptation, may be set within the Divine Service, Matins or Morning Prayer, Vespers or Evening Prayer, where it will follow the Sermon. It may also be used as a separate service.

2. The Propers are those appointed on pages 124—26.

Stand

3. When the wedding party has come to the foot of the altar, the pastor says:

P **In the name of the Father and of the ✠ Son and of the Holy Spirit.**

C Amen

P **We are gathered here in the sight of God and of his Church to witness and bless the joining together of this man and this woman in holy marriage. This is an honorable estate, which God himself has instituted and blessed, and by which he gives us a picture of the very communion of Christ and his bride, the Church. God has both established and sanctified marriage and has promised to bless therein all who love and trust in him and who seek to give him their faithful worship and service, for the sake of our Lord Jesus Christ.**

The union of husband and wife in heart, body, and mind is intended by God for their mutual joy, for the help and comfort given one another in prosperity and adversity, and, when it is God's will, for the procreation of children and their nurture in the knowledge and love of the Lord. Therefore marriage is not to be entered into inadvisedly or lightly, but reverently, deliberately, and in accordance with the purposes for which it was instituted by God.
Sit

4. Appropriate portions of Holy Scripture are read.

P **The Lord God said, "It is not good for the man to be alone. I will make a helper suitable for him." Now the Lord God had formed out of the ground all the beasts of the field and all the birds of the air. He brought them to the man to see what he would name them; and whatever the man called each living creature, that was its name. So the man gave names to all the livestock, the birds of the air and all the beasts of the field. But for Adam no suitable helper was found. So the Lord God caused the man to fall into a deep sleep; and while he was sleeping, he took one of the man's ribs and closed up the place with flesh. Then the Lord God made a woman from the rib he had taken out of the man, and he brought her to the man. The man said, "This is now bone of my bones and flesh of my flesh; she shall be called 'woman,' for she was taken out of man." For this reason a man will leave his father and mother and be united to his wife, and they will become one flesh.** (Gen. 2:18-24)

Submit to one another out of reverence for Christ. Wives, submit to your husbands as to the Lord. For the husband is the head of the wife as Christ is the head of the church, his body, of which he is the Savior. Now as the church submits to Christ, so also wives should submit to their husbands in everything. Husbands, love your wives, just as Christ loved the church and gave himself up for her to make her holy, cleansing her by the washing with water through the word, and to present her to himself as a radiant church, without stain or wrinkle or any other blemish, but holy and blameless. In this same way, husbands ought to love their wives as their own bodies. He who loves his wife loves himself. After all, no one ever hated his own body, but he feeds and cares for it, just as Christ does the church—for we are members of his body. "For this reason a man will leave his father and mother and be united to his wife, and the two will become one flesh." This is a profound mystery—but I am talking about Christ and the church. However, each one of you also must love his wife as he loves himself, and the wife must respect her husband. (Eph. 5:21-33)

[Jesus replied to the Pharisees, "Have you not read that] at the beginning the Creator 'made them male and female,' and said, 'For this reason a man will leave his father and mother and be united to his wife, and the two will become one flesh'? So they are no longer two, but one. Therefore what God has joined together, let man not separate." (Matt. 19:4-6)

5. An address may follow. A hymn may be sung.

6. If the bride and bridegroom have been seated for an address and/or a hymn, they now stand. The pastor asks the bridegroom:
P **___name___, will you have this woman to be your wife, to live with her in holy marriage according to the Word of God? Will you love her, comfort her, honor her, and keep her in sickness and in health and, forsaking all others, be husband to her as long as you both shall live?**

B I will.

7. The pastor asks the bride:

P **___name___, will you have this man to be your husband, to live with him in holy marriage according to the Word of God? Will you love him, comfort him, honor him, obey him, and keep him in sickness and in health and forsaking all others, be wife to him as long as you both shall live?**

R I will.

8. The pastor leads the bride and bridegroom to the altar.

9. The bridegroom, taking the right hand of the bride and facing her, says after the pastor:

I, ____name____ , in the presence of God and these witnesses, take you, ____name____ , to be my wife, to have and to hold from this day forward, for better, for worse, for richer, for poorer, in sickness and in health, to love and to cherish, until death parts us, and I pledge you my faithfulness.

10. The bride, in the same way, says after the pastor:

I, ____name____ , in the presence of God and these witnesses, take you, ____name____ , to be my husband, to have and to hold from this day forward, for better, for worse, for richer, for poorer, in sickness and in health, to love and to cherish, until death parts us, and I pledge you my faithfulness.

11. The bride and bridegroom exchange rings, saying:

Receive this ring as a pledge and token of wedded love and faithfulness.

12. The pastor may speak a blessing upon the pledging of their love with the exchange of rings.

P **Grant your blessing, O Lord, to your servants ____name____ and ____name____ that they may be ever mindful of their solemn pledge and, trusting in your mercy, abound evermore in love all their days; through Jesus Christ, our Lord.** ‹264›

R Amen

13. The bride and bridegroom kneel, and the pastor says:

P **Now that ____name____ and ____name____ have consented together in holy marriage, have given themselves to each other by their solemn pledges, and have declared the same before God and these witnesses, I pronounce them to be husband and wife, in the name of the Father and of the ✠ Son and of the Holy Spirit.**

What God has joined together, let no one put asunder.

C Amen

P **The almighty and gracious God abundantly grant you his favor and sanctify and bless you with the blessing given our first parents in paradise that you may please him in both body and soul and live together in holy love until your life's end.**

C Amen

Stand

P **Let us pray.**

Almighty, everlasting God, our heavenly Father, grant that by your blessing ____name____ and ____name____ may live together according to your Word and promise. Strengthen them in faithfulness and love toward each other. Sustain and defend them in all trial and temptation. Help them to live in faith toward you in the communion of your holy Church and in loving service to each other that they may ever enjoy your heavenly blessing; through Jesus Christ, your Son, our Lord, who lives and reigns with you and the Holy Spirit, one God, now and forever. ‹265›

C Amen

C Our Father who art in heaven,
hallowed be thy name,
thy kingdom come,
thy will be done
on earth as it is in heaven.
Give us this day our daily bread;
and forgive us our trespasses
as we forgive those
who trespass against us;
and lead us not into temptation,
but deliver us from evil.
For thine is the kingdom
and the power and the glory
forever and ever. Amen

OR

C Our Father in heaven,
hallowed be your name,
your kingdom come,
your will be done
on earth as in heaven.
Give us today our daily bread.
Forgive us our sins
as we forgive those
who sin against us.
Lead us not into temptation,
but deliver us from evil.
For the kingdom, the power,
and the glory are yours
now and forever. Amen

14. The pastor pronounces the Blessing.

P **The eternal God, the Father of our Lord Jesus Christ, grant you his Holy Spirit, be with you, and richly bless you now and forever.**

C Amen

(Marriage service from *Lutheran Worship Agenda,* Concordia Publishing House © 1984.)

For this reason a man will leave his father and mother and be united to his wife, and the two will become one flesh.

6. What about Divorce?

Preserve the vow these two shall make,
This circle round their life,
This golden ring that none may break
Which makes them man and wife.
Your daily mercies let them share,
All threats of harm destroy;
By this their vow divide their care
And double all their joy.

Lutheran Worship 252:2.
(Concordia Publishing House © 1982.)

A marriage ceremony, honeymoon, and setting up a home are such mountaintop experiences for most people that it is hard not to feel a letdown sometimes when the real work of building a marriage begins. For those who have sought God's guidance and established their marriage on sound foundations, the marriage relationship will provide much love and enrich their lives.

Yet the marriage statistics tell us that the mate selection process is not working well in our society. The divorce rate in the United States is far higher than in any other country in the world. One marriage out of eight ends in divorce. (This includes people married decades ago; the divorce rate has been much higher among recent marriages.) Some of those who remain married will not share much joy or intimacy. The average marriage lasts 9.4 years.

These statistics fail to mention all the pain, heartbreak, and disillusionment caused by a broken marriage. Some of those who suffer most are the many children who are innocently caught up in the painful and bewildering break-ups of their parents' marriages. Sixty percent of the children born this year will spend at least part of their childhood in a single-parent family. Many of us have lived through this experience. All of us know people to whom it has occurred.

From our confirmation instruction and our own life experiences we have learned that we face three powerful forces which tempt us to sin: our own sinful natures, the world, and the devil. These powerful forces are always present in our lives—and in the lives of our spouses too. When people succumb to temptations from these forces and make bad decisions or act in unloving ways, broken relationships result.

Many failed marriages were in trouble from the beginning. Some people simply sought the wrong person to marry, or married for the wrong reasons. Many did not have any spiritual bond from which to draw strength. In other cases one of the spouses changed so much during the course of the marriage that he or she was no longer the same.

Why Marriages Fail

Why do so many marriages fail? One or more of several factors contribute to most marital breakdowns.

> Marriages fail because of
>
> - lack of common bonds;
> - inability to forgive;
> - unrealistic expectations;
> - lack of readiness for marriage;
> - lack of mature love;
> - personality problems;
> - poor communication;
> - no support system;
> - inability to accept change.

1. Lack of common bonds. Religious beliefs and values were not shared. As we have already discussed, unity on this point is essential! If you believe it is important for husband and wife to pray together, to work together in the church, and to raise your children to love the Lord, but your partner feels these are not important, you face a potential area of conflict that may never be resolved.

2. Inability to forgive. The couple fails to share the forgiveness they have received from God. Jesus put it this way: **"Apart from Me you can do nothing" (John 15:5).** Couples who fail to draw from the strength which God provides must rely only on themselves to maintain their relationship. The basic selfishness of our human nature always gets in the way of love. We need an ongoing source of love if we are to go on loving.

3. Unrealistic expections. One or both partners believe the marriage and their partner should meet all their needs and expectations. After a couple break up, one spouse will often say something like, "I knew before we were married that we had some serious problems in our relationship, but I thought we would work them out after we got married."

As mentioned earlier in the chapter, some couples marry for the wrong reasons. They may feel that marriage will help them meet all their needs. It will make them feel good about themselves, solve a lot of their emotional (or other) problems, and provide all the love they will ever need.

If self-esteem is a problem for one or both of the partners, the chances for a successful marriage diminish. Waiting until after marriage to work out these problems is too late.

Many of our expectations and ideas of marriage are based upon our family of origin. Since each of us comes from a different background, each of us will have different ideas about how things should be done. We may grow up with the idea that we are entitled to all the good things in life—but may not have learned that we are not in this world just to serve ourselves. Unless and until we learn to be thoughtful of others and to work cooperatively with them to meet the needs of family and others, we will not have the caring sensitivity to the other person's needs and feelings that make a marriage endure.

4. Lack of readiness for marriage. The couple is not ready to marry. Perhaps one or the other has dated few other people and does not have a clear understanding of what type of spouse is suited for him or her. Some couples get married too quickly, without giving the relationship enough time to mature and develop so they will know if they are really suited for each other. Most people need at least a year or two of knowing each other before they are ready to commit for a lifetime.

Other couples marry too young. Statistics show that the younger the newlyweds, the less likely the marriage will last. The divorce rate for those in the 21–22 age bracket is twice as high as for those in the 24–25 age group. And the divorce rate for couples under 20 is incredibly high. Many people in our society have not developed full maturity and independence until their mid-20's. How can they be ready to choose a life partner when they have not yet established their own identities? How can they know themselves well enough to understand the strengths and weaknesses they will bring to a marriage? The qualities that make a marriage endure—generosity, sensitivity to the feelings and needs of the other, shared interests and common goals—develop with maturity.

5. Lack of mature love. The decision to marry is made largely on an emotional basis. The pleasures of romantic love are thrilling—but a marriage needs more to endure. Married couples must deal with some tough realities—they need a tough relationship, one based upon more than candlelit dinners and daydreams. A loving married couple will want to keep romance in their marriage—but they will need to build other bonds as well to weather the problems and challenges of a lifetime.

6. Personality problems. One or both partners have doubts about the personality of the other. A lot of people marry someone they don't wholeheartedly like—because they are infatuated, or they want to be married, or they think everything will work out after the wedding.

Many a broken-hearted spouse has spoken the words, "But I thought he [or she] would change." They expected that love and marriage would break the other person's drinking habit; dispel the other person's uncontrollable temper; make the flighty, unreliable person suddenly trustworthy; or transform the stubborn, uncompromising personality into someone who is easy to talk to and willing to change. A person's basic personality traits almost *never* change when he or she marries. What you see is what you get! Unless a person is willing to live with those traits for a lifetime, he or she must work through these problams with the partner *before* marriage.

7. Poor communication. The couple lack good communication skills. If you are afraid to tell your partner what you really feel, if your partner doesn't listen to you or understand how you feel, if you cannot resolve conflicts in a way that builds understanding, you may face a lifetime of anger and frustration. Without good communication skills, you will not have the tools to resolve the conflicts and problems you will face.

8. No support system. The couple lack a support system of family and friends. Every couple needs friends and family to stand by them at times, to share the joys and sorrows. If friends and family do not support your choice of a marriage partner, you may have no network of support. If your relatives and friends do not value marriage, their attitudes may influence you to be careless about your own marriage relationship. Christian family members, a caring church family, and Christian friends support our vows. No married couple is an island; all are part of a community and need the support of other people.

9. Inability to accept change. One or both persons fail to understand or cannot adapt to the stages and changes of their individual development, or the stages and changes that occur within the marriage. A young mother may no longer have the energy to dance all night. A husband who missed a promotion may not be ready to take the family vacation that was planned. Each of us will experience many changes within our lifetime; if we are unable or unwilling to accept these changes, our marriage will suffer. The changes and seasons of marriage will be discussed further in chapter 7.

Adapted from *Finding the Love Of Your Life* by Neil Clark Warren, © 1992 by Focus On The Family Publishing.

Discussion Questions

1. Which of these reasons do you think create the most marriage breakdowns? What other reasons, if any, would you add to the list?
2. Choose the two reasons that you think are the biggest reasons for marital problems and examine them from the following perspectives:
   a. Give an example of how and why they contribute to marriage breakdown. If you know someone whose marriage was dissolved because of these reasons, you may use their situation for an example, but do not use their names.
   b. Discuss how a couple could prevent these problems. How could they deal with the problems if they already exist?
3. Review the signs of readiness for marriage in section 1. How many of the signs of readiness can be used to predict marriage problems listed above? How many marriage breakdowns do you think can be predicted from the beginning of the marriage?
4. Marriage is a process, not a destination. The marriage relationship is constantly changing throughout a lifetime together. What motivates a Christian to treat his or her partner with tenderness and understanding? What power does a Christian possess that a non-Christian does not have?

Establishing a Good Marriage

How can a person find the answers to establishing a good marriage?

- Pray faithfully and often for God's guidance!
- Receive God's power through daily devotions, worship, and the Lord's Supper.
- Allow time for the relationship to grow; don't let anyone pressure you into marriage.
- Evaluate the relationship as honestly as you can, without glossing over the trouble spots.
- If you have serious doubts about whether the relationship can work, have the courage to say so! If you don't feel ready to make a commitment, you're not.
- If you feel the relationship can grow with some help and counseling prior to marriage, make a mutual commitment to get the help you need.

The institution of marriage is central to a healthy society. It nurtures the future and provides support for the present. It is more than a private agreement. Marriage is a public declaration of commitment to another person which is part of the fabric of our extended families, the church, the community, and society at large.

God has given us the power to love others. With it, we can build marriages that will work for our benefit and His glory. God uses wise preparation for marriage to bring us those blessings. No athlete, man or woman, would dream of entering competition without some preparation. She (or he) will train carefully to make sure her body is in the best physical condition. She will take care of herself to assure an optimum mental outlook. She will identify her weaknesses and practice long and hard to correct them—all this just to win a game or a match. Surely we should give equal or greater attention to preparing ourselves for a lifetime commitment!

> Marriage is not so much finding the right person as it is *being* the right person.
>
> —*Charlie Shedd*

1. What are some things you can do now that will make you a better marriage partner?
2. Discuss: Is marriage worth the risk? Is it worth the investment of self?

When a Marriage Fails

In marriage God teaches us what commitment to another person really involves. God uses marriage to help us grow in our commitment to the needs of others. He did not guarantee that the commitment would always be easy or pleasant. (Jesus' commitment to us led to His death.) Marriage gives us the opportunity to be faithful to one person—as God is faithful to us.

When this commitment breaks down, marriages fail. This breakdown occurs because of our selfish natures. Perhaps it was a mistake to marry this person. The breakdown may have come in not seeking help when the marriage was in trouble. It may have come from not seeking God's strength and power to heal the rifts in the relationship. It may have come as the couple were unable to forgive each other and go on loving. Human selfishness is always a threat to marriage.

The sign that hung in the window of a Hollywood jewelry store says a lot about the esteem in which marriage is held by the world around us. It read:

1. What is society's attitude toward divorce? Give some examples from the media or from people you know.

2. Is God's attitude toward divorce the same as society's? How do you know?

3. Who does more following when it comes to divorce: Christians following the world or the world following Christians?

4. The Pharisees confronted Jesus on the issue of divorce several times, for they knew it was a sticky problem in their day. Read **Matt. 19:3–9.** What does Jesus say about divorce? Why did Moses permit divorce? Is divorce a sin?

5. Read **1 Cor. 6:15–17.** As God points out through Paul, what happens when a man and a woman have sexual intercourse? When that act occurs outside the marriage union, how does it affect the guilty party's relationship with his or her spouse? with God?

6. Read **1 John 5:17a.** Is divorce a greater sin than other types of sins? What dangers, however, accompany divorce?

7. Read **Luke 5:31, 1 John 2:1–2,** and **1 John 1:7.** If a divorce does occur, how should the divorced person deal with it? What consequences of divorce might a guilty person still face after he or she has received assurance of God's forgiveness?

8. Read **John 8:1–7** and **Luke 17:3–4.** Why would it be wrong to use the words of Jesus in these passages to say that He *excuses* sin? What, however, *did* He do? How does He want us to treat other Christians, including those who are divorced?

9. Where can divorced persons and children whose parents have divorced find help in dealing with their pain and the adjustments which are required?

10. Do you think persons whose parents had an unhappy marriage or were divorced find it more difficult to establish a happy marriage? Why or why not?

11. How can the church minister to divorced persons? to children whose parents have divorced?

12. What promise of God do we have that covers even bad experiences such as the breaking up of a marriage? See **Rom. 8:28.**

Divorce has always been an accommodation to human weakness. It was never God's plan for the marriage relationship. It became necessary to bring order in a society that had disregarded God's will, but it was not God's intention for man and woman. Moses did not make divorce acceptable—he simply dealt with its consequences.

We can picture divorce as something like cutting up a living body. It is more than ending a business partnership. It is the destruction of a one flesh relationship. We cannot adopt or accept society's views that divorce is simply a way to rearrange marriage partners. The chaotic changes that have rocked the American family in the past several decades have dulled our sensitivity to many of the evils around us.

If one out of eight major businesses failed, or one out of eight schools closed, we would be in a panic. Yet we may accept those statistics (and much worse statistics among people married in recent years) for broken marriages without too much thought. We may begin to lower our own standards for how God wants us to live. When it becomes too difficult for us to live God's way, we often follow in the path the world has set.

Adultery is the only grounds for divorce in Scripture. That does not mean, however, that the partner who was not adulterous *must* seek divorce. Sometimes forgiveness and counseling can save the marriage. We cannot fulfill God's plan for marriage if we give up whenever our desires and wishes encourage us to do so—or if we just resign ourselves to an unhappy relationship. If through God's power we recommit ourselves to our vows, a marriage may be transformed.

But pastors are likely also to confront marriages in which one spouse has deserted another and there is no chance for reconciliation. Some marriages cannot be preserved, even after long and serious attempts to do so. When that happens, we need to draw upon the power of God's forgiveness to heal the scars of the past and to give us the strength to build new relationships. Jesus' formula for dealing with sinners was very simple: love the sinner in spite of his sin.

Whenever a relationship ends, people go through a process of grieving similar to the grieving that occurs when a loved one dies. They may feel a crushing sense of failure. If children are involved, the conflicts may continue to wear away their peace long after the divorce. Until a divorced person deals with the anger and pain caused by the end of a marriage, he or she will not be emotionally whole. Any new marriage is likely to suffer the consequences of these unresolved emotions.

Dealing with the pain requires the person to say good-bye to the past, to work through the loss, and to grow to be able to invest in other relationships once again. Children whose parents have divorced must deal with their feelings as well; if they do not, all the pain and bad feelings may later be brought into their own marriages, making a healthy marriage extremely difficult.

The good news is that for divorce, as for every other sin, **"The blood of Jesus, His Son, purifies us from all sin" (1 John 1:7)!** No sin is so shockingly bad that it blocks God's forgiveness. But no sin is so trivial that it does not require repentance and forgiveness. Divorced people can be forgiven and go on to establish new relationships to serve God and others.

Chapter Summary

God instituted marriage for three purposes: companionship, the procreation of children, and the restraint of sin.

Though marriage customs and arrangements have changed throughout history, God's design for the marriage relationship has not.

The marriage vow calls upon God's power as the only resource that can strengthen us for a lifetime commitment.

God forgives all sin, including the sin of divorce, and renews us so we may again serve Him and others.

We Christians have available to us the power and presence of the living Lord. We receive it through God's Word, Baptism, and the Lord's Supper. We draw on the prayer support of others in the family of God. We possess the inner working of the Holy Spirit. We have the divinely inspired handbook of instruction on marriage and the home. With these blessings, we can live out our marriage commitments to the glory of God in mutual happiness and love.

Jesus replied, "Moses permitted you to divorce your wives because your hearts were hard. But it was not this way from the beginning. I tell you that anyone who divorces his wife, except for marital unfaithfulness, and marries another woman commits adultery."

Matt. 19:8–9

Chapter 6

Unity in Marriage

Chapter Preview

Chapter 6 will help you answer the following questions:

- How does a newly married couple lay the foundation for a lifetime of loving and living together?
- How can a couple build strong unity within their marriage?
- How do a husband and wife nurture a satisfying intimacy in their relationship?

1. A New Way of Life

Cal and Donna had just returned from their honeymoon when Donna went to the bank to pick up information for opening new accounts. After Donna was shown to the proper desk, the bank officer rose to greet her. "Good morning, Mrs. Hawkins," said the officer, glancing down at the information sheet Donna had filled out. "How may I help you?"

For a moment Donna failed to reply. Then she realized *she* was Mrs. Hawkins. It was the first time anyone has called her by her married name.

Oh, the thrill of being a newlywed! Beautiful wedding gifts furnish your new home. Wonderful memories result from the resolution of your first argument and from your first Christmas together.

Because change and stress go hand in hand, being a newlywed is also a stressful time. Married persons can no longer function as they did before, and it takes effort and energy to develop new ways of functioning that will allow them to adapt to changes. Change produces growth, but the process is rarely painless.

When a couple are married, every aspect of their life changes to some degree. They must now learn to function as a couple rather than as separate individuals. They must make the gigantic adjustment of learning how to live as husband and wife. Each will have to sacrifice some independence and personal desires for the good of the marriage.

Before marriage, they were free to go where they wanted, spend their money as they chose, and make their own decisions about all aspects of their lives. Now they are committed to each other and must consider the other person's wishes and needs equally with their own. In a godly marriage, our heavenly Father can mold and shape individuals, who become less self-serving and more and more self-giving.

Do you agree with this statement: *The style of a marriage usually is set within one year of the wedding, remaining constant and predictable unless the couple enter therapy to change it?*

Tell why you agree or disagree.

Cal and Donna have just celebrated their one-month anniversary. During the month, they have had disagreements over the following situations:

- He ignored her at a party.
- They ran out of milk and bread three times.
- She smokes even though he objects.
- They can't decide whose parents to invite for dinner first.
- She wrote a large check and forgot to confer with him about it.
- He spends his weekend afternoons watching sports events on TV.

Which of these issues do you think might cause disagreement in your own marriage if you had been married just one month? What other issues might cause disagreement? List as many as you can think of. (You may find it fascinating to talk with someone who was married recently to discover what disagreements they had early in their marriage.)

Studies have demonstrated that the style of a couple's interaction is established during the first year of marriage, during which time they lay the foundation for their life together. Once these patterns are set they become difficult to change. For example, two persons who learned early in the marriage to forgive each other, and are able to put aside their egos and ask for forgiveness, have established a foundation on which to build for a lifetime.

Spouses who from the beginning of the marriage, set a pattern of worshiping, praying, and hav-

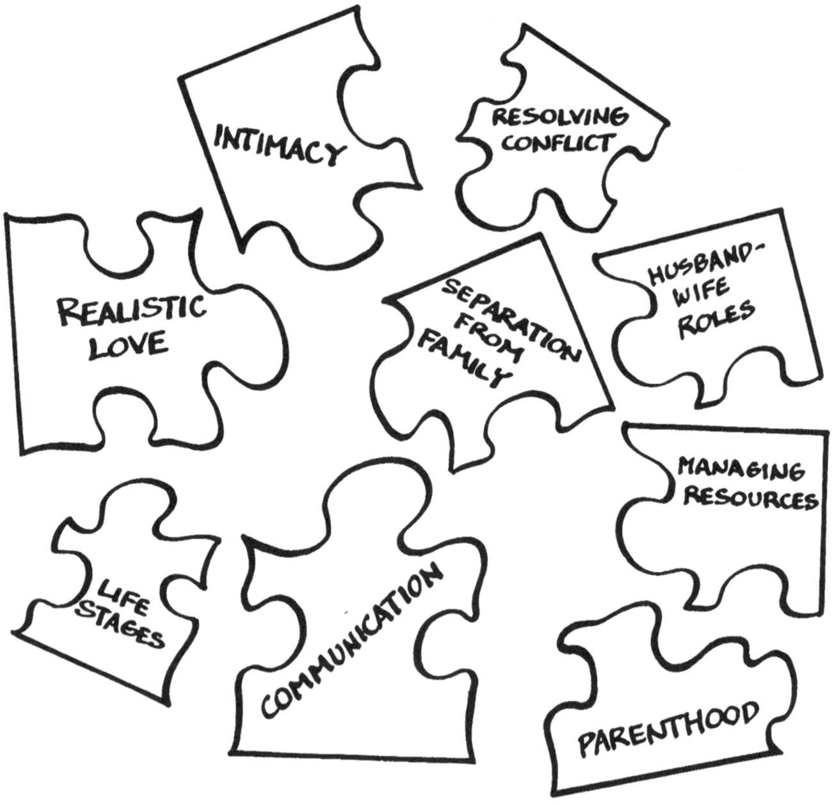

BUILDING A GOOD MARRIAGE

ing devotions together regularly have established a structure which will strengthen them year after year. A good marriage doesn't result from luck or from being made for each other. Rather, it develops day by day as husband and wife give of themselves to each other. Newlyweds have some very important tasks to face as they begin their life together!

Read **Deut. 24:5.** What was God's word through Moses to the newlyweds of his day? Why do you think God gave that decree? What does the decree have to say about the marriage relationship?

Tasks of the Newly Married

When a couple marry, they face certain basic tasks—work which must be done to build a lifetime partnership. The tasks they must accomplish focus on all aspects of their life together. These tasks establish the foundation for the marriage. A newly married husband and wife must

1. separate from family of origin;
2. develop a realistic view of love;
3. develop emotional, spiritual, and physical intimacy;
4. work out husband/wife roles;
5. establish effective patterns of communication;
6. learn how to resolve differences;
7. prepare for future life stages;
8. learn how to manage their resources cooperatively;
9. decide whether to have children, and prepare for parenthood if they choose to do so.

(Adapted from *Newly Married and Before* by Wayne Rickerson. Used with permission. © 1985 David C. Cook Publishing Co..)

In your own words, what do you think each of these tasks involves?

Each of these tasks will be discussed in this and succeeding chapters. This chapter will discuss how a couple build *unity* in their marriage through separating from their families of origin, developing a realistic view of love, and creating intimacy. The next chapter will focus on tasks 4 through 7 as it looks at the marriage partnership. Chapter 8 will deal with managing resources and chapter 9 will take a look at parenthood.

Discussion Questions

1. How would you define *unity* in marriage?
2. Why do you think it is (or is not) important?
3. What is the opposite of unity?
4. Give one example of something a couple could do which would build unity in their relationship.
5. Give one example of something a couple could do which would weaken or destroy unity in their relationship.

These nine tasks, of course, cannot be undertaken one at a time. Most of them will be going on simultaneously. As a couple begins their marriage, they have important and exciting work ahead.

The Honeymoon

The marriage relationship begins with the honeymoon period. Many couples take a trip together; some do not. No matter how long a couple have courted, the honeymoon period is still likely to bring some surprises. The intimacy of living together day after day will reveal things about your spouse that you didn't know before.

Some couples are unwilling or unable to go off together on a honeymoon, usually because of financial or job pressures. But every couple will benefit from time spent alone together as they begin their marriage. Investing time and effort in their marriage at the beginning of the relationship will pay dividends later.

The honeymoon serves some very important functions for a newly married couple:

1. Recuperation. It allows them to recuperate from the fatigue of the wedding preparations. As everyone who has been married knows, even a simple wedding requires a great amount of energy and planning.

2. Acquaintance. It provides time and opportunity for them to get to know each other on a deeper level, away from the distractions of jobs and other people.

3. Adjustment. It gives them experience in adapting to each other spiritually, emotionally, and sexually as they begin to respond to each other as partners. What better time than on the honeymoon, for example, for a married couple to begin their family devotional life?

Keeping these three functions in mind, with a student partner, plan a potential honeymoon. Consider also the following factors:

a. What kind of atmosphere do you want?

b. Where will you go? (Who will make the decision about the location? Who will make the arrangements? How will you get there? How much will it cost? Whose money will be used to pay for the honeymoon expenses?)

c. How much time will you have? How will you spend your time while on the honeymoon? (No couple, no matter how deeply in love they are, can spend 24 hours a day making love.) What other activities will you plan? Have you included some time for partners to spend alone? (Too much closeness or constant togetherness may lead to friction for some couples; have you allowed "breathing space" in your plans?)

If you have done your planning well, you have probably arranged a honeymoon that took into account several things.

- You chose a place that provides anonymity and privacy.
- You chose something you both like to do.
- You planned something free from fatigue and nervous tension.
- You kept it affordable.

What advice would you offer to a friend who has arranged for a very elaborate "dream" wedding but will have no money left for a honeymoon?

What advice would you offer to a friend who is planning an exotic honeymoon trip to a faraway place (e.g. a safari in Africa, backpacking in Alaska, a deep-sea fishing expedition, etc.)?

What advice would you offer a friend who is planning an expensive honeymoon but will have to go in debt to do so?

May your fountain be blessed, and may you rejoice in the wife of your youth.

Prov. 5:18

2. Becoming "We"

We all enter marriage with "unfinished business" from previous relationships, parents, and other family members. More than physical separation, leaving our family of origin also includes an emotional departure.

In marriage, two people must develop couple unity; they must forge a new identity as a family, separate from their original families. Now primary loyalty must be to each other, not to old friends and not to families. If either spouse remains dependent on the family of origin or on a network of old friends, it will be impossible to create an independent new family.

Separating from their families of origin is one of the first important tasks which a newly married couple must accomplish to build unity within their marriage. *Severance* or separation from our family of origin is a necessary part of establishing a marriage. When we identified the four essential elements of marriage according to God's plan in **Gen. 2:24–26,** severance was the first of these. (Permanence, a second necessary part, was discussed in the previous chapter. Unity and intimacy will be developed further in this chapter.)

For persons who are mature, who live some distance away from their families, and who have lived independently from them prior to marriage, separating from them may be relatively easy. But marriage counselors agree that problems with families and in-laws are one of the three major sources of friction in marriage (sex and money, the other two, will be discussed later).

No matter how well suited husband and wife are to each other, each marriage partner comes with a list of "shoulds" based on his or her own background. Here are a few examples. Answer them according to your own feelings about them.

- Who should balance the checkbook?
- Who should take care of the car?

- Who should fix things that are broken?
- Where and with whom should a couple spend holidays?
- What should partners do after an argument?

Even when we think we are doing things in a way entirely different from our family of origin, our first instinct will usually be to repeat certain behaviors from our previous family. To create a strong new family unit, the mixture of the old (family of origin) with the new (husband and wife) must be carefully balanced. Some persons might say, "I'm not going to make the same mistakes my parents made." Others might feel "I want to have the same kind of marriage and home my parents have." When couples recognize what old patterns they are repeating, they can evaluate whether they want to continue these patterns in their new family.

From day one, Christian marriages possess the most powerful resource available to anyone. In Christ, you and your spouse can find a complete and mighty unity. With God at work in your lives, partners in a godly marriage have the power to recognize that often in differences of opinion neither way is necessarily right nor wrong. In love you can resolve your differences by compromising on a new system that will work for the two of you.

In chapter 2, you examined the varied influences your family of origin has had upon you. Think for a moment about yourself as a marriage partner.

■ *What are the greatest strengths from your family of origin that you would want to incorporate into your marriage?*

■ *What things from your family background would you wish to change within your new family?*

Discussion Questions

1. You will see the word *compromise* occurring frequently in these chapters. Why is compromise important to marriage?
2. What does the word mean to you? Give some synonyms for it.
3. Is compromise the same as giving in? Why or why not?
4. Is compromise a Christian principle of action? Why or why not? Support your answer with Scripture.

When a married couple separate from their families of origin, they begin to create the unity which is one of the "musts" for a good marriage. As they adapt to each other and to their new status as a couple, they begin to develop a sense of being "we." They are no longer two separate individuals. Becoming a "we" doesn't happen immediately. It grows out of the situations and experiences married persons share as they live together as husband and wife.

How would you handle each of the following situations?

1. Every time you have an argument, your wife calls her mother for sympathy and advice.
2. Your husband goes out after work with his old buddies several nights a week.
3. Your car has been breaking down a lot. Your wife's father offers to buy you a new one.
4. Your parents have a way of dropping in at inconvenient times without calling first.
5. Your parents bring extravagant gifts for each of you on special occasions. Your spouse's parents cannot afford to provide you with the same kind of treatment.

A newly married couple must now build a new relationship with their parents, a relationship based on their new, independent family unit. They must decide how much time is appropriate to spend with parents. They will need to discuss when parental help is appropriate, and when it is not. Families can be a tremendous resource for a new marriage. But too much dependency prevents newlyweds from accomplishing their own goals.

Parents may become good friends, but they are not part of the marriage. Separating from their families of origin, while still maintaining loving relationships with family members, may present a challenge for the newly married. But once the relationship with parents has been defined and established, parents may provide a supporting foundation upon which the married couple can rely for years to come.

Ways to Build Unity in Marriage

What are some other things newly married persons can do to separate from their pasts and forge a new family unit?

1. Create new traditions. They can begin new traditions for themselves, traditions that will bind them together in the future. Examples of occasions around which traditions may be built include Christmas and other holidays, anniversaries, birthdays, and other special events. Religious traditions such as worshiping together regularly, daily devotions, mealtime prayers, and sharing words of faith are also an important part of this process.

What are some family traditions you would wish to establish if you marry? List at least three and describe briefly how you would develop them with your partner.

2. Share activities and interests. Another necessity for developing unity is sharing activities and interests. While no two people will ever share all the same interests, the couple who find enjoyable experiences to share, such as church activities or good times with friends and family, will strengthen their marriage bond.

What are some interests and activities you would hope to share with a marriage partner?

3. Establish roots. Couples also build unity as they establish roots. As they share their experiences of building their own social network—with friends, in the community, within the church—they develop a greater sense of closeness and of belonging together.

What is one way you could begin to establish roots with your marriage partner?

4. Share dreams. Sharing dreams also builds unity. When two people who love each other plan a future together and then work to make that future happen, they create a bond that keeps on growing.

What is one dream of yours that you would like to be able to share with a spouse?

Talk with a happily married couple you know. What traditions have they established? What interests and activities do they share? How have they put down roots? What dreams do they share? Do they think these experiences contribute to the strength of their marriage? Why or why not?

Enjoy life with your wife, whom you love.
Eccl. 9:9a

JUST BECAUSE A MAN DOESN'T BRING YOU ROSES, WRITE POETRY, OR ACT ROMANTIC, DOESN'T MEAN HE DOESN'T LOVE YOU.

3. If That's Not Love, What Is?

Imagine yourself in the following situation: Today is your seven-month anniversary. You went in to work early so you could leave early and prepare a special dinner for the two of you. At 6:30, the time your spouse usually gets home, you dim the lights, put on soft music and wait. At 8:30 p.m. you are still waiting. Are you likely to

- call your spouse's office to let him or her know how angry you are?
- throw the meal in the garbage and go out, leaving a nasty note on the table?
- call the local hospital to see if your spouse has been in an accident?
- choose a different course of action? If so, tell what you would do.

In a memorable scene from *Fiddler on the Roof,* Tevye, the Jewish father, is trying to come to terms with the fact that his daughters are marrying and leaving home. All their talk about love starts him thinking about his own marriage to Golda. So he proceeds to ask the question, "Golda, do you love me?" Golda is startled, and for a moment she doesn't know how to reply.

She and Tevye are not accustomed to talking about their feelings. Then she answers, "For 24 years I've washed your clothes . . . " and goes on to list the things she has done for him in their marriage. She concludes with a question of her own. "If that's not love, what is?"

But Tevye is not satisfied. He asks her again, "Golda, do you love me?" He waits for her to say the words. Though he recognizes all she has contributed to the family, he wants to hear her declare that she loves him, the person.

A second basic task of the newly married is to establish a realistic view of love. Maintaining a love relationship for a lifetime does not happen automatically. Our partner will feel loved when we do two things:

- Say the words
- Demonstrate love through our actions

We communicate our feelings both verbally and nonverbally—and both are important. Assuming that love exists is not the same as firsthand evidence! How easily we are able to communicate love, both verbally and nonverbally, will depend on our personality and background. But whether or not it comes easily, each of us can grow in our ability to communicate love. Every new behavior feels awkward the first time; the more we do it, the easier it becomes. As we learned in chapter 1, we demonstrate love when we are in tune to the other person's needs and willing to give of ourselves to meet those needs.

Discussion Questions

1. If you were the waiting spouse in the example above, what needs might your partner have when he or she finally arrived home?
2. What needs would you have?
3. Could both your needs be met at the same time? Why or why not?
4. Can any relationship always meet both persons' needs at the same time?
5. What do you need in order to feel loved by another person?
6. How can married couples meet each other's needs in ways that would strengthen their unity?

We all enter a marriage with idealistic expectations. We are determined not to make the same mistakes we may have seen other people make. How will we expect our partner to demonstrate his or her love for us? Will we expect him to drop whatever he is doing whenever we call? Will we expect her to handle all the cooking and shopping because that is what our mother used to do? How will *you* expect *your* marriage partner to demonstrate love for you?

Realistic expectations help to build unity in a marriage. Unrealistic expectations create friction and strife.

What Should I Expect?

Write the letters *a* through *l* on a piece of paper. Then consider the following list, which gives a variety of expectations and ideas which people often bring to marriage. If a statement describes something which you believe you can expect from your spouse, write *yes* after that letter on your paper. If a statement describes something which you determine not realistic to expect from your spouse, write *no* after it. If you are uncertain, write *maybe*.

a. My spouse will be honest and truthful.
b. We will always agree on all important issues.
c. I will have no more insecurities and fears.
d. He/she will show tolerance for personality differences.
e. We will each have freedom to grow and change.
f. He/she will show equal respect for my needs and opinions.
g. My spouse will demonstrate warmth and affection.
h. We will share basic agreement on worship and church commitments.
i. He/she will provide financial security.
j. We will enjoy complete sexual harmony at all times.
k. We will agree how to spend money.
l. I will be protected from sorrow and pain.

Be ready to explain *why* you think each expectation is either appropriate or unrealistic.

If we enter marriage with many unrealistic expectations, we are likely to feel hurt and angry if our partner does not measure up. When our expectations are realistic, we are more likely to value our partner as a unique person with qualities different from our own.

Some people enter marriage thinking they can demonstrate love by trying to "improve" their partner. They hope to change the other person so that he or she will conform more closely to their ideal. Others think that in order to be loved for a lifetime, they must make themselves over in order to suit their partner. But God created each of us to be unique, to be like no one else He has ever or will ever create. When we attempt to change someone to fit our mold—or allow the other person to change us into their image—our value as a unique person is lost.

As we discovered already in chapter 1, each of us was created by God with unique gifts. When we recognize and share each other's gifts, a relationship flourishes.

What are some gifts and abilities that *you* will bring to your marriage?

Marriage should involve mutual recognition and sharing of gifts for the benefit of both partners, rather than trying to make our spouse like us. Conflicts are negotiable within a marriage; demanding personality change is not. Our differences and changes add variety and depth to the relationship. If we manipulate a loved one to suit our own purposes, or sacrifice our personal dignity to allow someone to exploit us, anger and resentment will usually follow. Such feelings are the enemy of love and gradually work to destroy a relationship.

Couples build unity when they share those things and activities both of them enjoy—and value and tolerate differences in areas where they do not agree. In a Christian marriage God's power can be relied upon to create the best marriage possible from the raw materials of two sinful human beings with two entirely different personalities.

Humanly speaking, we cannot change others. However, every one of Jesus' followers, from New Testament times until now, has been changed through a personal relationship with Him. In fact, then, we don't change ourselves or other people; God changes us.

A popular slogan says, "Please be patient—God isn't finished with me yet." If God isn't finished with us, then He isn't finished with those close to us either. Therefore, it's not the job of a husband or wife to "make" their spouse into a better person or to assist God in the process with their comments and suggestions.

In one sense, however, believers do "help" God to change themselves—and their spouses. This happens when they draw upon the means of grace—God's Word and the sacraments. The Holy Spirit works through these means to make us new persons. Imagine what marvelous blessings come to a marriage through these means!

Love means acceptance of who and what the other person is now, not who we think we can make him or her to be. In other words, we need to love *the whole person*—not just his or her beauty, or body, or the extra paycheck. With God's help, we can see our partner as a unique and precious complement (completer) to ourselves. This kind of total acceptance creates a powerful bond between people. It allows a spouse to remember the qualities in the other person that caused him or her to fall in love. It provides the reason to keep alive within yourself the qualities which made your spouse fall in love with you.

In an atmosphere of God's accepting love for us, we sinners are able, through the power of the Spirit, to grow to be the persons God intends for us to be. The same is true in marriage. An atmosphere of accepting love will allow our partner to grow to be the kind of person God intends him or her to be. To accept what cannot be changed brings us peace of mind and allows our partner the freedom to be the person God made. (Surprisingly, we often discover that when we change our own attitudes or actions, the other person will change, too, in response to us. The change may occur, not because we demanded it, but because the love we demonstrated provided the motivation.)

Give some examples of situations in which changing *yourself,* with God's help, would improve a relationship.

In a nurturing marriage, each person feels "free to be me," but not at the other person's expense. Ironically, some people try to change the very characteristics that they found attractive when first they met the other person. A partner's flaws may have been part of his or her charm when the relationship began. Perhaps you've heard the saying, "opposites attract." Often we are attracted to people who have qualities we lack. For example, a quiet, studious person may be charmed by someone who is outgoing and carefree. Or, a frivolous spender may admire the self-discipline of someone who manages money well.

Personality traits may be charming or humorous—until a person has to live with them every day. Then those same qualities may become grating and annoying. A partner's flaws may seem like huge rocks on a beach while our own flaws are likely to seem as tiny pebbles. If someone enters a marriage believing their partner's little flaws and irritating habits would disappear, they will quickly become disillusioned when they do not. Sometimes people become so annoyed by the petty irritations that they overlook entirely all the other good qualities in the other person. When this happens, the problem often lies not so much with the partner as with the unrealistic expectations his or her spouse brought into the marriage.

No one person will ever have all the qualities we want. Therefore maturity and *knowing ourselves* are vital prerequisites to marriage. (What qualities are essential to *you* in the person you marry?)

Equally important is *knowing our partner* well before marriage. (Does this person have the qualities which will bond us together for a lifetime?)

More about Personalities

Though you do not yet know what qualities your future marriage partner may possess, you can look at the traits you possess. Listed below are some opposites. For each pair listed, find a place on the line which describes you.

Saver	Spender
Private, Quiet	Outgoing
Participator	Spectator
Optimist	Pessimist
Ambitious	Complacent
Planner	Impulsive
Traveler	Homebody
Morning Person	Night Owl
Worrier	Happy-Go-Lucky
Sports Nut	Book Lover
Neat, Precise	Disorganized
Realist	Idealist
Strong Christian	Doubter
Compassionate	Unsympathetic

If you marry someone whose personality is very different from yours, how will you establish unity in your marriage?

Questions for Reflection

As you think about acceptance and unity in marriage, ask yourself the following questions:

■ *Does marriage change people? How do you think marriage would change you?*

■ *What are some changes you need to make within yourself, with God's help, to "be the right person" for someone else?*

Discussion Questions

1. What traits would you find it difficult to accept in a partner? What would you do if you discovered those traits in a person you were dating? What would you do if you discovered those traits in your spouse after marriage?

2. How is it possible for two personalities to become "one flesh"?

3. How were people changed when they met Jesus? Give an example from the New Testament; include the place where that story can be found.

4. How have you been changed since you came to faith in Jesus?

5. Describe the power for change which the Gospel provides **(Eph. 2:1–10).**

6. Will you be a more loving, accepting marriage partner because you know Jesus? Why or why not?

Talk with a married person you know well. Ask him or her to share several of the ways he or she has changed since being married. What are two things each partner has had to accept about the other?

Conquering Love

Perhaps you've heard the slogan "Love conquers all." Do you agree with the slogan? Does every kind of love have conquering power?

As we discovered in chapter 1, there are many ideas and definitions and concepts of love floating around in our culture. Movie and TV plots, for example, usually depict love as a mysterious, magical feeling beyond the control of the person in love. People "fall in love" and seem to lose all powers of reason or self-control. For a marriage to endure, however, we know that love must be more than magical feelings. Read **Gal. 5:19–26** and think about how the fruit of the Spirit would apply to our ability to love.

Real Love

Write the numbers 1 through 9 on another piece of paper. After studying the list below which contains some ideas about love, write *yes* after the number of each statement which describes a Biblical concept of love and *no* after each statement which does not.

1. If love "stops," there is nothing we can do to recapture it.
2. We can learn how to love.
3. Loving is easy; just do what comes naturally.
4. Love is a mysterious, irrational force.
5. Loving requires self-discipline.
6. Love is a feeling beyond our control.
7. We can understand what love is through the Word of God.
8. We can act loving even when we don't feel loving.
9. There is room for selfishness in love.

On the basis of this exercise, describe the kind of love you believe can "conquer all." Does your description share any common ideas with **1 Peter 4:8** or **Eph. 4:32?** Where do we receive the power to love our spouses with a conquering love?

Love cares about the other person as much as about self. The blessing of love reaches both ways. We feel more "in love" when we actively give love to our partner, rather than waiting to receive it from him or her. In a love relationship giving is usually contagious, encouraging a like response from the one we love.

When we looked at the three Greek words for love in chapter 1, we discovered that marriage partners share all three! Their relationship includes

- friendship, trust and mutual respect *(phileo);*
- sexual and romantic attraction *(eros);*
- self-giving devotion *(agape).*

When these three kinds of love are present within a marriage, marital unity can be achieved and spouses are able to love each other's whole person. When a marriage partner asks "What can I do for you?" rather than "What will you do for me?", marital unity becomes a reality.

Above all, love each other deeply, because love covers over a multitude of sins.

1 Peter 4:8

4. Developing Intimacy (Part 1)

Did you hear about the doctor who threw a party for 400 of her most *intimate* friends?

Have you seen the ads for *intimate apparel?* Intimacy is another of those words, like love, which we hear tossed about so much that the sharpness of its meaning has been lost. How do *you* define the word *intimacy?* What is the opposite of intimacy?

Developing intimacy is another of the critical tasks which newlyweds confront. Like separating from family of origin and developing a realistic view of love, developing intimacy is essential to the building of unity within a marriage. Of course couples who have dated long enough to know each other well have already developed some understanding and intimacy. But a lifelong marriage commitment requires the development of a deeper intimacy in all areas of the relationship—*emotional, spiritual,* and *physical.*

Though we will discuss each of these types of intimacy individually, the three types of intimacy are interrelated, as are the three types of love. Spiritual intimacy lays the foundation for the intimacy with God which nurtures the love we bring to our partner. Emotional intimacy intensifies physical intimacy, and vice versa. Lack of intimacy in any one area will affect intimacy in the others as well.

For each of us, there are different levels of knowing and being known. As the illustration below explains, these levels are determined by how much of ourselves we reveal to others. Three different levels of self-revelation are likely within our relationships.

1. Our superficial selves, or surface personalities, are known by many. This level includes our ideas, thoughts, and some of our values. These are

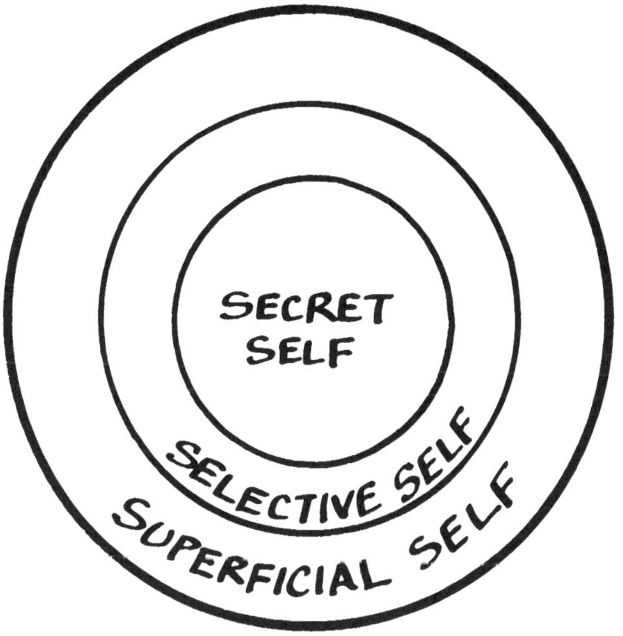

seen by most of our acquaintances. What are some things many people know about you?

2. Our selective selves are known by fewer people, those with whom we share our closely held thoughts, feelings, and values. We are more selective with this type of sharing, limiting it to those we trust. What are some things about you which are known only to people you trust?

3. Our secret selves contain the things we choose not to share with anyone, including our secret feelings, resentments, guilt, fears, hurts, and our true relationship with God. What are some things about you which are known only to you?

How much we are willing and able to reveal about ourselves determines the level of intimacy within a relationship.

A. Emotional Intimacy

Every marriage has its own individual character, its own ways of meeting the needs of both. Emotional intimacy may be different for each couple. For some people, intimacy seems natural and easy; for others, especially those who grew up in a family that did not have much intimacy, being open involves risk.

Many people, especially many men, have not grown up with the experience of sharing their feelings. For them, the ability to share intimate thoughts and feelings may develop gradually. But develop it they must if marriage is to become all that God intended.

Almost always present in strong marriages, intimacy is almost always absent in marriages that are in trouble. If our marriage relationship allows for the sharing of only our superficial selves, or only a small part of our selective selves, true intimacy is impossible. The more we open our selective selves to our partners, the deeper our intimacy can become. Some couples are able to build intimacy which includes portions of even their secret selves. These couples share their deepest emotions freely, confident that the accepting love of their partner will understand those parts of themselves which they do not wish the rest of the world to see.

Based on these three levels of self-revelation, we can describe marriages according to how much intimacy exists between the partners.

1. The first type of marriage, the *superficial marriage,* has little or no sharing of the true self. Marriage partners are afraid to reveal their real thoughts, values, and feelings. They may operate more like business partners than intimate companions. Consequently, such a marriage cannot meet the emotional and spiritual needs of the marriage partners. They are unfulfilled within the relationship because it lacks true intimacy at all three levels—emotional, spiritual, and physical.

2. The second type of marriage, the *intimate marriage,* has greater intimacy. Couples share emotions freely and openly discuss values and thoughts. Partners feel free to reveal who they really are. Each trusts the love and acceptance of the other. Such a marriage meets many needs of the couple much of the time, because there are bonds of emotional, spiritual, and physical intimacy.

3. The third type of marriage, the *deeply intimate marriage,* has the greatest depth of intimacy. It creates the freedom to share the tenderest emotions, to discuss openly all values, and to participate fully in each other's spiritual lives. Not all of the secret self is disclosed, of course—but each spouse feels free to discuss whatever is beneficial to the growth of the relationship without holding back.

(Adapted from "Newly Married and Before" by Wayne Rickerson. Used with permission. © 1985 David C. Cook Publishing Co.)

Central to any emotional intimacy is the sharing of one's self and one's needs. When we share the personal and private parts of ourselves with someone, we feel closest to them. Intimacy requires honesty, letting down our guard, communicating feelings, showing affection, and sharing goals and dreams. The commitment of marriage creates the bond of trust which makes this intimacy possible.

As emotional intimacy between husband and wife grows, love grows with it. The woven-together experience of intimacy produces relationships that endure. When the Bible uses the word "know" to describe total intimacy between husband and wife, it reminds us that intimacy is possible only when we truly know our partner and are truly known in return.

The relationship between God and His people has an intimacy which provides a model for the intimacy between husband and wife. Just as husband and wife grow to know each other through revealing themselves in the intimacy of marriage, so God revealed Himself to us in Christ Jesus. We see God's innermost self and the total commitment of His love in the hanging of Jesus on the cross, crying out "My God, My God, why have You forsaken me?" God truly went all the way to make us His own! We did not find Jesus—He found us. He knows the very worst about us—yet He chose us anyway!

The forgiveness Jesus earned for us now allows us to know God in a loving personal relationship. It makes it possible for us to open ourselves in love to other people. Because God shared everything He is when Jesus came to live among us, we have become new creatures who no longer have to hide our sins and faults. We can confess them, be forgiven, and share with each other the fullness of accepting love.

How is intimacy built in to everyday life? Each couple must work out the degree of togetherness and separateness which is comfortable for both, keeping in mind the need to grow in intimacy. Intimacy does not require that we be our spouse's shadow 24 hours a day. Some marriage partners believe they must be together all the time, as much as possible. In fact, "smother love" can destroy intimacy.

If David is a nut for antique car shows but his wife thinks they're a waste of time, will it enhance their intimacy if she feels obligated to go with him every time? Some newly married couples tend to stifle each other, perhaps because they think they must always be together, or because they have not yet grown to fully trust each other. But jealousy or possessiveness show conditional love at its worst. A stronger unity is created when spouses feel free to be themselves.

Persons who enjoy the freedom to be themselves within their marriage may still care as deeply about their partner as they do about themselves, but they continue to function as individuals and maintain personal interests. Marriage does not eliminate the need for persons to form relationships with people other than their mates. These friendships are different from those they enjoyed before marriage because of the central place their mate now occupies in their lives. Allowing some space in the togetherness encourages personal growth.

What about the opposite extreme, couples who have lots of space but little togetherness? Unless partners spend time with each other, they will not know what is happening in each other's lives and will be unable to share true intimacy. Spouses need to nurture companionship. In the face of all the pressures from jobs, children, and friends, they need to give priority to their marriage relationship. Developing emotional intimacy takes an investment of time and trust; it demands a willingness to be open and to share feelings and needs. But compromise and a willingness to grow in intimacy can make it happen.

Discussion Questions

1. Do you suppose most couples have superficial marriages, intimate marriages, or deeply intimate marriages?
2. Which marriages are most likely to endure for a lifetime? Why?
3. Which type of marriage fulfills best God's design for marriage in **Gen. 2:24–25?**
4. What factors would be necessary for you to establish a deeply intimate marriage?
5. What are some good things for marriage partners to do together?
6. What are some activities marriage partners might enjoy apart from each other?
7. How much time do you feel partners should spend together? How much time do you feel they should spend apart?

B. Spiritual Intimacy

The second type of intimacy, spiritual intimacy, brings to marriage a special unity for which nothing else can substitute. Yet, for most newly married couples, this form of intimacy is the most difficult. Persons who find it difficult to talk about their deepest emotions usually find it even more threatening to share their relationship with Jesus. To reveal our innermost convictions, our doubts and questions, and the ways God has worked in our lives requires courage.

It's easy to find excuses. Which of these have you heard (or used)?

- ☐ We're too busy to find time to read the Bible or pray together.
- ☐ We're at different places in our Christian lives; I don't want him or her to know my doubts and fears.
- ☐ We've tried to have devotions or pray together—it just didn't work out.
- ☐ We don't agree about how to live the Christian life—why ask for trouble by bringing it up?
- ☐ He thinks he's such a good Christian—he is always trying to reform me.
- ☐ It's too hard to talk about this.
- ☐ We have enough things to resolve—we don't need another.

Satan can use all of these excuses—and more—to prevent Christians from developing spiritual intimacy in their marriages. Yet a personal relationship with Jesus Christ is the cornerstone of Christian marriage. It gives meaning and purpose to every other aspect of life. We know whose we are and what our role in life is to be: to **"declare the**

praises of Him who called you out of darkness into His wonderful light" (1 Peter 2:9). Without God's help, how many of us could make it on our own—in our marriages, in our jobs, in our day-to-day lives? We need His power if spiritual intimacy is ever to become a reality in our relationships.

Spiritual intimacy is built in many ways. Whenever we nurture the Christian growth of our partner, we are also building spiritual intimacy. This occurs when we

- share our faith with each other and witness to each other in our everyday life;
- pray with each other and for each other;
- worship and partake of Holy Communion together;
- read and study the Word together, as a couple or as part of a Bible study group;
- have family devotions together.

Establishing a family altar—worshiping together in family devotions—is one important way to develop spiritual intimacy. It allows a couple to do many of the things listed above which build spiritual intimacy: share their faith with each other, pray together, read and study the Word.

Discussion Questions

1. What elements are necessary if family devotions are to be successful? List as many as you can. What encouragement does St. Paul give in **1 Thess. 5:11?**
2. What kind of devotions would work best for a couple without children?
3. If you were a parent, how would you need to change your style of devotions if you had
   - young children?
   - children with a wide age range (toddlers to teens)?
   - different work shifts for husband and wife?
   - visitors in your home?
   - an elderly parent who is not a Christian living with you?

There are many types of resources available for family devotions. Bring to class one or more with which you are familiar.

Spiritual intimacy, like emotional intimacy, requires an investment of time and trust. When marriage partners realize they were created by God for a purpose, they begin to share their spiritual life. How would spiritual intimacy help a couple deal with each of the following situations?

- You are afraid you will be laid off at your job.
- Your father is facing open-heart surgery.
- You had a disagreement with someone at church—and haven't been to a church service in the past month.
- You just got a raise and are reorganizing your family budget.
- Your child was caught cheating on an important exam at school.
- Your church needs Christian couples to provide leadership for some important new programs.

Spiritual intimacy rests upon forgiveness. We cannot be loving or open to someone when we are feeling hurt and angry with him or her. When husband and wife recognize that they are both sinners who have received freely God's gift of forgiveness, they are able to forgive each other and grow in their ability to encourage each other's spiritual growth.

God established marriage as a way to bring joy and happiness into our lives. Our self-centered sinfulness shatters that joy. But God's forgiveness reconciles us to Him and to each other.

For where two or three come together in My name, there am I with them.

Matt. 18:20

5. Developing Intimacy (Part 2)

C. Physical Intimacy

Two fourth-grade girls were discussing what they thought marriage would be like. One of them said she planned to ask her husband's mother for all his favorite recipes so she could learn to cook to please him. The other stated that she planned never to let her husband see her looking anything but her best. "I'd never want the man I love to see me brushing my teeth," she declared.

Those idealistic notions may be fine for fourth-graders, but they won't work for two people who plan to share a lifetime. Does that mean we should not make an effort to please our spouse or to look and be our best? Of course not. But we must also be prepared to accept each other at times of sickness and running to the bathroom, when appearances change through a loss or gain of weight, and even when hair starts to thin and skin begins to sag. All of these are experienced through the years as part of physical intimacy, of knowing and being known.

The intimacy of the sexual relationship adds a vital dimension to the ways in which husband and wife "know" each other. But it too is clouded by many myths. Listed below are a number of statements about the sexual bond. Once again number a sheet of paper appropriately and then indicate after the number of each statement whether you believe it is a fact (F) or a myth (M).

1. In a good marriage, sex must always be overwhelming, exciting, perfect.

2. Sex is a technique, a skill; it must be performed well if it is to be a pleasurable experience.
3. A good sexual relationship demands that we understand that sex is a good gift of God.
4. Commitment allows a sexual relationship to flourish.
5. A couple's sexual performance is the most important part of their marriage.
6. A good sexual experience means that both partners must come to orgasm.
7. Intercourse is only one of numerous physical acts which cement the bond between husband and wife.
8. Sexual satisfaction is unrelated to the other aspects of the marriage relationship.
9. God intends sexuality to be a special way for husband and wife to *complete* each other.
10. If husband and wife really love each other, they will always agree on the frequency and manner of intercourse.
11. Sexual desire helps to create unity and intimacy in marriage.
12. Sexual experience before marriage will make a person a better lover after marriage.

The sexual bond is an integral part of the total intimacy of marriage. *Eros,* with its feelings of sensual, romantic, and physical attraction, helps to make married love full and rich.

Sensitivity to the other person's needs is a prerequisite for all intimacy including the sexual relationship enjoyed by married persons. For some couples, the pleasures of sexual satisfaction may make it easy for spouses to satisfy each other's needs. But as the marriage goes on and couples experience pregnancy, children, job changes, illness, and the like, the sexual needs of one partner may become out of sync with the needs of the other. Compromise and sensitivity become necessary again to preserve and increase unity.

Sexual feelings alone are not love. The way we handle those feelings is a measure of our love and commitment. As we attempt to meet the sexual needs of our partner, we cannot assume he or she will have the same sexual responses as we have. What turns us on may turn our spouse off. The same individual differences which exist in our personalities exist also in our sexual responses. Unless partners enjoy mutually established methods and frequency of love-making, marital unity will be undermined.

Though many of us find it difficult to talk about sex comfortably, we can learn to be open with the one we love. When spouses openly communicate their likes and dislikes in love-making, each is given information which will enable him or her to respond in ways that will heighten mutual enjoyment and cause sexual intimacy to grow.

Married persons must be willing to respond to the needs of their spouses. When persons love their spouses as themselves, they want to know and do what pleases them in all aspects of the relationship including sexual intimacy.

Discussion Questions

1. Why are communication and the desire to please your spouse necessary for true sexual intimacy?
2. **1 Cor. 7:3–5** provides guidelines for sexual intimacy. Read the passage and then state in your own words what the Bible says about sexual intimacy.
3. What should a couple do if they have disagreements about their sexual relationship?

What Is Physical Intimacy?

Discuss these situations:

■ A woman friend comes to you with the private complaint that her husband is insensitive to her feelings when they make love. What would you tell her?

■ At a party you are attending, a newly married man jokes that his wife (sitting nearby) must have great night vision, because she always prefers to make love in the dark. How would you handle this comment?

Physical intimacy goes beyond love-making, extending into the ordinary events of everyday life. Touch is often thought to be the most powerful means of human communication. When a spouse feels hurt or discouraged, a hug, a caress, or a simple touch can be a greater expression of love than sexual intercourse.

Whenever a spouse responds to his or her partner's person and needs with loving words and actions, he or she is building physical intimacy. A wife expresses loving physical intimacy when she appreciates the many facets of her husband's male sexuality and shows that appreciation through word or gesture. Likewise, a husband demonstrates loving physical intimacy when he sees his wife as a beautiful person and expresses his feelings through word or gesture.

How would you as a loving partner respond to the following situations?

- Your spouse put on 20 pounds as a result of bad eating habits compounded by stress at his job.
- Your spouse was in a serious car accident and now has to wear a back brace for at least six months.
- Your spouse must take medication which has a side effect—her face and hands swell and become puffy.

The joy of loving intimately—and of being intimately loved—is beautifully expressed in the **Song of Songs,** a unique book of the Bible. Here, the writer, by divine inspiration, describes marital love, with all its physical and emotional beauty, in poetic detail. The relationship between the lovers also provides a beautiful picture of the love of God for his covenant people Israel, and Jesus' totally giving love for His bride, the church.

The voice of love in the poem is a woman. Her intense experience of love, both as a person who loves and as one who is deeply loved, presents an unsurpassed imagery of physical intimacy. In the dialogue between the woman (beloved) and the man (lover), the intimacy between them is expressed with many images from nature.

If you are a woman, read **Song of Songs 2:3–13** in which the woman describes the man she loves. Rewrite **verses 3–5** the way a poet of our time would write it.

If you are a man, read **Song of Songs 4:1–15.** in which the man describes his beloved. Rewrite **verses 9–11.** Use words and images a modern poet might use.

What do these passages say about God's gift of sexuality?

What words or images are used to show the intimacy which the lovers share?

Bring to class an example of imagery from a contemporary love song or poem, if possible.

As the **Song of Songs** makes clear, God intended marriage to be characterized by romance. In a loving marriage, the joy of sex lies in the fact that the love relationship enhances the sexual bond, even as the sexual bond enhances the total relationship. With God's blessing, love gives meaning to sexual intimacy and sexual intimacy strengthens love.

Tenderness, love, and trust help to create sexual fulfillment. God has blessed marriage with something truly wonderful in the gift of sex. In sexual intercourse, husbands and wives are doing much more than satisfying a physical urge; they are building unity and intimacy. Sexual intercourse usually involves both verbal and nonverbal expressions of love—no wonder it provides a wonderful feeling of being truly cared for and valued.

The sexual relationship between husband and wife has three important, interrelated functions within the marriage:

- It builds unity and intimacy.
- It provides joy and pleasure in each other.
- It is the means God uses to bring children into the world.

For these reasons, God has commanded faithfulness to the marriage vow. Adultery is no longer a fashionable word; "affairs" and "flings" are words more often used to describe marital infidelity. The world has never had, and will never have, Christian standards of conduct. But more easily accepted words do not change sin in the eyes of God.

Discussion Questions

1. Read **Heb. 13:4** and **Matt. 5:27–30.** What do these passages say about sexual intimacy?
2. What happens to unity in a marriage when one or both partners are unfaithful?
3. What are some of the reasons the world uses to justify adultery?
4. What are the consequences of marital infidelity?
5. What are the blessings of remaining faithful to the marriage vow?

As with every other command of God, the commandment not to commit adultery was given, not to make our lives *less,* but to give them *more.* God knew that the pain caused by rejection and unfaithfulness does permanent damage to people's lives.

Men and women who break their marriage vows of faithfulness often do so because of the problems in their relationship. Rather than working together to solve the problem, they go searching for a new relationship. But breaking these vows harms everyone involved. No matter how desirable or pleasurable or harmless the world makes adultery seem, it is always destructive.

Infidelity destroys intimacy and trust when the intimacy meant to be shared with a spouse is given to another. Even if the innocent spouse never finds out, he or she has been cheated of the love that was promised. And the person who was unfaithful feels guilty and dishonest.

Honor and loyalty are essential to a loving relationship. Faithfulness to the marriage vow helps a marriage to reach its true potential. God created us for relationships. He created us first for relationship with Him, our highest priority. He created us also for relationships with others. The marriage relationship has second highest priority. God gave us the good gift of sexual union to make the marriage relationship different from any other. Adam's love song when God brought Eve to him, **"This is now bone of my bones and flesh of my flesh" (Gen. 2:23),** reveals the joy with which husband and wife unite with each other.

One sociologist has compared dating to window shopping. Courtship then becomes the process of negotiating the transaction. Early in a marriage, partners may still be wearing masks. When the mask comes off (intimacy), then the marriage really begins to grow. The courage to grow and change are essential to developing both unity and intimacy.

When a couple have established emotional, spiritual, and physical intimacy, their marriage has some important strengths:

- Willingness to forgive
- Desire to please the other person (which results in less need for reconciliation and forgiveness)

- Valuing the total person God has made the spouse to be

Chapter Summary

Married couples build unity in their marriage as they accomplish the three tasks discussed in this chapter:

- Separate from family of origin
- Develop a realistic view of love
- Build emotional, spiritual and physical intimacy

Love grows in marriage when the couple's love is rooted in God's love and nurtured continually.

In a Christian marriage, two people are totally committed to the person of Jesus Christ and to each other. Such a marriage is a blessing both to the spouses and to all the other people who come into contact with them, for the love which radiates from God to them is reflected to all the lives they touch.

How beautiful you are, my darling!
Oh, how beautiful!
Your eyes are doves.
How handsome you are, my lover!
Oh, how charming!
And our bed is verdant.
The beams of our house are cedars;
our rafters are firs.
Song of Songs 1:15–17

Chapter 7

Partnership and Daily Life

Chapter Preview

Chapter 7 will help you answer the following questions:

- What is the role of a Christian wife in marriage?
- What is the role of a Christian husband in marriage?
- What does it take to be able to communicate effectively?
- Is it possible to learn how to improve communication skills?
- Is it possible for people to resolve conflicts in such a way that everyone will be satisfied?
- What should I expect in future stages of my life?

1. How Does It Work?

During a flight to visit an old friend, Mr. Wright found himself sitting next to a friendly, middle-aged woman. She told him she was traveling to her daughter's wedding.

"My congratulations to your daughter!" Mr. Wright exclaimed.

The woman gave a small smile. "Well," she said, "this is my daughter's third wedding. She has a good job and is an intelligent, pleasant young woman. But here she is at age 27 getting married for the third time. It's a strange feeling to go to your daughter's wedding and think, 'Maybe it will work and maybe it won't.' "

During the last two or three decades, the word *maybe* has become part of the American concept of marriage. We hear all kinds of maybes. Maybe I'd be happier if I weren't married. Maybe I made a mistake. Maybe this partner isn't good enough for me. Maybe I'd be happier married to a different person. Maybe we're growing in different directions and no longer have much in common.

Approaching marriage with a mental "maybe" demonstrates a weak pledge of commitment. If a marriage has difficult times, many people assume ending the marriage to be the logical solution. But difficulties bring growth. How sad that many couples never wait around for that growth to happen! Instead they end the marriage and often take their problems right along with them into the next relationship.

Many fail to anticipate the painful consequences of a broken marriage: loneliness; guilt; financial problems; giving up a home, neighbors, or friends; the grief of lost and broken dreams; the confusion and pain divorce causes their children. Few things create greater insecurity in a child than worrying about whether his or her home is about to be "rent asunder."

Because so many people around us no longer choose to remain faithful to their wedding vows, we Christians may be tempted to adopt a "maybe" mentality, too. Only when we return to the Designer of the marriage relationship and seek His power will we be able to build committed marriages.

After reading about marital unity in chapter 6, you may be wondering if all these ideals for marriage can really work. What about all the ups and downs of everyday life? How can a couple keep it together? This chapter will discuss the four tasks of the newly married which deal with the everyday workings of a marriage partnership:

- Working out husband/wife roles
- Communication
- Learning how to resolve conflict
- Preparing for life stages

The actions you and your spouse take and the decisions you make as you develop your marriage partnership will greatly influence the success and happiness of your marriage. What can you do to make it a lifelong blessing for both of you?

Whose Job Is It?

A generation or two ago, when a man and woman married, they usually knew what their roles in the marriage would be. The man would be the breadwinner. The woman would be the caregiver, responsible for family and home. Having children was an important part of family life, and the woman who bore those children usually assumed most of the responsibility of caring for and raising them. Though this divison of responsibility still exists in many families, there are many others in which the responsibilities must be negotiated or modified, for the traditional roles do not work for that family.

Most sexual roles are learned; we imitate what we see the men and women around us do. When men and women formerly divided the family responsibilities in the traditional way, society supported their roles. Men were supposed to provide for their families; women were supposed to bring up the children. Traditions formerly suggested that women were to be caring, compassionate, and emotionally expressive. Men, on the other hand, were expected to be ambitious, rational, and achievement-oriented. These sexual stereotypes were culturally determined, not Biblically based.

What is a *stereotype?* What are some stereotyped ideas about how men should behave? What are some stereotypical ideas about how women should behave? This traditional system is no longer strongly supported by society. Many families need two wage-earners to survive. Many women want to use their God-given talents in the workplace.

Unfortunately, society has not yet developed a system of clear values and roles to sort out all these changes. Mothers who work outside the home are often exhausted from trying to do their best on the job and barely have the time and energy left over to care for their families. Women who choose to stay home to raise their children are often given less respect than women in the workplace. Many husbands who come from families in which the father was sole breadwinner are not prepared to share the responsibilities of home and family. They may lack a role model to help them divide responsibilities with their wives. They may have little or no experience with children. When a couple marry, they are taking on-the-job training in their new roles as husband and wife. Each is becoming something he or she has never been before. They must learn to negotiate the responsibilities and develop a workable partnership.

When children enter a family, role segregation often increases. Mothers usually care for children, fathers handle cars, home repairs, yard chores, etc. As a result of society's changes and the changes which may occur within a family, confusion and conflict may occur as married couples try to work out the division of responsibilities in their family at different periods of family life. Certain roles may be better suited to one partner than another, but this depends on the needs of the individual and the family. Role changes require new flexibility and compromises. For the success and happiness of the couple, the husband and wife must work out their respectives roles in the marriage.

Sexual Roles

How do *you* define the sexual roles of men and women? On a separate sheet of paper, respond to each of the following statements by identifying it as applying to men, women, or either partner in a marriage.

a. _____ should have goals in life.
b. _____ should be able to express feelings.
c. _____ should be sensitive to the needs of others
d. _____ should be able and willing to care for children.
e. _____ should be self-reliant.
f. _____ should be a good money manager.
g. _____ should bring home the larger paycheck.
h. _____ should be allowed to go back to school.
i. _____ should express affection to family members.
j. _____ should be the listening partner.
k. _____ should say "I love you" first.
l. _____ should discipline the children.
m. _____ should make breakfast on weekends.
n. _____ should do the shopping.

(You might find it fascinating to give this list to your mother and/or father to answer. On which statements do you agree? On which do you disagree? What reasons might explain areas of disagreement?)

A rigid, inflexible approach to husband and wife roles can create great strain in a marriage. What if

the husband becomes disabled? who will provide the family income? What if the wife is unhappy about giving up her job to care for children, yet wants them to have the best possible loving environment? The women's movement which began in the 1960s has raised questions about many of these issues. Being sensitive to our partner's needs and feelings requires that each couple work through these questions in a loving, responsible way.

The differences between men and women are a vital part of this equation. Men and women are different in anatomy, emotions, hormones, sexuality, and social relationships. Because men and women carry different chromosomal patterns, they are literally different in every cell in their bodies. This male-female difference was God's design for fellowship and family, to unite husband and wife.

Society has opened many opportunities for women within the past generation. As a result women hear many conflicting messages. A woman who desires a career is often forced to arrange child care for her children at a very young age, because the workplace does not often make provisions for a career woman to remain at home to nurture her child.

A woman who chooses to be at home to raise her children may suffer a loss of self-esteem if she is made to feel that her role is less important than that of a wage earner. She may feel lonely and isolated if she is home alone with her children day after day. A father who requests time off from his job to help care for his newborn child, or who takes a day off to care for a sick child, may be thought to lack dedication to his job.

Yet children are our investment in the future, the future of our families, the future of our nation. They are a special blessing of God to a family. For them to grow up to be loving, responsible adults, they must receive Christian nurture as children, and Christian nurture requires an investment of time. There is no easy formula to resolve these questions.

In addition to the differences between men and women, every man is different from every other man, and every woman is different from every other woman. We all have traditionally "male" and "female" characteristics in our persons.

A well-rounded person generally has both types of traits. And so, as parents teach their children about sexual roles, Christian families can teach their sons to be caring and nurturing. Similarly, they can teach their daughters to make good use of the talents God has given them. If both parents work outside the home, it is especially necessary that both work together *in* the home to share chores and responsibilities.

As our culture has changed, there is much less emphasis on all men or all women conforming to a standard pattern. Marriage partners have discovered that stereotypical roles often create great friction and alienate their partners. In a good marriage, each person is loved and accepted for who he or she is. Such Christian love may have great diversity in the style in which it is demonstrated within the institution of marriage.

How marriage partners choose to divide their responsibilities is sure to continue to remain an important area to resolve within marriages. What does the Bible say about the roles of men and women and how husband and wife are to relate to each other in the family?

As we discovered in our history of marriage, the Jews were patriarchal. The husband established the status and social patterns for the family. A Jewish man would not speak to a woman in public. Because many men in Jesus' day were condescending and insensitive to women, Jesus' words and actions stood out in sharp contrast to their attitudes. He freely engaged women in conversations, disregarding the conventions of society so He could communicate His purpose for coming into the world.

Jesus encouraged women to take the extraordinary step of following Him, a striking breach of the custom of the day. How did Jesus treat women in the following two examples?

- **John 4:7–30**
- **Matt. 15:21–28**

Jesus always practiced what He preached. When the question of who should have the most power and privilege came up with His disciples, His answer was clear: **"You know that the rulers of the Gentiles lord it over them, and their high officials exercise authority over them. *Not so with you* [italics added]. Instead, whoever wants to become great among you must be your servant, and whoever wants to be first must be your slave—just as the Son of Man did not come to be served, but to serve, and to give His life as a ransom for many" (Matt. 20:25–28).**

The words of our Lord are clear and to the point: Christian men and women are to serve others. The natural place for service to others to begin is with those closest to us.

Jesus warmly accepted and included women in His life. Some of His dearest friends (Mary, Martha, Mary Magdalene) were women. He respected their intelligence and their faith and gladly received their help and ministry **(Mark 15:40–41).** On the day of His death, He was comforted by the constant, faithful presence of the women who were His friends and family members. To them came the first announcement of His resurrection on the third day **(Mark 16:1–9),** Jesus' example laid the foundation for a new dignity and concern for all people, regardless of sex or social status.

As the newly formed church followed His example, women played a vital role in the beginnings and growth of the early Christian community. Dorcas **(Acts 9:36)** was noted for her good works. Priscilla and her husband Aquilla were helpers to the apostle Paul **(Acts 18:26).** Phoebe **(Rom. 16:1–2)** was a deaconess of the church at Cenchreae. Paul considered all those who labored with him in the cause of the Gospel as his equals, whether they were men or women: **"Help these women who have contended at my side in the cause of the Gospel . . . whose names are in the book of life" (Phil. 4:3).**

Whether they were male or female was not important. **"There is neither Jew nor Greek, slave nor free, male nor female, for you are all one in Christ Jesus" (Gal. 3:28).** What was important was the fact that they were devoted to the cause of the Gospel. Women and men are equally members of the priesthood of all believers by faith in Jesus Christ. Both were created in the image of God. And both are equal in having the same relationship to God and nature.

Unfortunately, for many generations Christian people neglected to follow Jesus' example and often failed to encourage women to fully use all their gifts to build the body of Christ, the church. When Christian men and women work together, each using the gifts they have received, by the grace of God, families and churches grow strong.

God gives Christian people the power to witness His redeeming love by the way they live.

When God created man, He made him in the likeness of God. He created them male and female and blessed them. And when they were created, He called them "man."

Gen. 5:1–2

2. Respect and Responsibility

If men and women are equal before God, does that mean they have the same roles in marriage? Equality does *not* mean sameness. Men and women have distinctive identities in their relation to each other. The differences do not imply inferiority or superiority. They are equal, but their roles are not the same.

There are several important Bible references which speak to the question of husband and wife roles.

1. Read **1 Peter 2:17** to establish context for Peter's words to husbands and wives. State the meaning of this passage in your own words. To which marriage partner do Peter's words apply?

2. Read **1 Peter 3:1–9.** On a sheet of paper, make two columns, one headed *Wives,* the other headed *Husbands.*

Under the appropriate columns, list the traits which wives are to display in their marriages. List the traits which husbands are to display.

3. The word *submissive* has often created confusion. Submission had a different meaning in Peter's day than it has today. It in no way implies inferiority or subservience—**verses 8** and **9** make that clear. Peter is here talking about the respect and consideration which wives are to show their husbands, both of which are necessary for a home to operate in a harmonious, orderly fashion. State the meaning of **verses 8** and **9** in your own words.

4. A second important passage dealing with husband and wife roles comes from St. Paul.

Read **Eph. 5:18** and **5:21** to establish context for Paul's words. What power is present in the Christian life **(v. 18)?** How does this affect the marriage relationship **(v. 21)?** State the meaning of **verse 21** in your own words. To which marriage partner(s) do these words apply?

5. Read **Eph. 5:22–33.** How is a wife to demonstrate her reverence for God and her love for her husband? How is a husband to demonstrate his reverence for God and his love for his wife? In which verses does Paul emphasize the mutual submission to each other which should characterize the roles of husbands and wives?

6. The word *submit* in **verse 22** means to surrender your own will in service to another, to yield your own rights in mutual love. How would a wife demonstrate this in marriage? How is submitting in mutual love different from submitting to someone with greater power?

7. Paul uses an analogy to describe how husbands are to love their wives **(v. 25).** According to the analogy, how far are husbands to go in loving their wives? (See also **v. 28.**)

When both husband and wife are subject first to God, with His power they will then be able to be mutually submissive to the needs of each other. Love will seek to treat the other person as an esteemed, cherished partner. If a husband, for example, is really committed to serving his wife, he will put *her* needs before his own.

Husband and wife are not interchangeable parts of a business partnership. *They are equal members of a union—each with a different role.* If husband and wife are not willing to complement (complete) each other, power struggles are likely to arise.

In many marriages, the question of who should have the most power in the relationship creates endless conflict. If the power struggle continues, they risk destroying the permanence and unity of their marriage. If one partner demonstrates an attitude of greater importance than the other, he or she contradicts Christian love. And when marriage partners relate to each other in the context of a power struggle ("I have more power than you; you must carry out my wishes"), they are demonstrating sinful selfishness.

Christian love is *never* about power. It is always about self*less*ness and devotion to the loved partner. When married couples seek to support each other—rather than upstaging or competing with each other—love grows. Competition sometimes destroys closeness. Love, as we have already learned, seeks to *serve,* to meet the other person's needs—not to acquire power for itself. Jesus Himself demonstrated love that serves in a most surprising way on the night before His death.

Read **John 13:1–17.**

What was the surprising thing which Jesus did? Why was it so unusual?

What was His purpose in doing this? (See especially **vv. 12–15.**)

In what ways are Christians to "wash one another's feet"?

How would marriage partners "wash one another's feet"? Give some real-life examples from people you know who have demonstrated this kind of committed Christian love.

How would a Christian marriage partner deal with a spouse who fails to live this way, or doesn't even want to?

Jesus had power, yet He *chose* service. As Jesus, the Head of the church, devoted Himself totally to its needs, so a husband is to devote himself to the needs of his wife. And as the church yields completely to the love, care, and direction of the Lord, so the wife yields to her husband.

Marriage was designed as an ordered relationship. God desires man to be the head of woman, and woman to complement man, but not because one is better in any respect than the other. Woman was created to be a suitable helper to man, not a servant or inferior. She was created to complete him, making a household and children possible. She supports her husband in his responsibility to care for the family. She thus accepts the same submissive role that the church takes as it submits to Jesus by faith according to the Bible.

Her husband in turn is to protect her, provide for her, and consider her part of himself, a partner in life. He is the head of the relationship, head of a relationship that is "one flesh," for the purpose of showing sacrificial love to his wife. The purpose of leadership is to serve as Jesus did. Man was woman's head from the moment of her creation, but after the fall into sin, selfishness distorted this relationship. Christ's redemption creates a way for sin to be forgiven, but it does not remove the selfish, self-seeking character of human beings.

Submission in marriage is not imposed by the man over the woman because of superior authority or power. Rather, it is rooted in the order instituted by God to which both are subject. God desires women to be respectful to their husbands and husbands to accept responsibility for their wives for the sake of orderliness and unity within the family. When both husband and wife submit themselves first to the Lord, they will each be able to treat their spouse as they themselves wish to be treated.

"The man is the head of the woman; Christ is the head of the man; God is the head of Christ. The 'head' is that which is prior, that which determines, that which leads" (CTCR document, p. 7a).

"It is the responsibility of the individual men and women to work together as equal, redeemed Christians, putting the welfare of the Kingdom ahead of prejudices, customs, or mind-sets. Women and men must realize that each Christian has a calling and a ministry and that the service of each individual is important and valuable to the life of the church" (CTCR document p. 12a).

(Adapted from "Women in The Church." *The Lutheran Witness,* May 1986, 2–4, 18–19; and *Women in The Church,* The Lutheran Church—Missouri Synod Commission on Theology and Church Relations, September 1985.)

Wives, submit to your husbands as to the Lord. For the husband is the head of the wife as Christ is the head of the church, His body, of which He is the Savior. Now as the church submits to Christ, so also wives should submit to their husbands in everything. Husbands, love your wives, just as Christ loved the church and gave Himself up for her.

Eph. 5:22–25

3. Communication

A second vital aspect to the partnership of a married couple is establishing good communication. The average person spends 75–80 percent of the waking hours involved in communication through either reading, writing, speaking, or listening. We spend approximately half (40 percent of our waking hours) in listening. For a student, that figure may be even higher.

One would think that in our age of communication, with satellites, TV, VCRs, radio, and CBs, we would know how to communicate effectively. Yet communication problems are a factor in 90 percent of divorces.

Communication is *the sharing of yourself in such a way that someone else can understand what you mean and how you feel.* Most of our communication patterns were learned from our family of origin. We probably communicate in a way similar to that of our father or mother. But what if the communication patterns we learned are not satisfying? Communication is a skill and skills can be learned. Therefore, we can grow in our ability to communicate with others.

Although much communication is verbal, we can also communicate without words. In order for communication to be effective, it must be two-way: we must be able to share our ideas and feelings, and the person with whom we are communicating must be able to listen and understand.

The poem "Please Hear What I'm Not Saying" provides some important insights about the sharing that is necessary if people are to understand each other.

Please Hear What I'm Not Saying

Don't be fooled by me.
Don't be fooled by the face I wear,
For I wear a mask, I wear a thousand masks.
Masks that I am afraid to take off.
But none of them are me.
Pretending is an art that's second nature to me.
But don't be fooled.

I give you the impression that I am secure,
That all is sunny and unruffled with me,
Within as well as without,
That confidence is my name and coolness my game,
And that I need no one.
Don't believe me, Please!

My surface may be smooth,
But my surface is my mask,
My varying and ever concealing mask.
Beneath lies no smugness,
No complacence.
Beneath dwells the real me,
In confusion and fear,
In loneliness.

I idly chatter with you in the suave tones of surface talk.
I tell you everything that's really nothing,
Of what's crying within me.
So, when I'm going through my routine,
Please don't be fooled by what I'm saying.
Please listen carefully, and try to hear what I'm *not* saying,
And what I'd like to be able to say,
What for survival I need to say,
But what I can't say.

Only you can call me into aliveness,
Each time you're kind, and gentle, and encouraging,
Each time you try to understand because you really care.
My heart begins to grow wings.
Very small wings, very feeble wings, but wings.

With your sympathy and sensitivity, and your power of understanding,
You can breathe life into me, I want you to know that.
I want you to know how important you are to me,
How you can be a creator of the person that is me if you choose to.
Please choose to.
Do not pass me by.
It will not be easy for you.
My long conviction of worthlessness builds strong walls.
The nearer you approach me, the blinder I may strike back.
I fight against the very thing I cry out for,
But I am told that love is stronger than strong walls.
In this lies my hope.
My only hope.

Who am I, you may wonder.
I am someone you know very well—
I am a hurting member of your family,
I am the person sitting beside you in this room,
I am every person you meet on the street.
Please don't believe my mask,
Please come behind it to glimpse the real me.
At least *recognize* me.
Please.
Because you care.

(Author unknown [condensed and modified by Gilbert Wrenn, taken from *Curriculum Guide for Student Peer Counseling Training*]. Used by permission)

Discussion Questions

1. What does the speaker in the poem want you to "please hear"? What is it he is "not saying"?
2. What do you think are the three most important things this poem says about communication?
3. Why do people wear masks? Give some examples of the kinds of masks worn by people you know.
4. Choose two lines that reflect your own feelings or experience. What insights do those lines provide into yourself and into your relationships with other people?
5. How can one person be for another "a creator of the person that is me"? Think of an example from Jesus' ministry of a time when He was a "creator" of new possibilities for another person. Find the Bible reference for that story.

6. Suggest one or two ways to respond to the person in the poem, based on the love that Christ has placed in your heart.
7. Think of the people in your life. Name one person who needs *you* to hear what he or she is not saying. How will you reach out to him or her?

Write a prayer for God's power as you seek to grow in this area of your life.

Listening—a Key to Caring Communication

Is hearing the same as listening? Not at all. We hear every sound that occurs around us, but we listen only to those sounds to which we really want to pay attention. Hearing is a mere physical act requiring no effort on our part. Listening, on the other hand, requires active involvement in the dialog with the other person.

Did you ever play the listening game as a child? In the game a group of people pass a story down the line by each whispering the story in the ear of the person next to them in line. The last person to hear the story repeats it aloud for all to hear. Often the story is totally unrecognizable by the end of the line! What does this game teach us about our ability to listen?

Think of several people you know who are good listeners. What makes them good listeners? For whom do *you* provide a listening ear when it's needed?

How well do your parents or other family members listen to you? (Do they ever listen to see if you'll say what they want?) How well do you listen to your parents or other family members? (Do you ever listen for others to get finished talking?) How do you feel when a parent or family member *really* listens to you? How do you think your parents or other family members feel when you really listen to them?

Rate yourself as a listener. Which of the following best describes you:

a. I am always able to stop and give full attention when needed.
b. I am usually able to give full attention to another's concern when needed.
c. Now and then I am able to give some attention to another's concern.
d. I hardly ever give another family member or friend my full attention.
e. I never give a family member or friend my full attention to deal with his or her concern.

Which of the following apply to you? *Some of the things I sometimes do that keep me from really listening are*

☐ I keep on doing whatever I was doing.
☐ I forget to face the person and look directly at him or her.
☐ I turn my back on the other person.
☐ I keep the radio or TV turned up.
☐ I tend to interrupt and say what I think.
☐ I let my mind wander to other things.

When I don't listen well to family members or friends it's usually because

☐ I'm too busy.
☐ I have too much on my mind.
☐ I just don't think about it.
☐ I've had a bad day.
☐ I get tired of listening to everyone.
☐ I'm too upset.
☐ I don't think they understand me.
☐ I didn't realize it was that important to them.

(If you have the courage, after you have evaluated your own listening, you might wish to ask a family member or friend to evaluate you, too, to get another perspective on how well other people feel you listen to them.)

Would you like to become a more effective listener? Would you like to be someone friends confide in? someone to whom your children may one day be able to unburden their problems? someone a spouse will trust enough to share feelings?

To really listen to another person is one of the greatest demonstrations of love we can give. Listening is a *skill,* a skill you can learn if you keep in mind the following ideas:

Listening is *not*
- talking;
- thinking ahead to plan the perfect reply;
- being passive, uninvolved;
- waiting while you discover the perfect solution for the other person;
- conquering the other person;
- saying, "You think that's bad? You should hear what happened to **me**!";

Listening *is*
- caring enough to give your very best (yourself);
- giving the other person full attention;
- taking him or her seriously;
- hearing *feelings* as well as facts or words;
- letting the other person lead the conversation;
- being willing to follow.

The key to really listening is to *listen to understand.* Words may not be enough to communicate all of what the other person is saying. We must also "hear" the emotions and feelings going on behind the words. And we must listen to what is being said—not what we think the other person means. If we jump to conclusions before the other person finishes speaking, we may never hear what he or she really needed to communicate. Someone once said, "God gave us two ears and one mouth as a way to tell us to listen twice as much as we speak."

How do we demonstrate love by listening? What role does listening play in working through conflicts and problems?

Identify one person who might need you to listen this week, and listen to them according to the suggestions above. Then share your experiences with the class.

Speak to one another with psalms, hymns and spiritual songs. Sing and make music in your heart to the Lord, always giving thanks to God the Father for everything, in the name of our Lord Jesus Christ. Submit to one another out of reverence for Christ.

Eph. 5:19–21

4. Speaking to Be Heard

Some time ago, a whole series of popular TV commercials was made about speaking to be heard. In each commercial, a person would come into a crowded place (around a swimming pool, at a party, on a golf course, in a subway car) and begin to speak. Immediately, all other conversation would cease and the total attention of everyone would be focused on the speaker. The advertising slogan declared, "When E. F. Hutton talks, people listen." We can't help but envy someone to whom everyone listens. We'd all like to be like E. F. Hutton, with people eager to hear what we want to say. How can we learn to improve our communication skills so people will listen to us?

Some great comedy scenes on television and in the movies have been built on breakdowns in communication. But when it happens to us, it's not comedy. The results are misunderstandings, and hurt feeling that result in the building of walls rather than bridges in our relationships with others. Let's look at an example.

Setting: Saturday night
Characters: You and a friend of the opposite sex
Place: In a car on the way to see a movie

You: I'm really looking forward to this movie. I'm glad we were able to get together.

Friend: Me too. I'm sorry I didn't get around to calling you this week like I said I would. You look great tonight. Your new haircut really looks good. How was your first week on the new job?

You: It was okay. My boss is really strange, but the rest of the people seem okay. How was your week?

Friend: Pretty good. I finally finished the big project I've been working on. I hope this movie is as good as the reviews said it would be.

You've probably had dozens of conversations similar to the one above. Is the conversation communication? That depends. Let's look at it more closely. Are you really sharing what is going on with you? Is your friend really listening? So often our conversations are very poor communication because both speaker and listener are reluctant to share what is going on beneath the surface. Or we are so engrossed in our own problems that we find it difficult to really listen to what is going on with someone else.

Perhaps you got the new haircut because you discovered during your first day on the new job that your old image just didn't seem to fit this new setting. Perhaps you really needed this job but are becoming worried about whether this job is right for you. Perhaps you've heard rumors and already seen evidence that your boss plays favorites. His personal friends get the best assignments and privileges; to the rest of the people he is rude and overbearing. You are conscientious and hard-working, but are not willing to play the boss's game by fawning over him or treating him like a god. You say "okay" when your friend asks about the job, but you know things are far from okay.

And what is really going on with your friend? Did his or her project turn out well or not? Why didn't he or she call as promised? Is he or she really glad to see you? Good communication between two people is a necessity if a relationship is to grow and be satisfying.

Why do people so often find it hard to communicate?

There are several reasons:

1. We may be afraid to share our real feelings or real selves.Men especially may fear that sharing their feelings is unmanly, a sign of weakness. (Did Jesus share His feelings?) Often we fear that if we said what we really felt we might be rejected, so we share an ideal self, rather than our real selves. Limiting our disclosures to our superficial self may reduce the risk of rejection—but it makes an intimate relationship impossible. Sometimes we do this even with God, thinking that if we "put up a front" He will find it easier to love and accept us.

2. Communication may seem like more trouble than it's worth. We know that once we open up discussion on a personal issue we will have to see it through. However, when we keep all our feelings bottled up, sooner or later we are likely to blow up in some way—and the conversations which result may be very destructive.

3. We may feel that we're no good at it. Perhaps you've never had much experience with sharing your feelings in your family. Or maybe you've been shot down when you tried to share something about yourself with a friend. As a result, you avoid anything but superficial conversation.

We were not born with the *skill* of communication. But most persons can learn to communicate. Effective communication can change a very superficial marriage or friendship into one that is deep, rich, and intimate.

Each of us communicates both verbally and nonverbally. How would you communicate each of the following emotions verbally? nonverbally?

anger	joy
sympathy	success
frustration	sadness
fatigue	

Effective communication is especially important when people have a misunderstanding to resolve. Because they feel uneasy about confronting those who have caused them problems, people sometimes begin their discussions with those who have wronged them by getting their attention.

Which of the items in the list below have you seen people you use to get the attention of others:

a. Name calling
b. Sarcasm, put-downs
c. Touching the person
d. Calling the person by his or her correct name
e. Using a special name (nickname or pet phrase)
f. Raising of voice
g. Using a different tone of voice

Read through the list again. Which of these items are *you* most likely to use when you want to get someone's attention. Which of these are likely to get attention in a way that will lead to understanding? Which are likely to get attention that will add to the misunderstanding?

The Levels of Communication

There are five levels of communication which we can observe in our own conversations and the conversations of those around us:

Small talk or cliche conversation is the fifth and easiest level on which to talk with another person! We use it all the time. Examples of fifth level communication include the following: "Hi, how are ya?" "Okay. How about you?" "I'm doing okay. How's school going?" "Same old stuff. How is yours?" "Kinda boring. I can't wait to get out. Well, I've gotta go. See ya." "Take it easy." What would happen if, the next time someone asks you how you are, you really told him or her? (Are you daring enough to try it? If so, share your experience with your classmates.)

The facts about others—fourth level. This is pretty easy too. It's easy to talk about other people; there's no risk at all. Other people's quirks are fertile ground for endless conversations; they are easy to talk about and we don't have to reveal anything about ourselves.

Opinions and ideas—third level. At this level, we are beginning to experience true communication, for we are sharing something of ourselves. If we get any negative feedback, we may of course back off and go back to being superficial or saying what we think the other person wants to hear. But when we are willing to share some of our thoughts, we are engaging in real communication.

Feelings and emotions—second level. When we are able to express the feelings and emotions that lie beneath our opinions and ideas, then we are truly sharing ourselves. We will most likely not choose to communicate on this level with casual acquaintances. But often we are afraid to share our feelings even with those we love. As a result, they may be left to wonder what is really going on with us, or even misunderstand why we did the things we did.

Open and honest sharing of ourselves—first level. This level of communication is not easy—but when two people love and trust each other enough to open themselves to each other in honest and open level one sharing, that relationship will flourish. When we know the other person loves and accepts us as we are, we no longer need to be afraid of rejection. This level of conversation will not come automatically; it takes time and relationship-building. But striving for level one communication will bring rich rewards in our most important relationships including our marriages.

An Exercise in Communication

Keep a log of your conversations for one day in the following way:

1. Chart your day at one-hour intervals. For each hour, list the name(s) of persons with whom you had a conversation. (You need not record the topic of conversation unless you wish. Limit your log to significant conversations, e.g., those which lasted a minute or more. You may need to make notes at the end of every hour or several hours to remind yourself of the conversations you had.)

2. After the name of the person with whom you conversed, write down which of the five levels of conversation you used (e.g., mother, levels five and three).

3. At the end of the day, evaluate your conversations:

a. What percentage of your conversations were conducted on each level?
b. Which conversations did you find it easiest to remember at the end of the day? Why?
c. Which levels of communication led to greater understanding between you and another person? Why?

4. Write a paragraph about your experiences.

Consider the following recommendations for good family communication. "Watch your words. Help understand the problem. Speak up for what you really want underneath." Think about these three items and what they might mean for your family. Then rank the three in terms of their importance to you as a member of your own family at this moment. (Use a 1 for the most important, and so on.)

a. Watch your words. (Don't use put-downs, sarcasm, or anger.)
b. Help understand the problem. (Try to understand the whole issue, not just your own little part of it.)
c. Speak up for what you really want underneath. (Let the members of your family know what you want or are concerned about.)

(Adapted from Lutheran Family Challenge, Inc. Elk Grove Village, Il. Used by permission.)

Discussion Questions

1. What levels of conversation do you hear most from other people during the course of a day?

2. What levels of conversation would help to build the unity and intimacy in marriage which we discussed in the previous chapter?

3. When you pray to God, what type of communication are you using?

4. When you share your Christian faith with another person, what type of communication are you using?

Roleplay what might happen when you use the various levels of communication to share your Christian faith.

5. Read again the poem "Please Hear What I'm Not Saying." When the speaker in the poem describes the communication going on around him or her, what levels of communication are being described? For what levels of communication does the speaker yearn? Why?

6. James put it this way: **"My dear brothers, take note of this: Everyone should be quick to listen, slow to speak and slow to become angry, for man's anger does not bring about the righteous life that God desires" (James 1:19–20).** What three suggestions for effective communication does James provide? Which is the greatest challenge for you to do?

7. List some of the main issues that you find yourself confronting (or needing to confront) in your family. (You need not "get personal." Just list the issue.) How might the three suggestions listed above be of help to you in dealing with these issues?

8. How could you use these suggestions when you must confront someone with the condemnation of God's law upon his sin?

9. How could you apply these suggestions when you wish to provide the comfort of the Gospel to someone who repents of his sin?

10. How can you grow in your ability to share yourself with others? How can you grow in your ability to really listen to what other people are saying?

I pray out of [God's] glorious riches He may strengthen you with power through His Spirit in your inner beings, so that Christ may dwell in your hearts through faith. And I pray that you, being rooted and established in love, may have power, together with all the saints, to grasp how wide and long and high and deep is the love of Christ, and to know this love that surpasses knowledge—that you may be filled to the measure of all the fullness of God.

Eph. 3:16–19

5. Handling Conflict

Mrs. Martin was taking her coffee break at work when her co-worker, Mrs. Robinson, sat down next to her with a worried look on her face. Before Mrs. Martin could even ask what was wrong, Mrs. Robinson began to blurt out her story, "My husband and I had a terrible fight this morning. He put down a deposit on a new car with the money I had planned to use to buy new living room furniture. How do you handle fights with your husband?"

Mrs. Martin looked unconcerned. "I really can't help you," she said. "My husband and I never fight."

Do you think Mrs. Martin is telling the truth? Why or why not?

Every marriage has conflicts which must be resolved. No two people will ever agree on everything. Becoming one flesh in marriage does not erase our differences in personality, feelings, thoughts, and communication patterns. Conflict is natural and, when handled constructively, can actually strengthen a relationship! Being able to resolve conflicts constructively builds strong marriages. But many couples find it difficult to develop conflict-resolution skills.

Usually a marriage in which both people share common faith, values, and goals will have fewer serious conflicts than a marriage in which these are not shared. If two people agree on many important issues, they will not need as many fights or disagreements to clear the air and settle their differences. Couples with good communication skills likewise will need fewer fights to settle issues. But some couples never fight because they are never able or willing to work out their differences. Their conflicts remain unresolved because of an unwillingness to do the work required to settle their disagreements.

Resolving conflict need not involve quarreling. When two people quarrel, they become angry and attack each other, instead of discussing the issues. Conflict which arises from the selfishness of one person often cannot be resolved constructively either, especially if the person is unable or unwilling to change. But conflicts which arise from the differences between two people can lead to greater understanding between the people involved—if they confront each other in a caring, honest way.

Working with a student partner, discuss how you and your partner would resolve the following conflict. One of you take the role of Mr. Major, the other roleplay Mrs. Major, and then work through the following situation as you think a married couple might.

Before they were married, Mrs. Major promised that she would go to church with Mr. Major even though she wasn't a member. As the months have gone by, however, more often than not she's been "too tired" or had "too much housework" to go to church. Last Sunday they had a huge argument, and they have hardly spoken all week.

How did you and your partner resolve the conflict? What other possible ways of settling the issue did other class members use?

Give two other examples of conflicts which married couples are likely to encounter. Describe the situations. How might these conflicts be resolved?

Methods of Dealing With Conflict

There are at least five basic ways in which conflicts can be dealt with:

1. Yield—one person can simply give in to the other. Sometimes, especially if the issue is not too important to one of the partners, this can work. If one person always gives in to the other, however, the anger which builds up may eventually come out in destructive ways.

2. Withdraw—one person can simply refuse to deal with the issue. If that person has had negative experiences in dealing with conflicts in the past, he or she may decide it's not worth the effort. The anger and resentment stay, however.

3. Win—one person may keep fighting until the other person finally gives in. The person who feels he or she must always win will have difficulty resolving conflict successfully, since winning has become more important than understanding the other person. (Is it more important to win an argument or to build a stronger relationship?) The person who loses will feel bitter and resentful.

4. Compromise—each gives up something he or she wanted, to achieve a solution with which both can live. Each person yields some demands to the settling of the issue. A compromise should not mean, however, that both people hate what is agreed upon.

5. Resolve—the persons find a way to settle the issue through direct, caring communication. Each shares his or her feelings and listens to the feelings of the other as they work toward mutual understanding.

Discussion Questions

1. Which of the five methods did you and your discussion partner use? Was it effective?

2. Which method do you use most often when you have differences to work through with another person? Which methods are used by other members of your family?

3. Which methods best reflect your Christian faith? Why?

Listed below are five statements, each of which signals one of the five methods of dealing with conflicts listed above.

Match method above with the statement below which best expresses the end result of using that method.

a. "I'm glad you finally realize why this is the best way to do it."
b. "Now that we've talked this through and understand each other, this doesn't need to be a problem anymore."
c. "Oh, all right. I'm tired of fighting. We'll do it your way."
d. "I don't want to discuss it. Just do whatever you want to do and leave me out of it."
e. "If you will be flexible about this part of the problem, I am willing to meet you halfway on the other part of the issue."

Being able to resolve conflicts successfully is a necessary skill for any two people who wish to live in harmony for a lifetime. Many of us approach conflict situations by reacting in the ways we learned from our family of origin. If our family had successful ways to resolve differences, these techniques may work well for us. Most of us, however, can grow as Christians by relying on God to help us learn new methods of dealing with conflict.

Four Steps to Resolving Conflicts

Successful conflict resolution usually results from a process that has four stages:

1. Ventilation. We confront the problem, state it clearly, and air our feelings about it;

2. Clarifying the issue. We try to determine what caused the problem and understand all the feelings, both ours and the other person's, which were created by the problem;

3. Explore possible solutions. Many people often feel there is only one "right" solution to a problem and as a result are unable to bring any creative thinking to their problems; yet the more possible solutions we are able to generate, the more choices we will have as we try to find a good solution;

4. Agreement. Having looked at all the possible solutions, we are now ready, together with the other person, to choose the best solution for everyone involved.

Contributing Factors

Does it sound easy? How easy—and how successful we will be—depends on many factors. Which of the following factors would make successful conflict resolution more difficult? Which would make it easier?

- You have a quick temper.
- The problem has been going on for a long time.
- The other person has had a bad day at work.
- You are able to admit that you contributed to the problem.
- You bring up the problem when other people are around.
- You prayed for understanding before you began the discussion.
- You realize that the other person is very sensitive about this issue, so you choose your words carefully.
- The other person usually brings other unresolved issues into the discussion.
- You are convinced that the other person's attitude is wrong.

Questions for Reflection

1. Think of a conflict you had recently with a parent, a friend, or a brother or sister. Was the conflict resolved successfully or is it still hanging on? What did you do to try to resolve the conflict? What did the other person do?

2. If the problem was settled, which of the five methods did you use? If it is still hanging on, what do you think should be your next step?

3. What new techniques could you learn that would make it easier for you to resolve problems with other people?

4. How would God's forgiveness make it easier for you to resolve problems with other people?

The Bible speaks to the question of how we are to treat others when we have a conflict with them to resolve.

1. Read the following passages and then write the principle of Christian conflict resolution which each presents:

   Matt. 7:1–5:
   Eph. 4:1–2, 15:
   1 Peter 4:8:
   Eph. 4:26–32:

   Choose the verse that would help you the most in future conflicts and commit it to memory.
2. Write a prayer that you could use when you have a problem to resolve with someone.

I urge you to live a life worthy of the calling you have received. Be completely humble and gentle; be patient, bearing with one another in love.

Eph. 4:1–2

6. Putting Principles into Practice

If we wish to maintain loving relationships, we must learn how to resolve conflicts successfully. Some people become aggressive and hurtful when they are angry. Others pretend problems don't exist, hoping thereby to avoid confronting them. Some are so critical of others they fail to admit their own mistakes. Underneath all these destructive attitudes is our own basic sinful selfishness. Our sinful self wants to be right. It wants revenge on the person who hurt us and it wants to look out for itself without caring about the needs or feelings of the other person.

Sometimes people with a conflict develop "tunnel vision"—a situation where their feelings are so aroused that they see only the negative traits and mistakes of the other person which led to the conflict. They totally lose sight of the other person's good qualities. Furthermore, they are likely to assign 99 percent of the responsibility for the problem to the other person, while owning only 1 percent themselves.

The following student-written drama depicts a young couple, who have been married for four months, having their first major conflict. As you read the drama, keep in mind what you have learned about resolving conflicts.

Crisis Point

Introduction: There is no such thing as a perfect marriage. Every marriage has its ups and downs. Alan and Katherine Jones have been married for

four months. He is a chef and she is a journalist with a top city newspaper, a job that takes the majority of her time.

Scene 1

Katherine comes home from work and collapses in a chair.

Alan (*storming out of the kitchen*): Kathy, you're late again!

Kathy: Alan, don't start with me. I'm tired and I don't want to hear it.

Alan: You said you would be home for dinner, so I got it all together. But no, you decide to be late—again.

Kathy: I didn't *decide* anything. It's not my fault that my job held me over.

Alan: Your job takes all your time. What about me? If you don't want to be a wife, why did you get married?

Kathy: Alan, you're being childish.

Alan: I am not. How would you feel if I never had time for you?

Kathy: But your job is different.

Alan: You bet it is! I only work there; I don't *live* there.

Kathy: I'm sorry, but that's just the way my job is.

Alan: Can't you change anything?

Kathy: No. Things are really going great. I'll make it up to you, okay?

Alan: Well, okay. Now, let's eat.

Scene 2

Two weeks later.

Kathy (*coming in the door*): Alan, I'm home!

Alan: Hey, you're home early.

Kathy: With good news. My boss just gave me some vacation time.

Alan: Great! Now we can spend some time together.

Kathy: It feels so good to relax. (*Walks into the bedroom.*) ALAN!

Alan: What's the matter?

Kathy: How can I relax in this mess? This place is a disaster! Your clothes are all over the place and the dust on the furniture is an inch thick!

Alan: Well, you're never home to clean the house.

Kathy: You have more time than I do, so what's your excuse? What do you do all day? Obviously, you don't clean up!

Alan: Hey, you don't do housework when you're supposed to, either.

Kathy: Well, I can't do everything. And you're starting to sound just like my mother. She's always been on my back about housework, too.

Alan: I don't like housework any more than you do.

Kathy: The least you could do is pick up your clothes.

Alan: Well, I cleaned the kitchen.

Kathy: That's the only place you ever clean.

Alan: Look, you've got some time off. Let's both dig in and clean up the place together. Then I'll try to keep up my part. But I'm not making any promises.

Kathy: Okay, I agree. Let's get started.

Scene 3

One week later.

Kathy (*walking into the kitchen*): Good morning, Alan.

Alan: Good morning. Want some coffee?

Kathy: Thank you. Why are you being so cooperative this morning?

Alan: Well, my wife has time off, and I thought maybe we could do something fun today. Now that we've finally got this place cleaned up.

Kathy: Why are you bringing that up again? I wish you'd quit complaining! You've always got something to complain about.

Alan: I do not.

Kathy: You do too. You're never satisfied. (*The phone rings.*)

Kathy: I've got it. "Hello. Oh, hi, Mother. Yes, I'm enjoying my little vacation. Yes, Alan is fine. Oh, okay. Saturday's fine. See you then. Bye.

Alan: Saturday's fine for what?

Kathy: Well, my parents are coming over.

Alan: In-laws. Just what I needed.

Kathy: What is that supposed to mean?

Alan: Well, do you enjoy their visits? Your mother is always criticizing the way we live. And your father just sits there. I can't talk to him.

Kathy: You could if you tried.

Alan: And then there's your brother, who's part computer and can only talk in 13-syllable words.

Kathy: That's not fair. He's a good football player, too, just like my father.

Alan: That's another thing. If you don't like football and don't care about computers, they don't know anything else to talk about. And I'm tired of your brother's sermons about how evil everything is in the world.

Kathy: There's nothing wrong with being religious.

Alan: Can't he just be a Christian without being a fanatic?

Kathy: You might learn something by listening to him. You won't win any prizes for Christian behavior the way you're acting!

Alan: Neither will you! Face it. You have an abnormal family. Your mother is a perfectionist, your father can't hold a decent conversation, and your brother is just plain weird.

Kathy: And I suppose you think you're perfect. I don't know why I married you. You're never satisfied and you are impossible to live with!

Alan: How would you know? You're never home to live with!

Kathy: I'm not going to listen to anymore of this stupid talk! If you don't like it here, why don't you just leave? I got along perfectly well without you before we were married! (*Grabs her coat and slams out the door.*)

Scene 4

Several hours later.

Katherine walks in the door with shopping bags in her hand.

Alan: Kathy, let's talk.

Kathy: What is there to talk about?

Alan: I'm sorry I insulted your family. I lost my temper.

Kathy: I'm sorry, too; sorry I shouted at you. You're not really impossible. I've just realized there are things we both have to live with.

Alan: I guess you have to live with my complaining, and I have to live with your family. I am glad I married you.

Kathy: So am I. Thanks for letting me be who I am.

Alan: Me too.

Kathy: And thanks in advance for being nice to my mother.

Alan: I can hardly wait!

(Adapted from a skit written by Kelli Smith and Eugene Schoop. Used by permission.)

Discussion Questions

1. Have Alan and Kathy learned how to resolve conflicts successfully? Do they demonstrate a healthy approach to dealing with differences?

2. Are conflicts inevitable in marriage? Why or why not? What things caused conflict in this marriage? What other things are likely to cause conflicts in marriage?

3. In chapter 1 we discovered that forgiveness is a three-part process: (a) admitting sin, (b) receiving forgiveness, and (c) offering forgiveness. Why are Alan and Kathy able to forgive each other in scene 4? What is one thing they could say to each other to witness to their Christian faith? (God calls us to be a witness to "others," and especially to those whom we love!)

4. Keeping in mind the principles of conflict resolution, work through the conflict situation you have received from your teacher. Do this with a student perhaps.

Share your experience with the class.

Any successful relationship requires that two people develop a process of working things out together. It is more rewarding—and God-pleasing—to resolve a conflict than to destroy a relationship. We cannot escape conflicts.

If we try to avoid conflict because we are afraid of losing the relationship, then the relationship cannot grow. A couple who never disagree probably have a very superficial relationship. The couple who learn to resolve their conflicts within an atmosphere of love and forgiveness are building strong bonds for the future of their relationship. Such couples deal with problems as they arise, rather than letting anger and resentment build up until they explode. If we wait until we reach a crisis point to resolve differences, it is sometimes too late.

Our sinful, selfish natures make conflict inevitable in our relationships. But God forgives us of all these selfish, destructive behaviors and creates new growth for us. No mistake is fatal; He uses our mistakes to help us grow. When He is present in our lives, we can learn to be humble, to avoid judging others, and to realize that all of us are sinners. We can admit we are wrong, and be strong enough to be humble (and perhaps not even say anything!) when we are right. We can recognize that most times we have contributed to the problem in some way.

An old Indian proverb says "Do not criticize a man until you have walked a mile in his moccasins." The power we receive from God allows us to do just that—to see a conflict from the other person's point of view. When we are able to see a problem from the other person's perspective, and are willing to forgive as we have been forgiven, then we can resolve conflicts successfully.

Instead, speaking the truth in love, we will in all things grow up into Him who is the Head, that is, Christ. From Him the whole body, joined and held together by every supporting ligament, grows and builds itself up in love, as each part does its work.

Eph. 4:15–16

7. Preparing for Life's Stages

Change is one of the givens of human life and an inevitable part of the marriage relationship. A married couple celebrating a first anniversary will have undergone many changes before they celebrate their silver anniversary 24 years later. Some people enter a marriage believing that the marriage and their partner will always stay the same. That expectation is, of course, totally unrealistic.

Picture yourself 25 years from now. How will you have changed?

Picture yourself in a marriage that has lasted for 25 years. How will the relationship have changed?

Flexibility and openness to change are important for every person's mental health. They are necessary for us to continue to serve God and others in all the times and places of our lives. Couples who prepare and plan for changes are less likely to be overwhelmed by the stress that any change creates in their lives. Change is essential to growth. If you stayed as you are now for the rest of your life, you would not grow as a person, for you would not have the experiences which are necessary to change you and cause growth to occur.

If you marry, how will your marriage change over the years? Most marriages follow a typical pattern or cycle similar to the one below:

- Twosome
- Parenthood—young children
- Parenthood—school age children
- Parenthood—adolescent children
- Launching children as adults
- Empty nest
- Retirement

Make a chart to think through what you would expect to experience in each phase of adult married life by listing each of the headings above across a sheet of paper. Then under each heading, add the following information:

1. What would you expect your *age* to be at this stage? Your spouse's age?
2. What are some *things you would expect to be happening* in your marriage and family at each stage?
3. Describe what you think *you would be like* in each stage.
4. Describe what you think *your spouse would be like* in each stage.
5. What would your *church participation* be like at each stage?
6. At what stage(s) do you think you would have to be most understanding of your spouse? Why?
7. Give an example of a person or family you know in each stage, who you think is typical of what people are like in that stage.

(Feel free to consult with parents and friends as you think through these stages to see if your expectations fit their experiences.)

Every marriage has seasons or stages. A marriage without children would be different from a marriage with children, but every marriage would still go through different phases. The experiences and relationship-building which go on during each phase prepare the way for much of what will occur during the phase to follow. A wise couple spends time talking about and preparing for what they will encounter in the next phase, rather than just waiting to see what will happen. Without some planning and preparation, many of their goals can never be achieved.

Spouses who cannot accept change, or who never communicate about the changes they are experiencing, often grow apart. It's not uncommon, for example, for a marriage to break up after the children are grown. Did the couple stay together just for the sake of their children? Sometimes. Many couples simply fail to keep the communication going and then sadly discover that they no longer have much in common. They have failed to really share their lives with each other over the years.

A lot of jokes have been made about the time

in a marriage when "the honeymoon is over." The fact is, a honeymoon cannot last a lifetime. That does not mean that a marriage goes downhill after the honeymoon. Couples who build strong marriages find themselves more in love as the years go by; the marriage bond has been strengthened by the experiences they have shared. It will no longer be a "honeymoon love," but it may be a deeper love, based on greater understanding and deeper intimacy than the love they experienced early in the marriage. Someone has said, "Love is what two people have been through together."

What should you expect from each stage of marriage? Your chart has probably included some of the following:

1. Twosome—in the honeymoon phase, the couple established intimacy and closeness and set patterns for the relationship; as they settled into the marriage, they probably began to establish goals and objectives for their life together.

2. Parenthood—during the child rearing years, a couple's relationship changes in many ways. The time and energy required to raise children may detract from the time available for companionship. Spouses may realign household tasks, take on new job responsibilities as they advance in the work force, and face a more complex family life as they attempt to juggle all the responsibilities of home life and job duties.

Young children require a great investment of time and care. School-age children require parental time to talk about the things happening with them as they grow. Adolescence can put a strain on family life, as the children grow to become more independent, yet still rely on family financial support. Many families also have to deal with the problems of aging parents during this time.

3. Launching children as adults requires further adjustments. Parents must let go of their children and establish a relationship with them as adults. A home may seem empty for a time after the children leave. Some children return as adults to live with parents, requiring new family patterns. The loss of a parent may bring new responsibilities.

4. During the empty nest years, a couple will again have time for togetherness, having been through a lot together. They may become grandparents, a very rich experience for most couples.

5. As they enter the retirement years, the marriage will change yet again. When people no longer go off to work each day, they must find new ways to organize their time. Being together all day every day may strain the relationship if couples cannot find productive outlets for their time and energy. Matters of health will likely consume more time and attention. If one spouse dies, the other will have to establish new ways of living.

Each phase of marriage is different from the previous phase. Each will bring changes in the relationship. Each has new opportunities for growth and new challenges which must be faced. A giving love can weather the changes in both the spouse and the relationship. Couples who are able to communicate well will be sensitive to each other's needs during changes. The couples who make time for each other, who share their feelings and problems, will, by the grace of God, continue to grow closer as the years go by.

Togetherness for such couples does not only mean sitting together in front of the TV. It involves sharing time, interests, and themselves with each other; investing time and energy in their relationship; and keeping "romance" alive through thoughtful, loving words and actions. Such a relationship draws upon the power of God working through Word, Sacrament and Christian fellowship, to sustain the Christian love that will bind them together for a lifetime.

Wise couples see marriage as a career. They seek out ways to continue to grow as persons and as spouses. They may do this through classes, books, worship, Bible study, trips, and many other ways. They invest time and energy in keeping the marriage growing. The love they invest in each other brings lifetime dividends.

The Stages of Life

Like marriages, individuals also go through phases. Research in recent years has identified some of the changes and life cycles of individuals. Sociologists speak of seven stages which occur during adult life. Each stage deals with certain typical issues:

1. Breaking loose (late teens)—a time of leaving home, emphasis on peer relationships, trying new life-styles, defining adult moral standards, loneliness, involvement in social issues.

2. Nest building (twenties)—great dreams and feelings of power, search for identity, intimate relationships which may lead to marriage, making commitments and taking on responsibilities, working toward goals, beginning a career.

3. Looking around (thirties)—recognizing personal limitations, moving up the career ladder, settling down, having children (may have already begun in the twenties), gathering possessions, raising questions about "What do I want to do with my life?"

4. Mid-life (around forty)—diminishing physical energy, awareness of mortality, parenting teenagers, conflicting pressures, possible career change, emotional turmoil which sometimes leads to broken or strained relationships.

5. Investing in life (fifties)—life reorganized, focus on people instead of power and possessions, building close friendships, children leaving home, more financial freedom, making peace with lost dreams.

6. Deepening wisdom (later years)—mellowing wisdom, steady commitments to self and to others, simplifying life, adjustment to limitations, lower energy, retirement, self-knowledge and self-acceptance, facing death.

7. Twilight years—loneliness, dependence on those who once depended on you, failing strength of mind and/or body, preparing for death, sense of peace and perspective.

(Reprinted with permission from *Kicking Your Stress Habits* copyright 1981, Donald A. Tubesing. Published by Whole Person Associates Inc., P.O. Box 3151, Duluth, Minnesota 55803 used by permission.)

These stages will of course vary with individuals, but most of us will go through a similar sequence.

Follow-up Activity

1. To understand these stages more clearly, identify a person or persons you know in each of the seven states. What is one important issue each of those persons is dealing with?

2. At what stage are your parents? What is one important issue they are dealing with? (If you're not sure, ask!)

3. Ask your parents what they remember most from the time when they were your age.

4. Write a paragraph on one of these topics: (a) How your life is similar to (or different from) the life your parents were living when they were your age. (b) What your parents' life is like now and how you think your life will be similar to (or different from) theirs when you are the age they are now.

5. Imagine that you are near the end of your life and are writing your autobiography. How will you title your autobiography? How many chapters will your life have? Write a chapter title for each stage of your life that would reflect something about your life in that stage. (You need not divide your life into the same seven stages listed above; you may devise your own pattern.)

Our individual life stages will of course affect all our relationships. One of the reasons adolescence is such a time of upheaval in many families, for example, is because dramatic life changes may be occurring with several members of the family. At the same time as the adolescent is "breaking loose," pushing away from parents and family to achieve greater independence, his or her parents may be going through a critical time of their own. Many parents experience a mid-life crisis around the same time a child is old enough to leave home. Parents may thus be attempting to sort through issues in their own life at the same time the adolescent is sorting out his or her future.

A mother may have mixed feelings about the independence of her child—and may be experiencing some of the complex physiological and psychological aspects of menopause at the same time. In addition, at the same time as their children are looking to loosen parental control over their lives, the parents may also have to deal with the problems of their aging parents, who suddenly start to become dependent and require extra attention. Is it any wonder that with all these changes occurring simultaneously, a simple family problem sometimes quickly escalates to become a powder keg?

Knowing what to expect in each stage of our life makes it easier to adjust to the changes we and our spouses will face. Many couples will go through these stages at somewhat the same time. The stages of a woman's life will in most cases also be strongly affected by the growth of her children if she is a mother. The seven stages may alert us to times of potential stress in a marriage. For example, mid-life crisis is more than a slogan, for many people it is a difficult time which may strain the marriage.

An understanding, loving spouse can be a tremendous blessing during a time of personal turmoil and change.

Discussion Questions

1. How might it affect a marriage if one spouse is in a life stage different from the other?
2. Based on these life stages, what stresses might occur in a marriage of people who are separated by ten years or more in age?
3. How might a person's individual life stage affect his marriage and family? How do individual life stages affect the stages of family life, and vice versa?
4. How can their Christian faith help people to adapt to the changes they will face in their lives?
5. How can we in the church help one another through these stages? Identify one special ministry to help people at each stage.
6. Who directs and governs our lives? **(Acts 17:26, 28)**. What does God tell us about Himself? **(Mal. 3:6)**.
7. For what purpose does the Christian live? **(Rom. 15:5–7)**. How can knowing his or her purpose in life help a Christian through times of stress and change?
8. What glory will the Christian one day experience? **(Matt. 13:40–43)**.

What Makes a Marriage Last?

How can a marriage survive so many changes over the years?

1. Knowing that God has forgiven us for Jesus' sake

2. Knowing that God's Spirit is alive and well and living in us
3. Knowing that God's Spirit will work within us to make us change and grow to become more and more the people God wants us to be
4. Believing that love can be present even when hate is being felt and expressed
5. Being willing to share ourselves openly with our spouse
6. Forgiving our spouse as often as needed—and then putting the past behind us
7. Remaining firm, with God's help, in our **commitment** to our spouse

The editor of this textbook put it this way: "My wife and I follow a very simple guideline for behavior in marriage: By the power of God working in us, I attempt to do what pleases her, and she attempts to do what pleases me. We like it!"

Chapter Summary

God's Word provides the guideline of Jesus' selfless love for how husband and wife can relate to each other in marriage.Strengthening our communication skills improves our relationships.

Conflicts can, with God's help, be resolved in ways that strengthen rather than weaken relationships. God will go with us through all the changes and stages of life which we will experience.

The God who created us, who conceived the idea of marriage as a blessing for our lives, who gave us the potential and the power to love, also gave us the pattern for our marriage partnerships in the image of Christ. Christ, the bridegroom, was willing to sacrifice even His life for the sake of his bride, the church (us!). Marriage partners who live within the framework of His forgiving love receive the power they need to grow in their relationships with each other and with their Lord.

Therefore, as God's chosen people, holy and dearly loved, clothe yourselves with compassion, kindness, humility, gentleness and patience. Bear with each other and forgive whatever grievances you may have against one another. Forgive as the Lord forgave you. And over all these virtues put on love, which binds them all together in perfect unity.

Col. 3:12–14

Chapter 8

Managing Your Resources

Chapter Preview

Chapter 8 will help you answer the following questions:

- How can Christians know where to invest their resources of time, talents and treasure?
- How much does it cost for a family to live comfortably in your community?
- Is stewardship something I need to know about?

1. Planning for the Future

Bob and Jan are in love and planning to get married in a few months, as soon as Bob finishes college. Though Jan will still have another year of college left, Jan's mother has offered that they could live with her until Jan graduates. Bob has about $6,000 in college loan debts, but is sure he will be able to find a good job. Though they may have to borrow money to do it, they are planning a big wedding and a trip to New York City for their honeymoon. They are very excited as they tell you all their plans.

As their friend, how would you respond?

How we manage our resources of time, talents, and money tells a lot about the kinds of persons we are. Learning to manage resources cooperatively is another important task for the newly married. Two people who have been making their own decisions about how to spend their time, how to use their talents, and what to do with their money must now develop a way to make these decisions together if they wish to have unity and harmony in their marriage. Let's begin with the topic of money management first. Money problems contribute to many failed marriages; they are one of the top three common marital problems. Managing our money means more than just paying bills. Money also means power to many people; it reflects values; it determines whether we can live comfortably or will feel the constant strain of not enough money to keep up with expenses. This chapter will help us develop a Biblical view of finances and learn practical methods for managing finances.

About Money

To examine some of your attitudes toward money study the following list. With which statements do you agree?

1. A husband should earn a higher salary than his wife.
2. A couple should not have any debts when they marry.
3. A husband should be in charge of family finances (e.g., checkbook, insurance, taxes, etc.).
4. Sacrifices may be necessary for a couple to save money.
5. Conflicts over money affect the total relationship between two people.
6. Couples should not make any financial plans until after they marry.
7. A significant amount of money each week should go to the Lord's work.
8. If a couple truly loves each other, they will agree on how to spend their money.
9. Parents or friends should help out a couple with financial problems.
10. A husband and wife should have separate bank accounts.
11. We develop our attitudes and ways of handling money from our families.
12. Money is a way to measure our value as a person.
13. Children should be paid for all the jobs they do around the house.
14. A wife who is a homemaker should receive a spending allowance from her husband.
15. If we make a regular financial contribution to our church, it's all right to spend the rest of our money however we please.
16. Salary is the most important factor to consider when choosing a career.

Every married couple must resolve how money will be handled in their family. If money values are not shared, endless conflicts result. Decisions which a couple make about money affect every aspect of their lives: children, housing, job choices, life-style.

Every couple must resolve the following basic questions:

- Who will be in charge of finances in our family?
- How is money to be handled—ours? yours? mine?
- What kind of lifestyle will we have?
- Can we make it financially?
- How does my relationship with God affect the way I handle my finances?

Discussion Questions

Think of yourself as newly married.

1. List in order the five things for which you feel it is most important to spend your money.
2. How do you feel about going into debt? Short term (credit cards, charge accounts, etc.)? Long term (mortgages, auto loans, etc.)?
3. What percentage of your income do you believe is appropriate to return to the Lord through church and charity?
4. What percentage do you feel it is appropriate to save?
5. Is it important in a marriage for each partner to have some money to spend as he or she likes, no questions asked? What amount per week would be appropriate for a husband? For a wife?
6. Who do you think will be responsible for financial planning and bill paying in your marriage, if you marry? Why?
7. How important do you think it is for a husband and wife to share similar values about money? Explain your answer.
8. How will you resolve conflicts about finances—for example, if you have spent all your money before payday arrives?

Money and Values

The way we manage our money reflects the values we place on things. As with many of our values, our family of origin was our training ground for money management. Listed below are 12 choices for spending your money. Rank them from 1 (most important) to 12 (least important).

_____ A savings account
_____ A large, up-to-date wardrobe
_____ Owning your own home
_____ Having new furniture and up-to-date appliances
_____ Giving generous gifts to family and friends
_____ A nice car
_____ Going to an exotic place for a vacation each year
_____ Eating out regularly in nice restaurants
_____ Setting aside a regular amount for church
_____ Keeping up a life-style similar to your friends and neighbors
_____ Helping out friends or family in need
_____ Keeping up in your field through courses and books

Discussion Questions

1. If you ranked one of the points in the list above a 1 or a 2, and the person you intended to marry ranked it 11 or 12, what would you do?

2. What difference, if any, would it make if you discovered this difference in values just before you announced your engagement? A year before the wedding? A month before the wedding?

3. How can you determine what values about money another person has?

4. Consider the following. At what point in a relationship should a couple discuss their money values?

☐ when they become engaged
☐ shortly before the wedding
☐ when the relationship begins to get serious
☐ not at all—just let it take care of itself
☐ after they are married

5. What aspect(s) of **your** personal money management would you need to change if you marry?

"Well done, good and faithful servant! You have been faithful with a few things; I will put you in charge of many things. Come and share your master's happiness!"

Matt. 25:23

2. Where Does the Money Go?

How much do you know about the facts of money management? financial facts?

On a sheet of paper identfy each of the following statements as either true or false.

1. A couple can safely spend about 50 percent of their monthly take-home pay on housing expenses.
2. The word *deductible* on an insurance policy means the amount you must pay for coverage.
3. When interviewing for a job, it is not important to ask about medical coverage; that can come later.
4. It is important for both husband and wife to have some discretionary money, an amount they can use for incidentals or other items as they wish.
5. Tithing (giving 10 percent of your income to the Lord's work) is a way to measure a Christian's commitment to God.
6. An emergency fund is not necessary if you're under 40.
7. Once you establish a budget, you should never change it.

8. Credit cards are a good way to spread out your payments.
9. A young married couple does not need a will.
10. God does not care how much a Christian gives to spread His kingdom as long as he or she gives something.
11. Having children need not affect a family budget very much.
12. It is not important to save for retirement; Social Security will take care of that.
13. God blesses us with money so that we can help others.

Discussion Questions

(You may consult with your parents or other knowledgeable sources to get the information you need to be prepared to discuss these questions.)

1. What items are included in the term *utilities?*
2. How many types of taxes will you be required to pay if you live in this state? What percentage of your income will be required to pay for taxes?
3. How much does it cost *per mile* to own and operate the average car?
4. What is the purpose of life insurance? Do you need it?
5. What is the current interest rate for home mortgages? What is the current interest rate for credit card purchases?
6. What is profit sharing? Should it influence your job choice?

Where Does My Money Go?

To understand how you presently manage your money, list the amount of your average income per week (from allowances, jobs, etc.). Then list all the

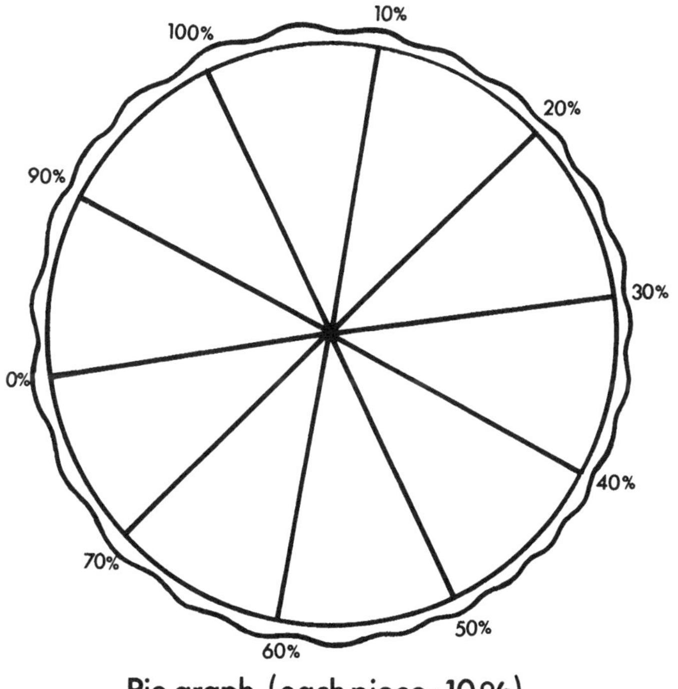

Pie graph (each piece = 10%)

things on which you usually use your money (food, clothing, entertainment, car expenses, savings, gifts, church offerings, etc.). Underline the five items on which you spend the most money. What percentage of your income do you use for each? "Slice" the pie graph to reflect the percentage of your income which is used for each of the five items you underlined.

Take another look at your pie graph. Imagine that you do not know the person who made the graph. How would you describe the person who made this graph on the basis of what you see there? Write a paragraph describing the kind of person you see when you look at this pie graph. Does the graph reflect the "real" you?

Setting up a Budget

For this activity, you and a classmate will work as partners. Thinking of yourself as a married couple, you will work out a family budget together, based on realistic costs for living in your community. Assume that you are budgeting for *a married couple with two children.* (You may set the ages.) You may use any resources you find helpful (parents, friends who are married, classified ads, phone calls to the company who would provide the goods or service, etc.).

Set up your budget *on a monthly basis* (or, if the item is not a regular monthly need, figure the

annual amount and divide by 12), using the following headings. Keep your figures realistic and be complete.

Occupation and income of husband ____
Occupation and income of wife ____
Ages of children____

	$ per month
FIXED EXPENSES	
My gift to the Lord (church and charities)	______
Housing (rent or mortage payments and maintenance)	______
Utilities	
Gas	______
Electricity	______
Phone	______
Water, garbage	______
Income Tax Deductions	
Federal	______
State	______
City	______
Social security deductions	______
Regular payments	
Loans or installments	______
Other	______
Insurance premiums	
Homeowners insurance	______
Medical insurance	______
Car insurance	______
Other insurance	______
Regular savings, profit sharing plans, etc.	______
Total $ per month	______

FLEXIBLE EXPENSES

Clothing	______
Food and household supplies	______
Medical and dental care	______
Education (continuing education,Parochial school tuition, books, and supplies)	______
Gifts and hobbies	______
Recreation (entertainment, vacation, restaurants, etc.)	______
Car upkeep (or public transportation)	______
Furniture and appliances	______
Laundry and cleaning	______
Books, newspapers, magazines	______
Personal expenses	______
Pets	______
Other expenses	______
Total	______
Total $ per month	______

Evaluate the budget you have drafted.

1. What is your estimated total monthly income? (Add incomes if both partners are working.)

2. Add fixed and flexible expenses together; what is your total monthly living cost?

3. Subtract item 2 from item 1. Is your budget realistic? Why or why not? What adjustments might need to be made? Working with your partner, revise where necessary and prepare a clean copy of your budget (to be handed in after step item 4.)

4. When you and your partner have completed your budget, ask a parent or other adult you know well to evaluate your budget and compare it with his or her own experience of living costs in the area.

Ask your evaluator to mark with a + every budget figure he or she sees as realistic; ask him or her to mark with a - every budget figure which is unrealistic. Substitute a more realistic number by writing a new figure to the *left* of your original number. (Please ask your resource person to sign his or her name and the date on the copy of your budget.)

Make any additional revisions that will be necessary to balance your budget in the light of the suggestions you received. (You may write the corrected figures to the *right* of your original numbers.) How many figures required change?

5. When all the steps above have been completed, write a brief summary of your budgeting experience and include it with your budget.

6. When all budgets have been submitted, compile a class budget showing the range of income and expenses anticipated in each category.

Finances need to be worked out together if a couple wishes to avoid endless conflict. A budget is a responsible way to stay out of financial trouble and avoid many arguments. Both husband and wife must agree on how money is to be spent. If one partner makes all the decisions, the other is likely to be resentful, and the couple may begin to work against each other, rather than pull together to reach their goals. Working together to build for the future strengthens the unity within a marriage.

Discussion Questions

1. What should a married couple do if one of them is a careful budgeter, the other an impulse spender?

2. What should a couple do if they argue regularly about money?

3. What should a couple do if one of them enjoys spending a lot on generous gifts to family members and friends, while the other person thinks it is more important to save?

Agreement on any of the issues within a marriage does not automatically fall into place when two people get married. Whether the issue is money management, husband-wife roles, separating from family of origin, or raising children, all the tasks of the newly married require practice. With God's help, we can actively work at being loving and understanding; thus we can learn to resolve differences in a spirit of mutual cooperation.

But seek first His kingdom and His righteousness, and all these things will be given to you as well.

Matt. 6:33

3. What is God's Money Plan?

How does our personal view of finances compare with God's directives for our lives? After reading each of the following passages, state in a sentence or two how God is asking you to manage your money.

Every Christian faces temptations when it comes to managing money. List three such temptations that you face or that face people you know.

What temptations are listed in each of the Bible passages below?

- **Luke 12:15:**
- **Ps. 73:3:**
- **Prov. 28:20,22:**
- **Matt. 6:1–4:**

Then rate yourself according to how well you are applying this principle in your daily life:

☐ Above Average
☐ Average
☐ Needs Improvement

(Do this privately—it's between you and God.)

1 Tim. 6:6–10
Luke 12:15–21
Matt. 6:19–34
Prov. 3:9–10
2 Cor. 8:1–5

Based on your study above, write a statement expressing your own philosophy of Christian money management. Write a prayer which reflects your philosophy.

Christians are not immune to temptations about money, for we too are influenced by the materialistic society around us. We, too, hear the me-first messages which say: "You owe it to yourself." "Look out for number one." "You only go around once in life, so grab all you can." Though it was meant to be a humorous commentary on our society, the phrase "He who dies with the most toys wins" often seems to reflect the goals of many people, Christians and non-Christians.

Discussion Questions

1. By what standards does the world measure greatness?

2. By what standards does a Christian measure greatness? (See **Matt. 23:11** if you are not sure.)

3. What made the churches in Macedonia so special according to Paul's letter to the **Corinthians** in **2 Cor. 8:1–15?** How does this apply to us?

When Christians think about money management, only one of the slogans above fits. When we Christians put God first in our lives, then we can "look out for number one," realizing that God is number One, not ourselves!

The church often uses the term *stewardship* to describe a Christian's response to the blessings God has given. But many Christians think of stewardship only in terms of offering envelopes and budget deficits. A true understanding of stewardship begins in a different place.

Principles of Christian Stewardship

True Christian stewardship incorporates the following principles:

1. By the grace of God, we have been given a new life. We did nothing to earn it. God's unconditional love made us His own in Jesus. We have literally been made new people, with a new hope and a revolutionary new way to manage our lives. Instead of living for ourselves, as we did before we were redeemed, we now live a life which is consecrated to Him **(2 Cor. 5:14–15).** Everything we have is a gift of God, who has promised to provide us with everything we need.

2. The Biblical word *oikonomia* (stewardship) means "management of a household." It means to be a responsible manager of *someone else's business* so that the business will benefit.

Stewardship is not giving; it is managing. God's "business" is bringing salvation to all peoples **(Matt. 28:18–20).** When we are His stewards, we manage our resources in such a way that God's business will be carried out. As God's instruments, spreading the Word is to be our highest priority in life, higher even than the necessities of earthly life, such as food, clothing, or shelter **(Matt. 6:31–33).** The object of our life—of all stewardship activity—is to use the resources God has entrusted to us in such a way that people will come to know and trust in the only true God.

3. God has given each of us different resources of time (the number of years we will be given to serve Him), personality, talents, spiritual gifts, opportunities and abilities, as well as material gifts such as money and possessions. All of these resources are *gifts*. We have done nothing to deserve even the gift of life.

All our money and possessions have come to us through the talents, abilities, and opportunities which were *God's* gifts for our lives. Some of our natural abilities and talents came to us at birth, and some were developed through the opportunities given to us by God.

Whether we have been given many gifts or few is not ours to control. Had we been born brain-damaged and severely retarded, for example, we would never be able to earn a living, but our life would still have value as God's gift. What we *can* control with God's power living in us, is how we *use* our gifts to His glory and for the common good.

4. God holds us accountable for how we use His gifts. In the parables on stewardship in the Bible, the master always returns and holds an accounting with the steward. Though we may hold (possess) certain things, God really owns everything we have, even our very lives! Since He already owns all, we can never really give anything to God. We can only determine how we will use it. We are only managers. Money is only a *means of exchange,* of providing for our needs with the abilities God has given us.

It is not money but the *love of money* that is the root of all evil. Money helps us meet our needs and share with others—it is merely a *tool* we use to manage our gifts from God. God gives us ability to work and opportunities to earn. With these we earn what we need by providing the goods and services that are helpful to others. We are accountable to God for how we manage every aspect of our lives. He forgives us when we give in to temptations to live for ourselves; He gives us His power so that we can become better stewards as we grow in service to Him and others.

5. It is not easy to practice Christian stewardship. Our selfish human natures and the temptations of our environment often cause us to fail. The world proclaims that living for and possessing material goods is *the* main purpose for life. Such an attitude, as we have seen, contradicts the will of God. But God has given us His forgiveness so that we may *grow* in our abilities to manage our lives so they will glorify Him **(Rom. 6:4–7).**

His power enables us to be good stewards of the gifts He has given us. When we have given our lives back to the Lord, our stewardship of His resources will follow His directives. Our giving will be *sacrificial* (not what is left over), *proportional* (we will want to return to Him a percentage of what He has given us), and a *clear* reflection of our priorities in life. Each of us is a "trust fund" for the resources we have been given. We need to ask ourselves two questions:

1. What have I been given?
2. How does God want me to use those resources? Thinking about these five principles of Christian stewardship, how would you answer someone who says the following?

- I need all my income to support my life-style.
- I give more to the church than a lot of people with higher incomes than mine.
- I've got to put something away for a rainy day. I work hard for what I have—I deserve the chance to enjoy it.
- God must love me a lot—He's given me a lot more blessings than other people.

Money is not the measure of our success in life.

The true measure, as Jesus makes clear, is whether we believe in Him; believing in Christ, we use our lives to the glory of God and welfare of others. Someone has said that "Contentment is not in having what you want, but in wanting what you have." Is this slogan in harmony with God's directives for our lives?

Jesus, the perfect steward, gave all that He had, including His very life. The question He addressed to the people of His day confronts each one of us as well: **"What good will it be for a man if he gains the whole world, yet forfeits his soul (Matt. 16:26)?** History is full of examples of people who tried to gain the whole world but lost their souls in the process.

A Modern Parable

Consider the following parable:

In 1923 eight of the world's wealthiest men met at the Edgewater Beach Hotel in Chicago. At the time they controlled more money than was contained in the United States Treasury. Consider the story of their lives:

Charles Schwab—president of the largest independent steel company—died broke.

Arthur Cutten—greatest wheat speculator—died abroad, bankrupt.

Richard Whitney—president of the New York Stock Exchange—died just after his release from prison.

Albert Fall—member of President Warren Harding's Cabinet—was pardoned from prison to die at home.

Jesse Livermore—greatest "bear" on Wall Street—committed suicide.

Leon Fraser—president of the Bank of International Settlements—committed suicide.

Ivan Krueger—head of the world's greatest monopoly—committed suicide.

(Adapted from *Stewardship,* November 1987. Parish Publications, Inc., 32401 Industrial Drive, Madison Heights. MI 48071.)

"Perhaps the real significance of giving is what it does to the steward. What matters to God is not the gift but the giver. Stewardship is God's invitation to a way of life. It helps us to overcome our selfishness and love of things. What we do with what we have been given is a sign to God and to the world of the depth and meaning of our commitment."

(From *Stewardship,* November 1987. Parish Publications, Inc., 32401 Industrial Drive, Madison Heights. MI 48071.)

Every married couple has dreams of how they would like their life to be. When our dreams include realistic expectations, are flexible, and are based on Biblical principles, they can help us set goals for our life. For most people, achieving a goal requires sacrifice. Owning your own home, for example, is a more difficult goal to attain today than it was a generation ago.

To own a home, a couple may have to sacrifice cars, expensive vacations, and restaurant meals. Because we live in an "I want it now" society, many people have difficulty disciplining themselves to work for future goals. They are so accustomed to hearing advertisers and television say, "You can have anything you want when you want it; you deserve to have all the very best; throw out what you have and buy what's new." Problems on TV are solved easily in a half hour or an hour. If we base our dreams on such an unrealistic view of life, we will find it very difficult to set worthwhile priorities for our lives.

My Future

Dream for a moment about your future life. On another piece of paper, write three dream goals for your future?

Now think about each goal and evaluate it on the basis of the following questions.

Questions for Reflection

1. Is this goal in harmony with what the Bible teaches?
2. Is this goal realistic?
3. What sacrifices might I need to make to reach this goal?
4. Is this goal worth the sacrifices required?
5. Revise any goals which, after evaluation, do not meet God's standards or are not worth the sacrifices.

Discussion Questions

1. What happens when we make bad decisions about our goals and begin serving only ourselves?

2. How does God empower us to live for eternity? Jesus often talked about the need to invest in those things that last. So many things on which we spend our money either break, go out of fashion, or are not worth what we spent to acquire them. They can be stolen from us by thieves or they can disappear during troublesome economic conditions. Will you make a commitment to live for the present? Or, living by the power of the Spirit, will you invest for eternity?

Do not store up for yourselves treasures on earth, where moth and rust destroy, and where thieves break in and steal. But store up for yourselves treasures in heaven, where moth and rust do not destroy, and where thieves do not break in and steal. For where your treasure is, there your heart will be also.

Matt. 6:19–21

4. Time and Talents

Where did the day go? Can the vacation be over already? I didn't realize it was so late!

How many such statements or questions about time have you heard recently?

In addition to the financial resources God has entrusted to each of us, He has also given us resources of time and talents. Thoreau once observed, "Men spend so much time thinking about how to spend their money, and so little thinking about how to spend their time." Most of us have already begun to realize the precious quality of time. When we juggle classes, schoolwork, extra-curricular activities, part-time jobs, and social life, we begin to discover how hard it can be to find time for everything we'd like to do. Time pressures are likely to be an issue in your marriage as well.

But time, too, is a resource we have been given, a resource we need to manage effectively if we want to avoid endless frustration. Overcrowded schedules are one of the biggest problems in family life today. The "do" list gets so long that many people have little or no time left for the really important things—such as building relationships with God, family, and friends.

Some couples invest so much time pursuing their careers that they meet their financial goals at the expense of becoming strangers to each other. What little time they spend with each other becomes devoted to the "business" talk of budgets and schedules. Maintaining relationships also requires an investment of time.

Minutes and hours which are wasted can never be reclaimed. By the time we reach the age of 70, we will have spent an average of 23 years sleeping, 11 years working, 8 years playing, 6 years eating, 5½ years grooming, 3 years being educated, 3 years reading, 3 years talking, and 7½ years on odds and ends. If we cut out 20 minutes a day of wasted time, we will have gained a whole year by the time we're 70.

(Reprint with permission from *Kicking Your Stress Habits*, copyright 1981, Donald A. Tubesing. Published by Whole Person Associates Inc., PO Box 3151, Duluth, MN 55803, (218) 728-6807.)

To manage time wisely, we must set priorities. We must decide what is really important. When we say "I have no time," we are really saying that we aren't managing our time well. Each of us has been given the same amount of time every day. But we need to make some decisions about how we manage it. For example, if we value keeping fit, we must set aside time for exercise. And if we value a relationship, we must arrange our schedule so that we have time to spend with the other person.

Time, Time, Time

To examine how you use your time, make a chart of your time usage in the following way (the chart is for your personal reflection—it need not be handed in):

1. List the five things which are most important in your life right now in a column down the left side of a sheet of paper, beginning with the most important and continuing to the least important. (Think about school, jobs, friendships, family, sports, worship, exercise, etc.)

2. After each item, write down how much time each day (on the average) is spent on that activity.

3. Think again about the importance of each item to your future goals. Look again at the time you spend on each. Then evaluate whether the time spent is in proper proportion to its importance. If you think you are spending the right amount of time on the activity, write "right amount"; if you are spending too much time, write "too much"; if you are spending too little, write "too little."

4. For any item on which you are spending too much or too little time, write out how you can achieve better time use for that item.

5. Write a paragraph summarizing your stewardship of time, based on what you have learned by completing the chart above. Your teacher may ask you to hand in your summary paragraphs.

6. What aspect(s) of *your* personal time management would you need to change if you marry?

Each of us needs to invest time in our relationships with God and with others; each of us also needs some time for ourselves. Reflect on the following questions:

- *Am I investing enough time in my relationship with God?* (If not, what changes do I need to make?)
- *Am I investing enough time in my relationships with loved ones?* (If not, what changes do I need to make?)
- *Am I allowing some time to nurture myself?* (If not, what changes do I need to make?)
- *Am I investing my time in things that matter, or am I wasting it on unimportant, trivial goals and pleasures?*

St. Paul writes, **"Be very careful, then, how you live—not as unwise but as wise, making the most of every opportunity" (Eph. 5: 15–16).** How can you apply these words to your life?

Talents and Abilities

When we discussed self-esteem in chapter 1, we talked about the uniqueness of every individual. Each of us was created with our own abilities, talents, and personality. God has given us different "trust funds" of characteristics, interests, and abilities to "invest" in our lives. When persons marry, they must "merge" their trust funds and work out complementary ways of using their abilities to serve each other, their children, and the other people whom God has placed in their lives.

One way to think about how you use your trust fund is to imagine yourself at the end of your life. Then ask yourself the question, *When I die, what must I have done to be satisfied with my life?*

Jot down at least five things that come to your mind when you answer that question. If the things you wrote down reflect the goals you listed previously, chances are you've established a satisfying direction for your life. On the basis of this question, are there any goals you would wish to add? Are there any you would wish to change? Read **Matt. 16:24–26.** State the meaning of this passage in a sentence or two.

What we want to accomplish in life should always reflect what God wants for our lives. True success in life comes when the Spirit gives us the power to turn our lives over to God for His direction. He has promised to hear and answer the prayers we offer asking for His direction in our lives!

Let's take a closer look at the "trust fund" of abilities and interests we have been given to invest in our lives. Our abilities and interests will usually fall into three categories:

People. Do you like working with people? talking and listening? helping? organizing? negotiating?

Information. Do you like facts? numbers? collecting information? applying facts? solving problems? finding answers?

Things. Do you like making things? repairing things? figuring out how things work?

1. Looking at these three categories, ask yourself the question, "What do I do *well?*" List at least three things you do well. The answer will give you insight into your *abilities.*

Describe one way in which you could use each ability to serve God and others.

2. Follow up with a second question. "What things do I really *like* to do?" List at least three things you really like to do. The answer will give you insight into your *interests.*

Describe one way in which you could use each interest to serve God and others.

3. What aspect(s) of *your* personal management of talents and abilities would you need to change if you marry?

4. Write a real-life resolution about how you plan to manage your resources of money, time, and talents both now and in the future:

With the help of God, I resolve . . .

Write a prayer asking God to help you keep your resolution.

Winston Churchill once said, "We make a living by what we get, but we make a life by what we give." Your abilities, interests, and aptitudes are all part of the person God has made you to be. They are part of the trust fund from which you give to others.

Chapter Summary

Each of us is a trust fund for the time, talents and treasure which God has given to us.

How we manage our trust fund clearly reflects our values and priorities.

By the power of the Spirit, we can grow to manage our trust funds to the glory of God and the benefit of the people He has placed in our lives.

Most people are happiest when their careers are compatible with their interests and abilities—and when they are able to share themselves in relationships with people they love. Christian stewardship includes managing our talents and aptitudes, our time and our resources wisely. When we use them according to God's will, He will be glorified, our neighbor will be served, and we will experience the joy that comes from knowing that God is working through us in His world.

So whether you eat or drink or whatever you do, do it all for the glory of God.

1 Cor. 10:31

Chapter 9

Parenting

Chapter Preview

Chapter 9 will help you answer the following questions:

- What makes people good parents?
- How does a couple prepare to become parents?
- What does God say about the role of Christian parents?
- What does God say about birth control and contraception?

1. From Child to Parent

Dear Mom and Dad,

I'll bet you never thought you'd get a letter like this. It's hard for me to say this, but I need your help. I know that I act as if I'm all grown up and ready to make my own decisions. But inside I'm scared.

You've always been there for me when I needed you in the past. I know you've prayed for me and worried over me, too. Don't give up on me, even when I seem to be pushing you away. I really do need your love. And though I hate to admit it, I need your guidance, too.

I face so many new decisions. And there are so many temptations around me. So many kids I know think it's all right to live only for yourself. When they talk about their futures, all they talk about is how much money they want to make, or the flashy cars they plan to buy. When they talk about their relationships, it seems all they care about is getting what they want for themselves. Many of them don't want to admit that God is real and has a plan for their lives.

How should I handle all these situations? Though I may act as if I don't need you, don't leave me all alone. Listen to me when I'm trying to sort things out. Share your faith with me. Remind me that with God's help I can do what is right, not just what is easy. I can't finish raising myself. It's a mixed-up world out there. Please give me the help I need to deal with it.

Your teenager

Do any of the ideas in this letter reflect your feelings? If so, write them down on another piece of paper. Is there anything you would like to add to a letter such as this? If so, write your own P.S.

Our relationship with our parents has shaped us in many ways. The parent-child relationship lays a foundation for our life that always remains as a part of us. Most of us are probably now in the process of becoming independent from our parents. We may still be dependent on them financially and in other ways, but we are already beginning to think about the lives we will make for ourselves as adults.

Brainstorm with your class. When you think of the word *parent,* what images come to mind? After you have listed all of these, circle those which describe the kind of parent *you* would like to become someday.

A License for Parenting?

Imagine for a moment that you live in a culture which requires licenses in order for people to become parents. People are permitted to become parents only if they meet the qualifications which will grant them a license.

1. List the qualities and abilities you think ought to be required for a person to get a license to become a parent.
2. Would *you* qualify for a license?
3. Would a license guarantee anything?
4. What are some characteristics of a good parent? of a poor parent?
5. Other than enough food and shelter, what do you want your children to have?
6. How many of the things you want for your children are things you didn't have?
7. Would you like your kids to be like you, or different from you?
8. Would you like to be the kind of parent your parents are? Or have you decided "I'm not going to make the same mistakes my parents made"?

As we have investigated the various tasks which newly married couples face, we have looked at many aspects of the relationship between husband

and wife. In this final chapter, we will examine what is involved when the two become three—or four, or more. How does a couple prepare to become parents? What makes people good parents? What does God say about the role of Christian parents? This chapter will look at some of these questions.

Listed below are some responsibilities of parenting. Rate each according to whether you think it is *very important, somewhat important,* or *not very important*. Which responsibility do you believe to be the most important of all?

☐ Being a good role model
☐ Providing food, clothing, shelter, health care
☐ Bringing your child to be baptized
☐ Building the child's self-esteem
☐ Providing love and security
☐ Teaching a child that Jesus loves him or her
☐ Helping a child become self-disciplined
☐ Providing a comfortable home
☐ Helping a child become independent
☐ Looking upon parenting as a relationship rather than a job

Becoming a parent is one of the most awesome responsibilities in the world. Many people underestimate the challenges—and the joys—of being a parent. Suddenly you are responsible for the welfare of another human being. That responsibility will last for 18 or more years and require continual commitment until that child is grown. (Sometimes, for parents of children who are born with handicaps, that responsiblity continues for the entire lifetime of the parent.) Parenthood is not something which can be taken lightly.

Each of us has many feelings, images, and expectations about what it will be like to be a parent; these are heavily influenced by our family of origin. Some of us may wish to parent as our parents did. Others of us may be determined to be very different from our own parents. Whatever our personal ideas of the kind of parents we would like to be, it is helpful to examine our own ideas and feelings about becoming a parent. The time to do this is *before* we have children!

A Five-Pound Baby

What is it like to have the responsibility for a child? To think through this question, each pair of student partners will bring to class a five-pound bag of sugar or flour. Working with your student partner, you will "adopt" this "five-pound baby" for a period of time assigned by your teacher. You will assume responsibility for your five-pound baby in the following ways:

1. The five-pound baby must be with either you or your student partner at all times, day and night, for the assigned time. Whenever this is not possible, you must make arrangements with family members or friends to "baby-sit," at which time the five-pound baby must be in their care. (No extended "day care" allowed!) The baby may not be left unattended at any time; you will be responsible to see that no injury or damage occurs to your "baby."

2. You and your partner should divide the responsibility fairly.

3. Give your five-pound baby a name, so you will think of it as a person rather than a thing.

4. Keep a log of your child care timetable.

5. Write a paragraph about your experiences.

Has not the Lord made them one? In flesh and spirit they are His. And why one? Because He was seeking godly offspring. So guard yourself in your spirit, and do not break faith with the wife of your youth.

Mal. 2:15

2. Becoming a Parent

Many of us may not yet know whether we will wish to have children after we marry. Nevertheless, children are a wonderful gift of God, and becoming a parent is one of the most educational experiences anyone can have. In the words of a folk hymn, "I've seen how little children help their parents grow." Parenthood teaches selflessness, commitment, forgiveness, and working together in ways few other experiences can. Parenthood also changes a marriage in many significant ways.

In order for parenthood to be the blessing God intends, we must be willing to undertake that responsibility for the right reasons. Husband and wife must be willing to work as a team to agree upon family rules and responsibilities; a united front and mutual respect between parents is a necessity for the child to feel secure.

A family is more than a place to raise children. It is a place where God shapes and molds the parents themselves. The family flourishes only when the selfish interests of parents are controlled by their commitment to the members of their family.

Imagine yourself trying to make a decision about whether or not you want to have children in your marriage. Then read each of the following statements. After numbering another piece of paper from 1 to 20, write *yes* after the number of every statement which reflects reasons you would want to have children. Write *no* after the number of any statement which does not reflect reasons you would want to have children.

1. I want a child who will look like me.
2. I want a child who will be successful.
3. I want someone to carry on the family name.
4. I want someone who will think I'm the greatest.

5. I want someone to whom I can leave my money and property when I die.
6. I want someone who will care for me when I am old.
7. I want a child to help me stay young at heart.
8. I will feel more fulfilled if I have a child.
9. A child would give me someone to love (especially if I don't have anyone else).
10. I want a child to help me make up for the unhappy family in which I was raised.
11. A child would help me feel more like a real man or woman.
12. A child could help me keep a troubled marriage together.
13. A child could help make up for job frustrations or lack of friends.
14. Having a child would help me be like everybody else.
15. My parents expect me to have a child.
16. People might think something is wrong with me if I don't have a child.
17. I want a child so I can help someone grow and develop.
18. I want the satisfaction of giving myself to someone else.
19. I want to share my values and faith with someone.
20. I want to give my love to a child.

People have children for many reasons. Some of these are valid; some are not. On the list above, go back and check those reasons which you feel are the *best* reasons to have children.

Most parents have a variety of reasons for having children, but often do not examine what the reasons were which led them to have children. Typical reasons for which people might want to have children usually reflect several types of motives:

1. Self-centered motives (reasons focused on what the child can do for us or how a child will increase our self-worth). Reasons 1 through 8 above are based primarily on self-centered motives. Are these good reasons to have children?

(Most parents, of course, will have some self-centered motives mixed in with all their other feelings about having children. Because we can never completely escape our sinful nature, none of us is capable of totally unselfish motives when it comes to having children or to any other aspect of our lives.)

2. Compensation motives (having a child to make up for what is missing in our own lives.) Reasons 9 through 12 above are these kinds of motives. Are these good reasons to have children?

It is sad but true that many teenage pregnancies are motivated by a desperate need for love on the part of the mother (or sometimes the father). What many such young people fail to realize, however, is that a baby requires a great deal of sacrificing love *from* them. A parent must be prepared to *give* more love than he or she receives in return. To have a child to make up for what is missing in our lives cheats the child and hardly ever works. Having a child cannot solve our personal problems or the problems within a marriage. Unless we are ready for parenthood, it may make those problems worse.

3. Pressure to conform (having a child to be like everyone else). Reasons 13 through 16 above derive from a wish to do what everyone else is doing (hardly a good reason to have a baby!).

4. Wanting to give love (wanting a child in order to share yourself and your love with that child). Reasons 17 through 20 above are healthy reasons for having a child, because they come from a desire to *give,* rather than a desire to get. Wanting to give love is always a good reason for a relationship!

(Adapted from *Newly Married and Before* by Wayne Rickerson. Used with permission. © 1985 David C. Cook Publishing Co.,)

Discussion Questions

1. What other reasons might there be for people to have children?

2. Are the motives listed in numbers 1 through 16 entirely bad?

3. Do you think any parent can escape some of the motives listed in numbers 1 through 16?

4. What was Jesus' relationship with children? See **Mark 10:13–16.** How does His relationship with them serve as an example for us?

The Bible talks about several reasons for having children:

a. To show God's glory. When God created the world and gave Adam and Eve the charge to manage it, He did so to reflect His glory. God's people are the means He uses to share His love from generation to generation. What does **Is. 43:6–7** say about God's creation?

b. To replenish the earth. Husbands and wives are the means God uses to nurture each new generation of human history. God directed Adam and Eve to do this already at the time of creation. Procreation of children is one of the three purposes of marriage. What does **Gen. 1:27–28** tell us about children?

c. To enjoy children. Children are a special gift of God to a marriage. As we nurture our children, God works through us in their lives. He also works in our lives as parents to help us grow into the kinds of persons He wants us to become. What does **Ps. 128:1–4** have to say about children and families?

Choosing Parenthood

How can a couple determine whether they are ready to have children? Questions such as the following are often asked by parent counseling services as they work with couples:

1. Do you like children? (Not just cuddly babies, but tantrum-throwing two-year-olds? gangly nine-year-olds? confused teenagers?)

2. When you think of having children, do you see them as an experience that will enrich your life? (Or do you see them as more of a burden?)

3. Are you able to give love without expecting an equal amount of love in return?

4. Are you willing to let a child develop according to his or her own abilities and personality—or will you expect him or her to be like you?

5. Do you have a realistic view of what being a parent involves? (Are you aware that there may be days when you wonder whether having children was the right decision?)

6. Can you accept the changes that children will bring to your marriage and to your lifestyle? (Raising children changes your life tremendously in terms of money, time, and personal goals.)

7. Are you willing to give up thinking about yourself first and be able to put a child's needs before your own?

8. Is your marriage strong enough to take on the responsibility of nurturing another person?

A First-Hand View

Interview someone whom you consider a good parent (it may be your own parent). Ask him or her to share with you

a. what he or she has learned by being a parent;
b. what joys parenthood has brought;
c. what problems he or she has had to face as a parent.

You might also wish to rephrase and incorporate some of the eight questions above (e.g, How did having children change your marriage? Did your children "turn out" the way you thought they would?).

Based on your interview, write a paragraph entitled "What It's Like to Be A Parent—One Person's View."

May the Lord bless you from Zion all the days of your life; may you see the prosperity of Jerusalem, and may you live to see your children's children.

Ps. 128:5–6

3. What Makes a Family Strong?

As we know only too well from the relationships in our own families, sin has had a negative effect on all our relationships. As we live out our Christian lives, all our relationships will always be affected by our sinfulness. But Christ has conquered sin, giving us the power to forgive and build one another up in Christ.

In spite of our sinfulness, God entrusts us with the care of children. Children belong to the Lord—they are *His* gift to us, not something we ourselves have created. **Ps. 127:3** calls children **"a heritage from the Lord . . . a reward from Him."** As Christians, we have the power to improve our family relationships. We can confess our past mistakes, forgive each other, and learn new skills which will improve our ability to relate to one another in helpful and healing ways.

A family need not be "traditional" (father, mother, two kids and a dog) to be strong. What makes a family strong is the way family members relate to each other—the way they demonstrate their faith in Jesus Christ. A family with only one parent and a child can be a very strong Christian family. A more traditional family, in contrast, may be troubled and weak if family members are unable to forgive and love each other.

Families face greater challenges than ever before in history. Only 7 percent of families today reflect the model we used to know: father as breadwinner and mother at home taking care of the children. Many families must deal with problems that are the consequences of sin: divorce, abuse, teenage pregnancies, irresponsibility, couples living together outside of marriage. Others must face the stresses created by two-career spouses, single-parent homes, and blended families resulting from remarriage.

The fact that our society offers so many choices today in terms of life-styles, careers, and social activities puts added pressure on many families. If we wish the families we create to be strong, we must nurture those qualities which make them strong. Characteristics of strong families include the following: They

1. share religious beliefs and convictions;
2. talk with and listen to each other;
3. support and affirm one another;
4. respect one another and teach respect for others;
5. trust each other;
6. are willing to share responsibilities;
7. have a clear sense of right and wrong;
8. have a sense of humor and value play and fun together;
9. establish a sense of family with family traditions and rituals;
10. include each family member in activities;
11. serve other people;
12. encourage family table time and talk and share free time;
13. admit problems and help one another with them.

Adapted from Family Life materials by Rev. Ron Brusius

Discussion Questions

1. Looking at this list, which of these strengths does your family have?

2. What are some things you could do now to strengthen your family?

3. Which characteristics would you most like to build into your future family?

4. What are some things you could do to develop these characteristics in your future family?

5. What can the church do to strengthen families and living units?

If we were to sum up all these characteristics, the one word *commitment* would probably serve well. Commitment, as we learned when we discussed the marriage vow, is the pledge of faithful, giving love we make to another person. God showed His commitment to us when He kept His promise to save us through the sacrifice of His only Son. He gives us the power to show our commitment to members of our families by relating to each other as His precious persons. **"Be devoted to one another in brotherly love. Honor one another above yourselves,"** St. Paul says in **Rom. 12:10.**

For this kind of commitment to exist, family members must support and help each other. After their relationship to God, they must put family first—and arrange job responsibilities and social and church activities to leave time for the family to be together. That does not mean giving up all activities. It does mean setting priorities about what is most important. Sometimes it means sacrifice—giving up something for the welfare of the family.

Some people get so caught up in trying to keep up with the Joneses or in acquiring all the trappings of success that they forget to nurture their own families. Families who share common goals and are involved in each other's lives can, with God's help, survive the many problems and pressures which all families face.

God has given parents important responsibilities. The Christian example of faith and life which they set greatly influences the lives of their children. Studies have found that family example influences whether or not children remain active in the church. Consider the following statistics:

Will Your Child Remain Active in the Church?

- If both Mom and Dad attend regularly, 72 percent remain faithful
- If only Dad attends regularly, 55 percent remain faithful
- If only Mom attends regularly, 15 percent remain faithful
- If neither attend regularly, 6 percent remain faithful

Discuss with your class: what do these statistics say about our responsibilities when we become parents?

Christian parents know that their children belong to the Lord. After giving them life, God brings them into His family through Holy Baptism and He has already prepared a place for them in heaven. Christian parents know they cannot to be the kind of parents God wants them to be without His help. They understand that the parent-child relationship has been given to them by God.

God's Word to Parents

The Bible speaks clearly about this parent-child relationship. It says:

1. Parents are responsible to God for their children. They have the obligation and privilege to bring their children to God in Holy Baptism. Through Baptism the Holy Sporit works the gift of faith. As children grow, parents have the responsibility to exercise authority, loving and disciplining them in such a way that, by the continued working of the Spirit, they will grow in their relationship to God. Parents answer to God for the way in which they deal with their children.

Authority is more than power. Authority means accepting responsibility to do what is best for a child, even if the child does not wish to accept the parent's guidance. What does **Heb. 12:7–11** say about parental responsibility and discipline?

2. Parents are responsible for teaching their children. Already in the Old Testament, God made it clear that his people were always to teach their children about Him; one translation uses the words, **"Impress [these commandments] on your children."** Every child is born sinful; every child needs to hear from his parent the truth about God's plan of salvation for him. What does **Deut. 6:4–7** say about the role of parents in teaching the faith?

3. Parents have the responsibility to pass on Christian morality and values to their children. Every person grows up with some moral standards. If Christian parents do not teach God's plan for living, their children will surely absorb the godless morals and values of the world around them. According to **2 Cor. 5:17,** what do parents need to share with their children?

4. Christian families are models for the world. They do not follow the world—they witness to the world the power of God's forgiveness in their lives. They demonstrate to each other the kind of commitment which God demonstrated to them when He sent Jesus.

Christian families face the same problems, heartaches, and temptations as everyone else, but thay have the power of the Spirit living within them. They know that only the Gospel—the good news of new life in Jesus—can provide the power and motivation for true Christian living. When parents fail in their responsibility to their children, or children fail to give parents the honor and respect that is due, they repent their mistakes, receive forgiveness, and go on loving. That makes all the difference! What does **Rom. 12:2** say about the role of Christians in the world?

How would a Christian home enable people to have a better family life?

(Adapted from Board for Parish Service Bulletin 70087, "Family Life Education in Your Congregation," St. Louis: The Lutheran Church—Missouri Synod Board for Parish Services.)

For the Lord is good and His love endures forever; His faithfulness continues through all generations.

Ps. 100:5

4. Preparing for Children

How can Christian couples prepare for the momentous changes parenthood will bring? It is important for every couple to realize that parenthood will have both positive and negative aspects.

There are some great joys. No experience quite compares with seeing your child take his or her first steps. When your child falls and gets hurt, no one else will be able to comfort and help as well as you, the parent. When your child grows into a fine Christian person, no joy can compare with knowing your child will be with you in eternity one day.

Parenthood also has great challenges associated with it. God expects us to take our commitment to our children seriously. If our children are to receive the Christian nurture that will help them grow in their relationship to God, we must invest the time and energy to provide that nurture.

People who have grown up living only for themselves may find it difficult to learn how to give love to their children. Consider the following examples:

1. One study showed that the average 5-year-old spends 25 minutes a week in close interaction with his father—but 25 hours a week in front of the TV set. How much time do you think a parent needs to spend with a child each week in order to build a nurturing relationship?

2. A successful middle-aged businessman—who drives a $60,000 Porsche and wears custom-made suits—didn't know the name of the high school his son attended. Where must children be on a parent's list of priorities if that parent wants to build a nurturing relationship?

The idea of sacrifice is no longer very popular among Americans. We want to have it all and have it now. But children aren't nurtured that way. Raising children takes great patience and perseverance. It requires loving when the child is being totally unlovable. It means caring enough to set boundaries even when you know you will have to face angry words or hostile behavior from a child. The results of our investment of time and love may not be seen for years; in fact, there is no guarantee that our children will ever give back to us even a portion of what we have invested in them.

Neither should we enter parenthood expecting to be repaid. To be a nurturing parent, we will have to live in a way that is entirely different from the standards of our look-out-for-number-one (myself) society. Only when we remember that God is really number one in our lives will we be able to invest in those things which last—our relationship with Him and our commitment to the people He has placed into our lives.

Dealing with the Change

John and Valerie had always expected that they would have children—someday. Both of them were very involved in their careers and led busy, happy lives. Unexpectedly, Valerie became pregnant shortly after they moved into a new house. She was able to continue work almost until her baby was born, and she planned to return after her six-weeks maternity leave was up. All went well with the birth of Ryan, and John and Valerie were thrilled with their new baby.

Valerie nursed the baby and felt her love for Ryan growing day by day. She started having second thoughts about going back to work so soon, but she knew their house payment was a large expense that needed to be met. John loved Ryan, too, but often felt left out now that Valerie was so busy with the baby. He was afraid that he might do something wrong with the baby, so most of the time he tried to help with the housework and left Valerie to care for Ryan.

When Valerie began to feed Ryan with bottles of baby formula instead of nursing him (something she knew would be necessary if she went back to work) he became fussy and fretful. Her pediatrician discovered that Ryan had an allergy to the formula and recommended that she continue breastfeeding the baby for several months more before trying again to introduce formula.

If you were Valerie or John, what would you do?

When children enter a family, many changes take place. The basic interaction between husband and wife changes, for now they can no longer give each other full attention; their child will require much attention for many years. The birth of a child is thus a period of dramatic adjustment for most parents.

Parents who do not have a realistic view of what parenting requires may find the adjustment especially difficult. We have all read the tragic stories of children who were abused because their immature or selfish parents did not understand normal childlike behavior, or were not able to get beyond their own problems to nurture their child.

Planning for a new baby is an exciting prospect. But many new mothers are not prepared for the exhaustion and insecurities they may face with the care of a newborn infant. They may feel helpless and inadequate, especially if the child is fussy or requires special attention. A loving, supportive husband can be a great source of strength. Friendships with other mothers and the support of other friends and family members can also be of great help for mothers adjusting to their new role.

New fathers also may face many adjustments. Some may feel neglected when their wife spends so much time with the baby. They may be envious of the special mother-child bond which grows so quickly. They may feel clumsy and awkward in attempting to care for their child.

As we mentioned earlier, having children changes a marriage in significant ways. A strong, committed marriage is the most important thing any parent can give to a child. Someone has said that the most important thing a father can do for his children is to love their mother. Studies have found a direct correlation between the kind of family a youngster lives in and the behavioral characteristics he or she is likely to have.

Children who grow up in an unstable home are likely to experience problems socially, academically, and psychologically. Children who receive love, tenderness, and guidance from two loving parents receive the nurture for which God designed the family.

Mothers and fathers relate to their children in different ways. Single parents may try to compensate for the missing parent by arranging for a friend or relative of the opposite sex to spend time with their children. A single mother, for example, may arrange with an uncle or a friend from church to do things with her son, providing him with male role models.

But the model of love for all parents is Jesus Christ. The love of Christian parents for their children is rooted in the love He has for them. **"Let us love one another, for love comes from God. Everyone who loves has been born of God and knows God. . . .We love because He first loved us" (1 John 4:7, 19).**

Even very young children receive the love of Christ through the words and actions of their parents. A child who does not receive love from his or her parents will find it hard to understand God's love. If a child's father is always angry or abuses the child emotionally or physically, the child will have a very negative image of the word *father.* What will be in that child's mind when he or she learns the Lord's Prayer and begins to pray "Our Father?" It is difficult for a child to learn to pray in trust to a heavenly Father when he or she has never experienced the love of an earthly father. The love which a child receives or does not receive from parents has a tremendous impact on the life of that child.

The first five or six years of a child's life are especially critical in the formation of values. If parents want their child to grow up with Christian values, then they must model those values for the child and be willing to spend time talking with and listening to their child. Traditionally, this was an important part of the mother's role. With so many women in the workplace, however, fathers and mothers need to find new ways to fill this need in the lives of their child.

If they spend 90 percent of their energy each day on the job, how much will be left for their families? Many parents who cannot spend "quantity" time with their children try to compensate with "quality" time. This does not always work, however. If a child has a serious problem or question, he or she may not be able to wait until the weekend for a solution. Parents must be available for and interested in their children. God has given them the responsibility to bring up their children to trust and love Him. He holds them responsible for the Christian training of their child—until that child reaches adulthood.

Parents are the role models for love. In the past, many children had grandparents and uncles and aunts whose families could provide role models of love if their own family was having problems. But far fewer children today have extended families living nearby to provide such role models. Thus the parents' role model is of vital importance.

One mother told of her preschool son speaking to his four-year-old friend. The friend asked, "Where's your daddy? I've never seen him!" The child replied, "Oh, he doesn't *live* here; he only *sleeps* here!" Can such a father provide the nurture his child needs?

A recent study on youth sexuality discovered that "the role of parents is critical to the development of teenage values. The love, guidance, and concern shown to the teenager by his/her parent is the single most important element in the manner in which he/she develops," more important even than peer pressure. The father plays an especially key role in the development of the teenager. The teens who were the most "stable" in a survey were those who had a solid relationship with their fathers.

Another study showed that children learn the personal relationship of the Christian faith primarily from their mothers—and the living out of their faith from the example of their fathers. A parent's influence can extend for a lifetime!

Sadly, many children today are being neglected. No one has time to listen to them, to share their little victories, to comfort and encourage them when they face disappointments. Many parents are simply too busy, too preoccupied, too wrapped up in their own lives. Some have severe personal problems of their own. Statistics show, for example, that one out of eight children have a parent who is alcoholic. Those children may never know the security of a stable homelife.

A child's ability to trust and be faithful depends upon the love he receives as a child, beginning with the the love he or she senses from the bond with his or her mother which begins at birth. If children are to grow up with the healthy self-image which is necessary for them to be able to love others, they must receive as children the love which will make that possible.

Being a Christian parent requires a firm commitment to God and to the people He has given us in our families. Few are those who at the end of their lives have said, "I wish I had spent more time on the job." Many people have deep regrets: "I wish I had spent more time with my family, with the people who mean the most to me." The most important thing parents can provide for their children is constant, accepting love that will enable them to experience Jesus' love *through* the love of their parents!

Discussion Questions

1. What are some effective ways in which parents can nurture the Christian growth of their children?

2. Should parents be prepared to make sacrifices to assist such Christian growth? What sacrifices would you be willing to make as a Christian parent?

3. When both parents work outside the home, does this have a positive or a negative effect on a family? Support your answer.

4. How could a single-parent household deal with the problems they must face because only one parent is available to nurture the child?

How can Christian parents face the enormous challenges of parenthood?

- By daily asking God's guidance and trusting His will for their lives
- By entrusting their children to His care rather than relying simply on their own knowledge and skill
- By telling their children over and over that Jesus loves them
- By telling their children over and over that they love them
- By demonstrating love through frequent gestures of affection ("Have you hugged your kid today?")
- By liberally praising their efforts ("One pat on the back is worth a dozen pats on the rear!" is how one mother put it.)
- By accepting them as unique creations of God and trusting Him to round off the rough edges

(Adapted from *Sexuality: God's Precious Gift to Parents and Children,* Book 6 in the Concordia Sex Education series. Copyright © 1982 Concordia Publishing House, revised 1988, *How to Talk Confidently with Your Child about Sex.)*

But from everlasting to everlasting the Lord's love is with those who fear Him, and His righteousness with their children's children.
Ps. 103:17

5. Family Planning

When we discussed the three purposes of marriage in chapter 5, we spoke of the procreation of children as one of those three purposes. Adam and Eve were instructed by God to be fruitful and increase in number, to fill the earth and subdue it **(Gen. 1:28).**

Husband and wife are privileged to give life to future generations. Children are one of God's good gifts to His people. God allows us actually to share His acts of creation! The very word *procreation* brings to mind the fact that we are sharing in God's creative acts. In their child, husband and wife bring forth a new life which celebrates their one-flesh relationship. Their child is part of both of them, carrying genes from each of them which become part of the creation of a unique individual.

Couples may, of course, remain childless. Some make a deliberate choice not to have children; some are unable to do so. Couples who do not have children still have a complete marriage; instead of sharing their love with children, they may share it with many other people who need love and concern.

This question of whether to have children or not has become especially significant over the past generation. Many Christians are confused about this question. Improved methods of contraception have in the past several decades given much greater freedom of choice in planning for children than was ever possible before.

Scripture does not prohibit contraception. It does, however, warn against the dangers of a self-serving life. The one-flesh union of a man and a woman is ordinarily expected to be fruitful, to have children. With the birth of a child, husband and wife come to share a common work.

They demonstrate that their union does not concentrate solely upon itself, but reaches out to the children God sends.

But there may be special circumstances with some couples which would lead them to decide that it would be more responsible and helpful to all concerned, under God, not to have children. Christians dare not take lightly their decisions about having children. Through prayer, they need to seek God's will for them, examining their motives honestly and completely to be certain that their reasons for having no children or few children are God-pleasing, and not based on selfish interests.

Valid Reasons

Listed below are some reasons couples often give for choosing not to have children. Evaluate each reason and tell whether, on the basis of God's Word, each reason is valid (V) or not valid (N). Be ready to support your answers.

1. Pregnancy would endanger the woman's life because of a medical condition she has.
2. Having a child would force the couple to make sacrifices in their life-style.
3. The world is such a mess—why bring any more children into it?
4. One parent carries a genetic defect which would endanger the life of any children he or she had.
5. The woman might lose a chance for a promotion at her job if she takes time off to give birth to a child.
6. The world is overpopulated.

Birth Control? Or Contraception?

Many people use the terms *birth control* and *contraception* interchangeably. They are not the same. Birth control includes *any technique or device which results in prevention of birth.* It thus includes techniques or devices which may destroy an already fertilized egg. Contraception is the use of *any technique or device which results in prevention of fertilization* of the egg. The word literally means, "against conception," anything which prevents conception from occurring. Contraception is thus one form of birth control.

But the term birth control also includes the destruction of a human life which may already have begun, through abortion or any other devices or actions which destroy an already fertilized egg. Since life is conceived when the egg is fertilized by the sperm, destroying an already fertilized egg is contrary to God's will.

Contraception prevents an egg from being fertilized, and thus does not destroy a potential human life. There are many methods of contraception, and scientific research is likely to produce more. Except for surgical sterilization, no methods of contraception are 100 percent reliable. Human error and/or defective devices are always a possibility, a fact which Christian parents will wish to keep in mind. Contraceptive methods include the following:

A. Artificial Methods
(Methods Based on the Use of Chemicals or Artificial Devices)

Females

The pill (which prevents ovulation)

The diaphragm (which prevents sperm from entering the uterus)

Spermicides (chemicals applied within the vagina which destroy sperm cells and thus prevent fertilization)

Males

The condom (which prevents sperm from entering the vagina and uniting with the egg; the condom is the only device which also protects against sexually transmitted diseases; a condom is also being developed for females)

B. Natural Methods
(Methods Based on Understanding of the Woman's Reproductive Cycles and Functions)

The rhythm method (determining a woman's fertile days, based on the time of ovulation in her menstrual cycle, and abstaining from intercourse on those days)

The temperature method (determining a woman's fertile days on the basis of normal temperature fluctuations which occur during the menstrual cycle, and abstaining from intercourse on fertile days)

C. Surgical Methods
(Methods which Prevent Fertilization through Surgery on Parts of the Reproductive system)

Males

Vasectomy (cutting the vas deferens tubes so that sperm will no longer be ejaculated; generally considered permanent)

Silicon plug (inserting a plug in the vas deferens tubes to prevent sperm from being released into the seminal fluids during ejaculation; reversible if a male should want children later)

Females

Tubal ligation (cutting and/or tying of the fallopian tubes to prevent eggs from being fertilized)

Hysterectomy (surgical removal of the uterus; though this surgery is not performed for contraceptive purposes, it makes childbearing no longer possible)

None of these methods listed above are prohibited by Scripture. Birth control methods which destroy an already fertilized egg are prohibited, however; these include the following:

- ☐ *Abortion*(whether by pill or by medical procedures);
- ☐ *The "morning after" pill* (which prevents an egg which may have been fertilized from attaching itself to the uterus);
- ☐ *The IUD* (any intra-uterine device which likewise prevents an egg which may have been fertilized from attaching itself to the uterus; most of these are now illegal).

Why are these methods of birth control prohibited?

1. The living but unborn are persons in the sight of God from the time of conception. (Did you know that before we were born we smiled and frowned; we made noises, hiccupped, and cried; we were able to distinguish our mother's voice from other voices around us; we slept, dreamed, played, and exercised; we could feel pain? In other words, *we were real people* even before our birth.)

The Bible says that each of us has a special relationship with God that began before we were born. God told Jeremiah that He already knew Jeremiah **"before I formed you in the womb" (Jer. 1:5).** David acknowledges that God **"knit me together in my mother's womb. . . . When I was woven together . . . Your eyes saw my unformed body." (Ps. 139:13–16)** If we believe, as Scripture teaches, that life is God's gift, then we do not have the choice of whether or not to keep a fetus that has been conceived.

2. As persons the unborn stand under the full protection of God's commandment against murder. God prohibits the taking of human life in the Fifth Commandment.

3. Since abortion takes a human life, it is not a moral option, except as a tragically unavoidable result of medical procedures necessary to prevent the death of the mother.

(Adapted from LYF Supplement, "Every Teen a Wanted Teen" (December 1983). Used by permission of Board For Youth Services, The Lutheran Church—Missouri Synod, 1333 S. Kirkwood Road, St. Louis, MO 63122-7295.)

Discussion Questions

1. What are some of the important concerns which a husband and wife should consider *before* choosing a method of birth control?

2. How should a Christian respond to a friend who has had an abortion?

3. Where can Christian couples get the information they need to make wise, God-pleasing decisions?

As they plan their families, Christian parents need to seek God's guidance. They also need reliable medical advice. Artificial and chemical methods of contraception may have serious side effects. Some are much more reliable than others. Some (natural methods) may require self-discipline which could strain the relationship. Some (the pill, for example) can be life-threatening to women with certain medical conditions. Some are expensive. All surgical procedures have at least some degree of risk. Making God-pleasing decisions is not easy!

Husbands and wives who search the Scriptures, receive Holy Communion regularly, pray together, and communicate with each other will, with God's help, be able to make good decisions about having and rearing children.

Chapter Summary

God has designed the Christian family to share in the creation of children and to provide nurture for the children who are His gifts to parents.

A mature Christian faith and life-style are essential if parents wish to nurture their children as God commands.

Christian families model to each other and to the world the love and forgiveness which they have received from God.

The world needs loving, caring Christian parents! It needs parents who can nurture healthy, loving, positive children—children who will grow to be instruments for God's love to reach out into the world. It needs parents who remain faithful to their commitments to their spouses and their children, and thus model the commitment which God made to us in Jesus. It needs parents who will provide Christian nurture for their children so those children will be equipped for the job every Christian has been called to do: **"Go and make disciples of all nations" (Matt. 28:19).**

Conclusion

A little girl was busily drawing a picture. When her mother asked her what she was drawing, she answered, "I'm drawing a picture of God."

"But no one knows what God looks like," her mother responded. The child's answer was clear and to the point. "Well, they will when I get through!"

This is the prayer of every religion teacher in every religion class: that the interaction of Spirit, students, teacher, and textbook will have helped both students and teachers to see God. When other people can see God through us, then our lives have both purpose and meaning. May God richly bless both our Christian students and our teachers that together we may witness to His glory!

When this school year concludes, some of us may not see each other again until eternity. But the bond of faith that we share will continue to be a blessing in our lives. May this benediction go with each of us:

Go out into the world in peace; have courage; hold to what is good; return no man evil for evil; strengthen the faint-hearted; support the weak; help the suffering; honor all men; love and serve the Lord, rejoicing in the power of the Holy Spirit. And may almighty God, the Father, the Son, and the Holy Spirit, bless you! Amen.

Before I formed you in the womb I knew you, before you were born I set you apart.

Jer. 1:5